THE
S1NGLE
EXPERIENCE

Other books by Keith Miller

The Taste of New Wine
A Second Touch
Habitation of Dragons
The Becomers
Please Love Me
With No Fear of Failure (with Tom J. Fatjo, Jr.)
The Edge of Adventure (with Bruce Larson)
Living the Adventure (with Bruce Larson)
The Passionate People (with Bruce Larson)

By Andrea Wells Miller

The Choir Director's Handbook

THE
S1NGLE
EXPERIENCE

Keith Miller
Andrea Wells Miller

WORD BOOKS
PUBLISHER
WACO, TEXAS

ISBN 0-8499-0286-X
Library of Congress catalog card number: 80-54551
Printed in the United States of America

Contents

Acknowledgments

Although there are many people to whom we are grateful for help and suggestions, the following men and women took time to read the manuscript and give us specific feedback which was invaluable: Glenn Bailey, Anne Christian Buchanan, Sharee Heatherley, Jerry Jones, Laura Kendall, Jo Ann King, Donna McMullen, Kristin Miller Provence and Clover Thomasson. Since we did not take all of their suggestions we can't blame them for any errors or ideas with which you may disagree in the final copy of the book.

Patty Smith and Laurie Casner typed and retyped the manuscript and kept our spirits up by their encouragement, as did our friend Doc Heatherley at Word.

Floyd Thatcher and Pat Wienandt are not only our editors but have been friends and advisors as we have gone through the process of trying to be sensitive and real in dealing with some areas of life which are emotionally loaded for many people.

To all of these people, we are very grateful.

Keith and Andrea Miller

For the Reader

This book is a distillation from our own experiences. During some long and lonely nights each of us has wondered if we were the only ones who faced the doubts and uncertainties about ourselves, the stark fears concerning the future, the frustrating ignorance about what to do concerning intimate relationships within and outside our families, and the numb and distant feelings about God when we faced some of the very personal issues of being a single person trying to live as a Christian.

We asked around, looked for books to read, and wrestled with some of the inner dragons barehanded and alone. Then we met. And cautiously we began to talk about what had been happening to us as single people. We had both been unprepared for what seemed to be a wild and unstructured world of men and women who were fascinating, lonely, selfish, aggressive and defensive. We saw these people searching in all kinds of ways for companionship, love, faith and stability—just as we were.

We saw fine Christians whose lives were being turned inside out by the powerful pressures of the single experience. The church didn't appear to understand the nature of the problem, and in many congregations singles had no place to go to feel at home with other Christians. Consequently some singles appeared to be "on vacation from God" while they worked out their lifestyles alone.

Ministers told us that they would really like to help but didn't know how. They had simply never been single in a world filled with divorced men and women, widows, widowers, and unbridled freedom. They frankly didn't understand the single experience any more. And single people who had never been married told us that when they got through school they felt like there was no longer a valid place for them in the church.

We participated in several seminars concerned with trying to live as single Christians. Then one day we got a call from our dear friend Francis (Doc) Heatherley at Word, Inc. He urged us to produce a course which would speak openly to the issues of the single experience from a Christian perspective. We wanted to do it, since we had looked unsuccessfully for books and courses which spoke to our own pressing personal problems. But we were also afraid.

Since the biblical standards concerning sexuality (for instance) are pretty clear, no one has written about the problems and choices people run into if they don't adhere to these standards. While we definitely want to encourage men and women who are keeping the biblical standards, we also want to help people in every area of their lives we can—regardless of how unwise or "unrighteous" their choices may seem to those who are married.

In 1980 we produced a twelve weeks' course called "Faith, Intimacy and Risk in the Single Life." We recorded a series of small group sessions in which we and the group discussed many of the subjects listed in the contents here. But that course was primarily for group use, and because of the cost, it was not as accessible to many individual singles as a book, for instance, would be.

When we came to the writing of this book we made a major decision which makes the book very different from the course. These pages represent an intimate sharing of *our own* personal encounters with the single experience. Here we are presenting a witness of what we have seen and heard personally as we have tried to come to grips with singleness and with God. Although our experience in *coming into* the singles' world as divorcees may be different from the experience of those who have lost a mate through death or who have never been married, we hope that much of the rest of our stories may relate to the experience of anyone who is single.

Andrea and Keith Miller
Waco, Texas

CHAPTER ONE

Beginning the Single Life

by KEITH MILLER

I suppose if I live to be a hundred I'll never forget the day I knew the marriage was over. Rain was coming down in sheets, waves of them running across the highway in front of the car as I drove toward the Gulf of Mexico. The windshield wiper opened momentary holes in the splashing deluge. My knuckles were white on the steering wheel. I felt numb, and I remember saying out loud, "It's finished. It's all finished!" Twenty-seven years of marriage, and now it was over. It seemed eerie, unreal. Surely this was a dream, and I'd wake up soon.

As I turned up the beach toward Port Aransas, my mind flashed back to my childhood. I remembered my mother and father, who'd been dead for twenty years, and tried to imagine their faces when they heard I was getting a divorce. I strained to see their expressions in the gray rain ahead. Then time disappeared as I drove silently through the blustering storm coming in from the Gulf.

The next thing I remember was sitting on the screened porch of our beach house, staring out at the whitecaps across the dunes. The palm trees in front of the porch were pirouetting in the storm. The wind howled. And my chest ached. Then I began to cry, and the tears kept coming. It was as if a giant, tightly wound spring lock in my chest had snapped and was uncoiling. And all the hot tears I hadn't been able to cry for years flowed up from the dark center of me and splashed into that stormy afternoon.

During the next few weeks I lived alone in a shadowy world of semi-reality. I spent hours staring out over the dunes, or walking on the beach, thinking how much I missed my daughters and Patrick, their big white Siberian Husky who used to run on the beach with me. Then I'd become aware of the tightness in my chest and stomach again, and say out loud to myself, "I *can't* be getting a divorce, not *me!*" But I was. Slowly I realized that I was. As the weeks went by, I began to shake my head and look around. And I started to realize that life was going to go on.

To keep my mind off what was happening, I tried to dig into the business matters that had to be taken care of with regard to the divorce. I blocked out many memories, good and bad, and stumbled through my schedule still trying to be God's person in the midst of my confusion and hurting. (I know that Christians who have never been through a separation or divorce may not be able to even comprehend the fact that it is possible to foul up your life that way and still love God very much and want to do His will. But I now know that this is a very common experience.)

The singles' jungle—Arriving in a strange land

As I began slowly to recover from the trauma and looked around in the singles' world I was now a part of, I couldn't believe what I saw and heard. It was as if I had been shipped to a foreign country with a different language and a new set of laws and social regulations.

Someone invited me to come to a singles' party. I felt ill at ease and excited at the same time. As I looked around and listened that night, I felt a little like Rip Van Winkle must have when he awakened and realized he'd been asleep for a generation or so. The ways I had learned to behave and relate in the world of dating had changed *drastically.*

Almost all of my former friends were married. They were nice to me and several invited me to dinner in their homes. And I took some of them out as couples. But it soon became awkward because I was an "extra." I became ill at ease with most of my married friends and didn't feel as if I fit anywhere. I had been married so long that I was embarrassed, for instance, to be seen taking a woman out to dinner. I still *felt* married. And often I just wanted to withdraw from social situations.

At church no one seemed to know what to do about me. I was the writer who had written and spoken about family life, and now I was divorced. Most people were polite, but they seemed to look at me in a strange way when I came down the hall after church. Where once we had found it easy and natural to talk about important things, now we only seemed to chat superficially—or so it seemed.

I know now that these are very normal experiences, but at the time it was as if almost everyone I knew wished I would just drop out of the world so they could be comfortable. And it didn't matter that I knew I was being paranoid and projecting my feelings onto them, or that I could understand their attitudes and behaviors. I still had the negative feelings and was often controlled by them.

The questions of singles

As I began to get to know other singles, I had the impression that almost every person I met was in some kind of identity crisis (probably because I was). And some of the problems and questions we shared seemed to be crying out for some attention. The resentment, loneliness, guilt and money problems kept people from being able to handle the difficulties relating to the broken relationships they experienced and their relations with parents and other family members.

But as I wrestled with these and other problems and questions, two seemed to rise above the others and demand my attention: I'd been such a people-pleaser that I had unconsciously discounted my own feelings and didn't really know who God had made me to be. So the first thing I wanted was to discover the *identity* He had given me. And the second thing was the question, "How can I learn to risk relating intimately and honestly with people close to me?" I longed to share some of the feelings and fears I'd been storing up inside. I wanted desperately to check myself out and get some honest feedback, but I was so afraid of being rejected and hurt.

And with these questions, I began my journey into the single experience.

Beginning the Single Life

by ANDREA WELLS MILLER

When I walked down the steps of the courthouse that hot July afternoon, after spending fifteen minutes in an office with a judge and a lawyer, I was angry. At twenty-six, I had just gotten a divorce after four and a half years of marriage. I wanted to go back to age twenty-one and pretend that none of it had happened.

I thought back to the scene five years earlier in which I had accepted the marriage proposal. As I replayed it, I was now wise and mature enough to see that I could have said "no" and avoided all this pain. But as it turned out, that first mistake was followed by more and more, and now here I was... a divorcee, scared, angry, proud, hurt, lonely ... and exhausted, both physically and emotionally.

My lawyer and I stopped by a restaurant for a cup of coffee to "celebrate," but I kept wanting to cry and beat on the table. I knew that if I did, I'd splash the coffee all over the tablecloth, and that thought kept me from giving in to those aching feelings.

Facing singleness and life... What do I do now?

As I drove home alone from the restaurant the realization of what had taken place came crashing in on me with full force. I was *divorced!* I began to get tough with myself—a sign (I learned through counseling) that I am feeling frightened and very inadequate for whatever is confronting me. The pain of wallowing in all those feelings of self-pity and helplessness was very uncomfortable. I recognized that I needed to begin to find out what had kept me from making good decisions. I

14

needed to overcome whatever I had to, and to become a happy, responsible, fulfilled individual who didn't need to rely on a relationship with a man to feel adequate.

The life I had planned

Up through the wedding, everything had gone according to the plan I had chosen for my life. Then things started being different from the script. But at least when I had married, I had a model in mind of what a marriage should be—however unrealistic the model may have been. After the divorce, however, I had the uneasy feeling that I was beginning to live a life for which I had *no* models at all. No one I knew well had ever gotten a divorce or even remained single beyond the age of twenty-four.

Friends who have never married have told me they wrestle with uneasy feelings about deciding when they should start living life as a single adult rather than "a recent college graduate" or a "soon-to-be-married" young person—twenty-one? Twenty-five? Thirty? Forty? But the day after my divorce was final, I knew I was now a single adult and had to start thinking of myself as one and to discover my own style of living.

The first two years

The next few years after the divorce were a mixture of nightmares and adventures, pain and joy, an incredible laboratory for learning about myself, life, and God.

I lived that first year realizing that for a while—I had no idea how long—I was going to be a wounded person in a healing process. I planned things to do on holidays, looked ahead and carefully tried to protect myself from having to handle too much at once. It was a reasonably comfortable year.

By the second year, I figured I should be "over it" by now, so I tried to be more outgoing and dated more. Yet the second year was more difficult than the first. I was often *surprised* by sudden painful feelings. Believing I'd made it through the worst part, I had evidently lowered my defenses, leaving me vulnerable to new kinds of emotional pain.

Veteran single

By the third and fourth years, the excitement had worn off. I began to feel restless and bored wherever I was. If I was with a date, I wished I were at home reading. If I was home with no social plans, reading seemed boring and television worse than boring. I had mental lists of things I needed to do—mending clothes, writing letters, paying bills, cleaning out drawers, tending plants, doing exercises, calling friends, working puzzles, cooking up batches of stew, and yet I almost constantly felt I had "nothing to do." I kept dreaming that an exotic vacation, job change, or new apartment would take care of the lonely boredom, but I didn't do anything about any of the dreams . . . except dream.

In my dreams my goal was to become responsible for myself financially, emotionally, spiritually, mentally and physically. Before I could even *consider* a permanent relationship with a man, I wanted to develop one with myself. And if I *never* had another marriage, I figured I could still be all right if I could become an authentic individual.

But my dreams only circled in my head, coming back to the question: "How can I get out of the dream world and in touch with the real life God has for me out there—somewhere?"

CHAPTER TWO

The Search for "Answers"

NOTES

Dear Keith,

I'm sitting at my desk, sharpening all my pencils and looking at our outline for this book. These chapter titles look <u>challenging</u>. And I've often wondered how <u>men</u> feel about so many of these things. Could I write you some questions about a man's point of view that you could try to deal with in your part of each chapter? It would help me, too, if you would send a few questions my way. By writing notes, we can keep working privately in our separate studies the way we've planned to and still have each other's input at hand.

For instance, after your divorce, how did you begin a fresh search to learn how to have close relationships with people and God as a single Christian?

What <u>is</u> intimacy? And if it is so important for a fulfilled life and we all want it, why don't we just start being intimate? Why is it so hard to do?

A.

"What do I want out of life?" I asked myself one day—for the hundredth time in three months—while waiting in my car in a ferry line to cross the ship channel. I was almost fifty years old and yet I felt frightened about the future in ways I never had before, and that unnerved me.

I knew that I wanted to be God's person, but I had failed. I'd gotten a divorce. And although in my head I believed that God loved me, I didn't feel good about myself as I thought about Him. So I pushed God away by not being regular in my prayers and church attendance and not reading the Bible much. This wouldn't seem unusual for some people, but I wrote and spoke professionally about living the Christian life. And I had prayed, gone to church and read the Bible regularly for almost twenty years.

Inside my life where no one could see, it was as if I had locked the door to the inner citadel of my heart and was manning the parapets night and day to make sure no one—including God—could get in to hurt me. I sort of hurled prayers out over the fortress walls to God to "help me know what to do!" "Help me to get my life straightened out!" and later, "Help me to find out why I seem to have so much trouble just being myself in my intimate relationships with You and with people close to me!" But at that time I didn't invite God or anyone *inside* the fortress with me. I was too afraid.

A fresh search for intimacy begins

When I had crossed the ferry and driven to the post office before going home, I found a letter from a woman I had met once several years earlier when she was recovering from a near fatal car wreck. This woman, whom I'll call Hedy Robinson, began to tell me about her life and her difficulties with the church and in some of her personal relationships. Later I talked to her. And as she continued her story I began to realize that in some ways her life provided a window into my own struggles to relate to my father and to have honest and intimate relations with God and with people.

Finally it hit me that this woman's life was the story of millions of us in America who wonder who we are as we search for, and yet run from, genuine intimacy. I began to get excited! Maybe through this woman's story I could discover something which would help me and other people find out about the search for closeness.

I stopped the work I was doing and wrote a book about Hedy Robinson's life and her search for openness and a way to be close to God and another human being.* And as I wrote, the book became a mirror in which I saw some aspects of my own life I'd avoided facing for years—all my life in fact. And as Hedy faced these problems and made new discoveries, I was forced to face the same issues in my own life. And I learned some amazing things about myself, and about close relationships. I began to read the Bible and everything I could find, searching for information about genuine closeness between persons.

What is closeness and how can it best be described?

For one thing, I discovered that one of the best words describing this kind of closeness is *intimacy.* And yet the meaning of intimacy, like so many other words, has been warped. Piet Heim, the Danish philosopher, said some years ago that words are like old houses at the beach with the windows broken out. New meanings blow in and out of them like the wind from the sea. There's a sense in which the word may still stand, but its inner meaning has changed, and we can hardly recognize it for what it was originally.

I had previously thought that intimacy referred to sexual relations. If someone said, "We were intimate last night," I would assume they meant they engaged in sexual intercourse. But when I looked in a dictionary, the first three definitions of *intimate* were: (1) "belonging to or characterizing one's deepest nature" or (2) "marked by a very close association or contact or familiarity" or (3) "marked by a warm friend-

---

Please Love Me (Waco, TX: Word Books, 1977).

ship developed through long associations suggesting informal warmth and privacy of a very personal nature." Only then was there a reference to "intimate" as referring to sex.

The psychological literature and other articles and books I found indicated that being intimate means relating closely without trying to manipulate the situation or the person being related to—just facing things as they really are with sensitive honesty. In an intimate relationship one feels safe to reveal hopes, dreams, fears, the past—including one's sins and mistakes. These things can be shared without the fear of being judged, condemned, or straightened out.*

As these definitions suggest, intimacy takes place in the deepest and most private areas of human experience. This is a very exciting and exotic jungle into which one must go, it seems, to discover the source and shape of his or her own masculinity, femininity, or personhood, the shape of friendship and its limits, what it means to "belong to another," what commitment means. And somewhere, hidden in the threatening undergrowth of these kinds of thoughts and feelings— which are so emotionally loaded for us—is the mystery of sex and also, paradoxically, the mystery of a close relationship to God.

Intimacy with God

As I thought about these things and read the Scriptures, I realized with a great deal of excitement that there was something very important about a relationship with God that was buried behind the experi-

---

*In this view sexual intercourse is the sacrament of that very basic intimacy between a man and woman in marriage. A sacrament is an outward and visible sign of an inward and spiritual truth. In an intimate relationship two people walk into each others' lives, up and down the hallways of each others' imaginations, each actually penetrating many of the secret places of the other's heart and mind. The longing for intimacy is a longing for union.

If you were an engineer designing human bodies to be inhabited by people in whom you had placed a deep longing for intimacy, can you think of a more beautiful and practical way to form them than male and female? In sexual intercourse two human beings are *actually* joined and temporarily mingled into one. At this point the couple is like God in that they actually participate in the creation of a new life, conceived in their oneness. That is one reason sexual intercourse is such a serious matter for Christians.

ence of intimacy. And I saw that what I've always longed for as a Christian was a genuinely intimate relationship with God *and with other people in the church.*

But so many times I have not had an open, close relationship with the people at church because I wouldn't come out of my inner fortress or let them in. And church became distant and irrelevant to where I lived my real life. I realized that when intimacy was not present in the church, when we were not open at a deep level, then we had unconsciously made the sacraments (the *outward signs* of intimacy with God) *the* thing. Being a Christian, then, became "going to church" and "going to communion" instead of relating intimately with the living God. And these things became boring instead of the exciting expression of the closeness each of us is *supposed* to experience firsthand with God and each other—or so I began to believe.

I became convinced that, as frightening as it is, the intimate no-hiding relationship is the model which God gave *all* of us, single or married, by which to relate to each other, to ourselves and to Him. I began to realize that the reason we long for intimacy in relationships is that this is a large part of the way we are made in God's image. He made us, unlike the other animals, to relate closely, openly, intimately. And part of our sinful condition is that we are afraid to relate that way. So we hide our true feelings from each other and feel separated and alone in the midst of a church filled with other hiding and lonely people who were also made for intimacy.

As I pored over the books I was studying and sifted through my thoughts and feelings, I felt more and more alone with my intense need to learn about intimacy. And I began to wonder how other single Christians faced the questions which seemed to be all around me.

NOTES

Dear Andrea,

    I think writing notes back and forth concerning the questions we've had on each chapter is a good idea.

    In this chapter how about telling a little of your own background as a Christian searching for answers about God? What happened to your spiritual journey as a result of your divorce? Also, where did your search for answers as a single Christian lead you (did you join a singles' group or read any good books, etc.)?

K.

The First Baptist Church of my hometown was my introduction to Chris- tianity. I was baptized at the age of nine. I remember the excitement of that Sunday afternoon. Mother had bought me a new white dress in which to be baptized. It was made of dotted swiss, and it had a big collar with a ruffle, big puff sleeves, a gathered skirt and a wide sash which tied in a big bow in back. She starched it and ironed it, and to me it looked marvelous.

But by the time I had walked into the baptistry and into the view of the congregation, the water was up to my neck and no one could even see my pretty dress, a wet, limp mass of material clinging to my body. A ripple of excitement went through me as I felt the pastor's hand on the back of my neck and saw the white handkerchief coming toward my nose. I was comfortable around water, so it was not a frightening thing to be gently laid back until I was totally submerged, held for a few seconds, then firmly placed back on my feet. I knew I had promised something big to God, but I was to spend the next twenty years trying to figure out what it was.

When I went away to college, I took a new look at "what I believe," and I concluded that while Christianity had some very good basic principles, there appeared to be a flaw: it seemed that we Christians were supposed to keep the rules and do other things for other people. Doing good things for others seemed admirable to me, but the *reason* for doing them appeared to be so that we could earn our "reward in heaven" or gold stars in our crowns or something. In my mind I called this the "lollipop theory" of Christianity and saw doing good as something Christians had to be almost bribed to do—in exchange for God's promise of goodies after death. In my lofty idealism I said to myself, "Anything which is done with such selfish motives as 'gold stars in crowns' can't be all that good," so I quit learning and trying to grow as

23

a Christian and put God on a shelf in my mind to think about later. Doing good was still a goal of mine, but Jesus Christ and God were not a part of this ideal.

Life went on—I graduated from college, married, realized the marriage wasn't going well, and turned to a church for help. I guess I still believed at a deep level in God and Christianity. And I recognized that I'm as selfish as anybody when it comes to needing help, that my motives were not as pure as I had thought.

The counselor I chose, an associate pastor at a small Baptist church, suggested I join a group of people who were going to become a "sharing group." I was the only single person in the group, and wasn't a member of the church, but they welcomed me anyway. After a couple of months I began to care about the church, the people I met, and the way it felt going to services again regularly. So I became a member of that congregation.

The search begins

At that time I acknowledged God as Creator, and as some kind of power, but I had no idea that I could have a personal relationship with Him. He was Someone who presided at church on Sunday, and since I had begun to go to church more, I thought I had a pretty good relationship with God.

I started looking for books to read to find out how to handle the seemingly irrational feelings of boredom, longing, fear, and emptiness that lurked behind my cool exterior—to get the magic keys to happiness, meaning, fulfillment, and love.

But the things I read didn't seem to relate to many of the real questions I faced, like, "What do I say to a guy when I don't want to go to bed with him, but I want to keep dating him?" "How can I relate to a close girlfriend when my favorite guy stops seeing me and starts dating her?" "How do I get my heart to quit pounding when a noise wakes me up in the middle of the night?" "How do I deal with having a better job than someone I'm dating?" "What is real intimacy?" "Does God really know what I'm going through, and how can I get in touch with Him?"

If there are books which address these questions, I didn't find them.

The church search

When my divorce actually happened, a few key people from that church were God's kind of love to me. For a while, the church was a haven. But then some harsh realities of the single life hit me and I began to feel different somehow—especially from these loving people. I felt that they, being safe in their marriages, would not understand my deep struggles inside with issues like dating, sexual choices, and loneliness, which might seem "cut and dried" to them. So I withdrew, attending church services once in a while but dropping out of Sunday school and choir.

This church did not have an active singles' group. And I didn't feel I could fit into any of the existing Sunday school classes. I was too old at twenty-six for the college/career class. So I began to feel strongly that I needed and wanted the support of a network of people who understood what being single was like and who didn't think it was weird to go to church. After some hesitation I finally made an appointment with the minister.

On the day of the appointment, I went to his office and told him about my struggles, my questions, and my need for a singles' group in the church. He listened very attentively, and then said, "I have to admit that I really don't know very much about the needs you're describing. I got married right out of college and we're still together and happy, so I guess I've never really been 'single' in that way. I'd be glad to commit some budget money, but I need your help in forming the content of the group. Would you recommend what we should do?"

I hadn't expected that development. I wanted the church to 'do it for me,' and then I could just walk in and be cool and distant and decide if I liked it or not. But since I could see the dilemma, I decided to give it a try. And I recommended three formats, one after the other: (1) a sharing group, (2) a social group, and (3) a study course.

The other single people in that church didn't respond to any of these. After a few initial group meetings, they simply did not show up any more. Frankly, I didn't like them very much myself. Even though we had sensitive and caring (though married) leaders, in the sharing group format we often tended to get morbid, playing "poor me." In the social format, many of us simply had more exciting things to do outside the church. And in the study course, the materials we found were not relevant to most of our more pressing questions and needs. We became very "brainy" and academic—and almost bored ourselves to death. I realized that for me there had to be a reason for getting together that was *vital* to living a more positive kind of life . . . something that dealt realistically with loneliness, hatred, sex, fulfillment, money, God, and lots of other subjects. I wanted something led by somebody who understood psychology, the Bible, and also had first-hand experience in the singles' world. I knew what I wanted to hear, but I couldn't find it. Neither could anyone I knew.

Accepting responsibility

During the fourth year, I met Keith. He was asking questions like, "Now that I'm single, what are the relationship rules like?" (he'd seen that they were obviously different), and several of the other questions I was stumped by. It seemed to me that he was having a struggle very similar to mine, only he was searching from a man's perspective. The more I got to know him, the more I realized how much valuable psychological and theological insight into the jungle he had.

Much later, Keith suggested that we speak at some singles' seminars together. I wanted to learn what he had to say, but I was afraid to actually take part as a speaker. Since, however, the same issues (i.e., dating, loneliness, etc.) often look different from a man's perspective than from a woman's, he insisted that someone needed to try to tell a woman's point of view. And I agreed. But did it have to be me?

And so I found myself sitting with my back to a fireplace in the game room of an apartment complex, next to Keith. The two of us were facing a group of about thirty to forty other single people, and Keith was explaining that we were going to try to discuss some of the really tough areas of the single life as honestly as we could. My heart pounded somewhere down in my stomach as I looked around the room. Some of the people had been my friends for months or years, others were strangers. How honest would it be possible for me to be? I didn't know. But by now I wanted to get at the truth so much that I was going to try to do whatever I could, butterflies in my stomach and all.

We spoke at seminars together a few more times after that, asking for anonymous questions written by the audience and trying to deal with them. At last, a discussion which included biblical insight and firsthand single experience was taking place.

The experience within my church and the subsequent seminars at which Keith and I spoke deeply affected me by helping focus many of the things I had experienced. I found that even though being single is not the easy, carefree, swinging life many people think it is, it can be a positive adventure of learning and growing. I began to see that it could even be possible for me to find a truly intimate and more natural relationship with God and perhaps even another human being. The only problem was, I felt I didn't know very much about how to be open without driving people away. How could I find out?

CHAPTER THREE
Handling Loneliness

NOTES

Dear Andrea,

Loneliness seems to affect some singles deeply and some hardly at all—at least on the surface. I've wondered if it's different for women than men. How about going inside yourself and describing what loneliness really feels like for a single woman?

What sorts of things did you find to do to cope with the various kinds of lonely feelings you experienced (holidays, weekend blahs, etc.)?

Also, how was your loneliness affected by your attitudes toward (and relations with) other people and God?

K.

The small commuter plane touched down on the runway and bounced twice before settling into a taxi pattern, the brakes rapidly slowing the speed of the plane. As I felt the seatbelt pressing against me, I watched the steadily falling sheets of rain dimly lit by the lights beside the runway. A sign on the side of a hangar said, "Waco, Texas—Home of the Baylor Bears." It was 9:00 P.M. and I was home at last from an exhausting business trip.

As the plane turned toward the terminal, the other three passengers began to pull their carry-on luggage out from under the seats in front of them. One was a college-age girl wearing jeans, loafers and a heavy sweater. Her long brown hair was caught at the back of her neck in a thick red rubber band. The other two passengers were business people, two men in sports coats and slacks, each one carrying a briefcase. They looked as tired as I felt.

No one spoke as the rear door of the plane opened, letting the sound of the rain into the cabin. No one had rain gear, so we would all have to make a hasty walk from the plane into the terminal, dodging raindrops in a hopeless effort to stay dry in the downpour.

Since I was seated nearest the door, I got off first and jog-walked to the shelter of the terminal door. Once inside, I noticed three people standing a few yards from the entrance straining to see through the dark rain-soaked glass wall—a bearded young man in jeans and a dark blue windbreaker; a trim woman in slacks, holding a man's black umbrella; and a heavy-set woman in a denim skirt, loafers and a beige raincoat, with a blue raincoat folded over her arm. My three fellow passengers would be greeted by smiles, kisses, and hugs, or all three.

I pressed my lips together in a businesslike way, raised one eyebrow briefly and hurried past them. No one even knew I was coming home tonight, much less cared enough to come out in this mess to meet me.

29

But I wasn't too disappointed. It was this way every time I traveled. I walked through the small lobby, out the front door and jogged to the parking lot to find my car. It was a good feeling to see it there, the bronze paint glistening in the rain, welcoming me home. I slipped my briefcase in the back seat, turned the ignition key, grateful that the motor started right up, and drove to the front door of the terminal under the shelter.

By the time I got back inside the terminal, my hair was wet and flat and my skin felt chilly and damp under my wet clothes. The luggage was just being delivered, and I scanned it anxiously, trying to see around the couples who stood arm in arm before the bin. Good! There it was! I lifted my two bags off the bin and lugged them outside to the rear of the car, thankful not to have to add to my familiarity with "lost baggage" claim forms.

The drive home was quiet and peaceful, the only sounds being the hiss of the tires on the wet streets and the rhythm of the windshield wipers. I left the radio off, savoring the quiet rainy night.

I pulled into the parking lot in front of my apartment building, parked as close as I could, got my bags and hauled them up the fifteen stairs. The automatic porch light was shining and I was glad to have its light as I searched for the door key on my crowded ring of keys.

Opening the door, I picked up the bags, walked in, set them down, closed the door, turned on a light and looked around. Only then did I feel it—the incredible wave of loneliness that washed over me every time I came home after a business trip. This particular night the feeling was tinged with sadness—because of the rain, the three couples at the airport, and the accomplishments I had achieved on my trip. I wanted to talk to somebody about how well things had gone, to collapse with a sigh on the couch and have somebody hand me a cup of hot coffee and ask me how it went.

But as I looked around, only my ivy plant looked back. The pillows on the sofa, the bedroom slippers out of place and askew on the floor, the dusty end table with a dirty coffee cup on it, all reminded me that I was alone. No one had bothered anything while I was away. Everything was just as I had left it.

I went the short distance from the entry hall to the kitchen. Everything was neat and clean, except the coffee percolator sitting alone on the cabinet where I had left it unplugged. I opened the lid and looked inside—green moldy splotches were floating on the half inch of coffee I had not poured out. It amazed me how quickly mold could grow. I had only been gone from Wednesday morning to Sunday night.

As I rinsed the coffee pot in hot soapy water, I glanced across the open counter, through the small dining area to the open bedroom door. The room looked inviting with the bed neatly made and the dresser top clear. As soon as I finished washing the percolator and filling it with fresh water and coffee, ready to plug it in the morning, I went into the bedroom and lay face down on top of the spread, pulling a pillow out and squashing it under my chin.

Just then a bright flash of lightning illumated the furniture for an instant, and a loud, rolling clap of thunder followed almost instantly. That sudden sound shook loose the last of my control, and I buried my face in the pillow and sobbed.

Preventive medicine for loneliness

Those occasions of coming home from a business trip were perhaps the loneliest times I can remember. To counteract that "empty apartment" feeling when I came home, I rearranged my living room so that there were a lamp and a stereo/radio both plugged into a wall socket connected to a light switch on the wall by the door. I left the radio on and the lamp on, but turned the wall switch to "off" when I left on a trip. Then, when I came home, I just flipped the switch—lights, music—I'm home! It also helped, if I had time, to really clean up, put fresh towels up in the bathroom, fresh sheets on the bed, and clean out the coffee pot. Those little touches helped me feel warm and welcomed when I returned from a trip.

There were also special times of day when I felt vulnerable to loneliness. The late afternoon time between 5:00 and 7:30 P.M.—that transition time from day to evening felt empty. I usually filled it by working late and then going by the grocery store or doing some other errand before going home. Sunday afternoons were usually filled with lying by the pool in the summer, and reading novels in the winter.

Holiday blahs

One of the first times I can remember encountering loneliness head-on and trying to cope with it was about sixteen months after my divorce. The shock had worn off, I guess, and my protective layer of numbness had begun to fade. This particular occasion was the second Thanksgiving after my divorce. I lived 950 miles from my parents, which was too far to drive for a short holiday. And I couldn't afford to fly home. All the friends I had were either going to be out of town or had family members coming to visit. When I realized this meant that I would be alone, I started planning things to do to fill the day.

In my apartment was a little desk which I had bought unfinished and had painted several years earlier. It was rather battered by now, so I decided that Thanksgiving Day would be a good day to repaint it. I decided on a new color and bought paint, brushes, sandpaper, turpentine—everything I would need to redo that desk. I also got the ingredients for a homemade pumpkin pie, just in case there might be some empty time. I was eager for the holiday by this time!

On most days, it is difficult for me to wake up and get going. In fact I have slept until noon on many Saturdays. But for some reason, on that particular day my eyelids flew open at 6:00 in the morning! I realized "The Big Day" was here—Thanksgiving, and I was all alone. I closed my eyes again, turned over and tried to go back to sleep. After two hours of tossing and turning, I gave up and got myself out of bed by 8:00.

I fixed a light breakfast, put on my old jeans and a work shirt and attacked the desk, grateful to have a major project to occupy my mind for the day. But by noon, the desk was all painted. The four drawers were outside my front door propped on their backs, fronts facing up. The main body of the desk stood drying on plastic laundry bags (which stuck to my bare feet as I walked around the desk) in the alcove I used as a dining area. There it was, shining and wet. I couldn't move it or even touch it. As I stood looking at the desk, I also looked at the fact that there was a long afternoon ahead of me, and I had nothing else planned to do.

I went into the tiny kitchen and baked the pumpkin pie, which represented my Thanksgiving dinner. I remember noticing the time—1:30 P.M.—and I began to feel frantic. In one of those instant fantasies, I imagined that time had stopped and I might have to live this awful moment forever.

I looked around the room, and it seemed that the walls were moving toward me and the room was getting smaller. I cut a slice of pie and ate it, faster than I meant to. Then I sat down on the sofa in the living room and looked around the room some more. The noise of the traffic outside got louder—a motorcycle went by, someone's tires squealed turning the corner, the engine noises of all the cars seemed louder than usual. I started getting angry and scared, and I wasn't sure at all how I was going to last all the way to midnight without going crazy.

I thought back on the Thanksgivings in my childhood—I could see the family gathered around as we ate and talked and then took naps. I had always had that kind of Thanksgiving.

Now I was so scared and depressed that even books I had been trying to find the time to read seemed boring, and afternoon television didn't interest me. As I sat in this dizzying whirlpool of feelings, it suddenly occurred to me "This is how it feels to be lonely." I took a deep breath and decided, "I am either going to die or I am going to survive, but I am going to *feel* 'lonely.'"

I spent several hours that afternoon sitting on that sofa and letting the lonely feelings wash over me. I listened to my heart beat, took in deep breaths of air and watched my hands shake. I listened to the traffic, the hum of the refrigerator, the sound of the furnace blowing on and off. I felt my eyes blink, and counted the number of seconds between blinks. And I thought about the ache in my chest and wondered where it came from and how long it would stay. I wondered if my chest would get so tight I couldn't breathe.

I think that afternoon was the first time I ever really got in touch with one of my own strong negative feelings. I had usually tried to concentrate on good feelings like happiness, motivation and inspiration. And I had put "bad" feelings like hate, anger, fear and loneliness somewhere else. Sometime during that afternoon, though, I really *felt* loneliness. And I saw that as deep as that loneliness was, I wasn't going to die from it. I was going to live until the next day and go back to work, and the cycle would pick up again.

It was not a pleasant afternoon, but I did manage to get to sleep that night at a reasonable hour like 10:00 or 11:00. And as I dropped off to sleep I breathed a prayer of gratitude because I had just found out I didn't have to be afraid of loneliness any more.

Some home remedies for lonely times

Even though I now knew that being lonely was not necessarily fatal, still I often found myself filled with that dreaded ache of loneliness, so great that it seemed to interfere with anything else I tried to do.

Sometimes I could cope with lonely feelings by planning very personal things to do for *me*—to care for myself. When I first heard this idea it seemed selfish—to care for myself. But then I read somewhere that a certain amount of tending to your own needs is a mark of maturity. So I thought about what I might do.

I started cooking myself an elegant dinner occasionally. I'd set a placemat, napkin and even a candle on the table. Then I'd take my time with dinner, both in preparing it and eating it. Afterwards I would treat myself to a luxurious evening of lying on the sofa reading a light, fun book or watching a television movie.

At other times when I was too keyed up to sleep, I'd run a steaming hot bubble bath, light a candle or two in the bathroom and relax for half an hour or so in the tub. The secret to this was when I'd get out, I would blow out the candles, dry off, slip into my gown and crawl into bed before I would wake up. (I *did not* clean out the tub before going to bed; it would only wake me up again!)

You may not like bubble baths or cooking and eating alone. That doesn't matter. The exciting thing to me is to think of the secret things *you* like to do—and do them. It may be writing poems, playing a guitar, sewing, building model airplanes, or working jigsaw puzzles. Think of activities that are soothing to you. They often require solitude to be enjoyed, and doing such fun things has helped me pass many long, lonely hours with less pain.

Loneliness and other people

One thing I have thought about a lot is the fact that I live in a world where almost any small wish I may have can be instantly granted. If I want entertainment, I can flip on the TV or play a record. If I need food, my car takes me to the store were I can buy almost anything I want. So, when I wanted companionship I had unconsciously expected a person to show up and be with me. When no one was there as I snapped my fingers, I felt irritated and inconvenienced. And I began to realize that *that* feeling of irritation when my friends were not available was a part of loneliness too.

As I thought about this and talked about these feelings in the sharing group, I came to see that my attitude toward people around me was not good at all. I was regarding my friends as objects for my own pleasure. So whenever I felt that irritation because no one was available to me, I tried to remind myself that people are not objects for me to use to meet my needs. Instead of resenting their absence, I began trying to see other people as persons who also wrestle with fears, loneliness and the needs for love and attention, and to try to reach out to them as fellow travelers on this trip through loneliness and life.

I'm sure that there will always be times when I will be alone, and I know now that if I can begin to relax in some of those times and use them as times of solitude, I can ease some of the pain of loneliness. There will of course be times when I'll need people. But I know now that I don't always have to panic if no one is available on my time schedule.

After my day alone at Thanksgiving, I realized it was perfectly understandable and "normal" for me to have felt intense loneliness. We expect to feel cold when we go out in the snow, hot when we go to the beach, yet that doesn't stop us from enjoying the rest of life—the skiing or the ocean surf. We get prepared and then go do whatever it is we want to do. And yet the fear of being lonely at parties or going out without an escort had often kept me from getting myself mentally prepared and going ahead.

I began to think of all the parties, dinners at the homes of friends, movies and concerts I could have enjoyed—even with a tinge of loneliness—if I had not let the fear of loneliness stop me from attending.

NOTES

Dear Keith,

   As I indicated, I've spent many lonely days
and nights which sometimes seemed to be endless!
And I've noticed that not all loneliness is the
same. Sometimes it is sad, sometimes frightening
and sometimes it's infuriating and frustrating.
Although being with other people often helped, at
other times people only seemed irritating to me.
   Did you experience these differences? If so,
what do you think is the reason for them? And can we
do anything about loneliness, or is it just an
emotional state we have to endure?
   At times I was so depressed during periods of
loneliness, I ran out of ideas about what to do and
got pretty tired of my own well-worn responses. I
hope you'll share some of the things you've found
helpful. (I'll tell mine if you'll tell yours!)

                                    A.

As a single person I soon learned that the way I reacted to being lonely had a lot to do with whether I was going to have a happy or miserable day (or week). Many times loneliness was just horrible and I found that I couldn't do anything but sit and cry and feel sorry for myself. But I began to see that loneliness, though very painful, can also be a very cleansing and positive experience of intimacy with myself.

Alone vs. lonely

Sometimes after the divorce when I was alone, I found I was relieved and thankful that I was not in conflict with another person. I remember listening to the silence. I could sometimes consciously slow my mental pace, relax my whole body, and let my mind stretch and roam. Sometimes I used periods of being alone to fantasize and dream creatively about the future, or to pray and listen to God. At other times I'd settle down with a good book. When these things happened, aloneness became a kind of private "place to go," a quiet island. I can remember winter nights when it was cold outside, propping myself up in bed and reading an adventure book and letting myself live the story. These were good times and were like mini-holidays for me. And I did not feel lonely at all. But besides these positive experiences of being alone, there came some very different kinds of aloneness. The kind called loneliness was sometimes very painful. And I soon learned that some kinds of loneliness can be dealt with much more easily than others.

"Social" loneliness

There is a loneliness which is strictly social, just a need to have someone to talk to. I would sometimes find myself lonely and just want to reach out and touch someone or talk to a friend. And when this happened I realized that I just needed to get out of my chair and call someone I knew. But often I've been strangely shy about calling people when I've been lonely. I've felt that my friends probably didn't want to be with me (or I didn't want to risk that they might not). When I felt that way, someone suggested that I could go see someone else who might be very lonely and whom I might have neglected.

At first, I rejected this idea because when I am down and feel like a misfit, the last thing I want to do is visit with another "loser." I'd rather see someone who is going to make *me* happy. But I decided to give "visiting" a try. The first time I tried going to see someone when I was feeling lonely, I went on raw faith. I didn't feel this person would reject me because I knew he was in worse shape than I was, and probably just as lonely. Finally I drove to his house.

As I walked up the front steps, I dreaded the next half hour. What would I say to a man who had always appeared to me to be sort of arrogant and defensive when I'd seen him at church? I'd pegged Bart as a "know it all" type who felt superior to the rest of the members of the church. He was not attractive to me in any way.

But I'd heard that Bart was hurting and he'd said he'd like to see me some time. He smiled in surprise as he opened the door—even though he'd known I was coming. It was an awkward moment as we both realized what he'd done. But when we sat down and began talking— after reviewing the weather that day—I began to feel a change in the atmosphere. The arrogance melted, and there sitting before me was a man just like me, afraid he really wasn't much good at relationships and yet not knowing what to do. He began to tell me about his life and what had happened to him. Sometimes he would pause for thirty seconds and stare at the floor as his story unfolded. Although he was a respected community and church leader, his marriage had been bad for years. Recently he'd had an affair and fallen in love with the other woman. Bart was really open in admitting his problems, mistakes and sins. And I found myself caring very much about him. An hour flew by. And when it was time to leave, I hated to go. I had gotten outside myself and really become involved in Bart's life. And as I had, he became more animated and interesting—whereas before I'd showed interest in him, he had been drab and boring. And I realized that *my* being bored sometimes when I had gone to see people before must have communicated itself at some level, and they had *become* passive and boring. But my listening and asking questions changed the experience for Bart and for me. We prayed together. And when I left, I found that my loneliness had evaporated for the rest of the evening.

Loneliness and fear

There is another kind of loneliness that is combined with the irrational fear that I'll be overwhelmed by it or by my problems. I can remember sitting alone at the breakfast bar in my kitchen one stormy winter evening. I had opened a can of ranch style beans, sliced a tomato on some lettuce and gotten out a couple of pieces of bread and a glass of milk. It was raining and cold outside and I felt a wave of loneliness come over me. I realized that if I dropped dead at the table, no one would know for days. I began to imagine the future and started to fantasize things like growing old all alone with no one to care for me. I could see myself bent, unkempt, and uncared-for in a dirty apartment. In a rising panic I tried to live out the rest of my life in an hour in a series of negative fantasies.

When loneliness strikes hard and lasts several days, the first thing I try to do is to call a good friend or pastor and talk out my feelings. But what I've often done instead of getting help is to start putting the pressure on my friends and children to love me, to pay attention to me. Unfortunately, when I run after people socially or cling to them possessively, my needs seem to scare them. And my intensity can drive them away. People tend to leave us alone when they are afraid they can't fill our irrational needs, so I sometimes cause the very thing I fear. My franticness to relate when I feel scared says loudly to everyone around me that my interest is in *me* and not in *them*. And then my chances of real intimacy are very small.

Depression, hatred, guilt, and loneliness

Another reaction to loneliness is depression. When loneliness descends, it's sometimes like a smothering wet blanket which drops on me out of nowhere. I wake up in the morning and I'm miserable—no specific reason. I may lie in bed and get morbidly introspective. My imagination starts replaying all the "selfish, thoughtless and unfair" things people have done to me.

As sick as it sounds, I have sometimes almost enjoyed this misery. There is a bittersweet self-justified aspect to this replaying the injuries done to me. For one thing, by doing this, I can keep a dead relationship alive and I'm not quite as alone for a few minutes. If I can recall the hatred and other bad feelings and keep reliving the pain, I can keep myself from getting over a bad relationship. *But* what this winds up doing for me is to make the subsequent loneliness more intense, because my stirred-up resentment often drowns my good feelings and leads to deeper depression.

Guilt is another reaction to loneliness. In this response, when you are lonely, you replay the bad things *you* have done *to other people* which caused *them* misery. The payoff of this kind of fantasizing game is the spiraling feeling of worthlessness and self-hate.

Both these feelings—self-pity and guilt—are sometimes the result of anger turned in on ourselves, either for "letting them do it to us" (in replaying injuries done to us) or for our "doing it to them." And the resulting anger, unconsciously turned in on ourselves, is sometimes what depression is.

Some alternative responses to loneliness

After some trying hours of introspection, panic, hatred, and guilt, I finally met someone who suggested a kind of prayer which really started to help me deal with the most poignant lonely times. This man said that he prayed with a pencil and paper before him. So at his suggestion I started saying, "Okay God, what would you like to say to me in this mess?" and then I'd be silent and listen.

I expected some profound "answers" to my problems. Instead I began to "hear" things like, "Pay your bills today, they're late," or "Answer your mail," or "Call your middle daughter." Since these weren't "spiritual" things, I started to ignore them. But my friend had said to write down any thoughts which came—even "bad" or "irrational" ones. Sometimes the thought would be, "Get up and go to work early today."

If I had illicit, lustful thoughts about someone, I'd pray about these and ask God to help me see the woman in question as a person, not a sex object.

After I finished praying I'd begin to do the things I'd written down. By doing this, I started getting out of my self-centered introspection. And I discovered in a new way that God wanted to talk to me about the ordinary things in my life. The bottom line was that the more concrete things I followed up on which came out of my prayer time, the more I got away from the fantasy world of introspection where depression thrives, since creative action is impossible.

Waiting quietly

Another response which has helped me when loneliness and desolation sweep over me came from the experience of the late Baron Friedrich von Hügel.

He put it this way. "I'm traveling on a camel across a huge desert. Windless days occur, and then all is well. But hurricanes of wind will come, unforeseen and tremendous. What to do then? It's very simple, but it takes a lot of practice to do it well at all. You dismount from the camel, fall prostrate face downward on the sand, covering your head with your cloak. And you lie there an hour, three hours, a day. The sandstorm will go and you will arise and continue your journey as if nothing had happened." But, von Hügel goes on to say that in such periods of lonely desolation there's a general rule of thumb that's really helpful to him: a person should form no conclusions, make no big decisions, nor change the course of his or her life during such crises. He particularly stresses not to try to force anything religious on one's self. He advises us to turn gently to other things and to maintain an attitude of acceptance of life and to be gentle with ourselves. I've found that when I can do this, the emotional crisis often goes by and I feel stronger for having weathered it without panic. But people who try to "fight the sandstorm" get lost and wind up far from their way.

And of course sometimes we've got to keep working and being with people. But by using von Hügel's attitude toward loneliness I've found I can give myself a rest from struggling in fruitless "hand-to-hand" combat with my fears. I take any concrete action I can to solve the problem. Then I tell God I'm going to relax, and I take my anxiety and put it on an imaginary conveyor belt and send it up to Him saying, "God, please handle this anxiety today. I'm going to rest a day till my windstorm is over." And then I get busy in a way that has proved very calming for me.

Doing little things

I have found that by turning big things over to God for a day, I can gain new strength. When I make the act of committing the problem to Him, I have to *do* something specific about some area of my life or I'll take the big worry right back and get stuck in the swamp of loneliness again. So I turn and get caught up on little things. I catch up on my mail, maybe calling or writing people I haven't written for a long time. I file note cards or read articles or books I'm behind on and perhaps mow and trim the yard, consciously turning the whole future over to God when I start mulling over "my problem" again.

One of my daughters washes her hair, does her laundry, gets her clothes in shape, and cleans her room when she sees this overwhelming loneliness coming. And since one can succeed at such little tasks (and they are not directly tied to acceptance or rejection by other people), it's amazing how much more quickly the "lonely frantics" are sometimes dissipated and go away.

And after such times, because I have in some sense put my house in order, I feel more ready to walk out of the pit of introspection and self-pity and begin life again.

Small groups, taking risks, and God

One of the best things I've found to help deal with loneliness and the problems which come with it is having a small group of people with whom I can share feelings like these we're looking at. When I can express these thoughts and feelings with people who also have them, I can sometimes begin to sense that what I am experiencing is natural and not the result of something that is wrong with me. This has really been helpful—especially in calming the various fears which can be greatly exaggerated by loneliness—like the fear of death, of never finding a mate, of becoming sick, etc.

When loneliness and depression have closed in for days and I haven't been able to share with a friend or pastor or group that I trust, I've found it's good to go to a competent professional counselor. By going to a counselor who isn't going to butter me up but will listen and really hear my feelings, I can often discover that my fear is not neurotic. Some of the fear just goes with being afloat in the depersonalization of modern life—and can't be blamed on being single. I tended to forget that I was sometimes lonely when I was married or in my parents' home before that. Many Christians won't go to counselors for help, being afraid of what they might discover about themselves. But to me that attitude is a little like having a strange rattle in the engine of your car and deciding not to go to a mechanic because he might find something that needs fixing. Counseling has been very helpful to me, and I've almost always been more comfortable and less lonely with the truths I've discovered in counseling—even the painful ones—than I was with the fear in not knowing what was the matter.

Taking risks

Something I never would have thought of, especially as a way of dealing with fear and loneliness, is the taking of personal risks. All kinds of outstanding people—poets, military leaders, and psychologists—have agreed that doing something extremely risky or participating in a cause greater than ourselves can help us get rid of fear. Several years ago I read an article in one of the psychological journals that some people use parachuting as a way to overcome their personal fears. If we have something scary to do we can sometimes forget our loneliness and our fear of people.

And for those of us who see the Christian life as an adventure, God has provided a way (and a loving group) whereby we can risk ourselves and our "fortunes" for God and other people. We are immersed in a lifelong venture of faith—which is the best deterrent I've found to fear and loneliness.

I think one of the reasons God's adventure is so absorbing is that, besides the excitement of being with people who have a common purpose and understanding of life, we begin to discover who *we are* and what our true identity is as we try to discover God's will for our lives.

CHAPTER FOUR

A Real Identity: It's Never Too Late

NOTES

Dear Keith,

One of the things you told me when we first met
was that you have been trying to find out for a long
time who God made you to be. What were some of
your thoughts as you searched? Did you feel any
differently about the search when you became
single?

Also, I think it would be good to talk about
how you felt the church viewed single people and
how that affected your identity.

Finally, I really understood your feelings
when you told me about the way you struggle to
believe other people when they affirm you, because
I struggle with that, and I bet a lot of other
people do too!

A.

"Who am *I?" I shouted into the salt spray as a wave hit the pilings below* me. I was standing alone on the end of an old wooden fishing pier watching the sun rise over the whitecapped waves which were sliding by on either side or crashing into the heavy pilings ten feet below me.

I had begun to wonder if I really was the person I'd seen myself to be all these years. From the time I was a small boy, I'd been loved and rewarded for being an extrovert-achiever at school and in extracurricular activities. I had always worked hard and repressed my shyness and fear of being a public person. I'd been affirmed first for "being honest," and the past few years for being a committed Christian. I was almost never hostile, and considered myself a real straight arrow morally and ethically.

But in the last three years before the divorce, I'd discovered some feelings I had never allowed myself to experience. Besides the rage which emerged "from nowhere," I'd begun doing things I'd prided myself on never doing, telling lies and hiding my unacceptable thoughts and behaviors.

But I wasn't comfortable with myself as a person as I was thinking about those things. As a matter of fact, the problem of my identity at that moment seemed to center in the question, "How can I accept myself now?" I felt guilt and a sense of failure as a divorced Christian.

And now, standing on the pier watching the June sun climb through the billowing white and gray clouds, I wondered who I really was. What did it mean as a forty-nine-year-old divorcé (the divorce would be final in fifteen days) to "have a sense of identity" as a person and as a Christian?

As I looked back over my life I realized that until the divorce my public "identity" had been pretty clear and well defined. I had been first a son, than a husband, a father, a businessman-turned-writer and a Christian speaker. But now I realized that these identification marks all had to do with *what I did,* not *who I was.*

As a young child I remember often being relieved in new situations when some adult would say, "Oh yes, you're Earle and Mabel Miller's son." When that happened I felt safe somehow, as if they would treat me well because my mother and father were honorable substantial people. But in that case my identity was dependent on my family, my name—and I'd had nothing to do with acquiring that either.

Who am I going to be now?

When I got back from the pier the telephone was ringing. It was a single woman friend of my soon-to-be-ex-wife's and mine. She said, "I just heard that you two are divorcing."

"Yes, that's right," I answered solemnly.

"Well, I'm sorry," she said, "and I know you're probably feeling very lonely and miserable right now."

"I'm doing okay," I replied. "I feel like I've been in a bad wreck and am still a little in shock, but I'm beginning to get things squared away."

There was a slight pause on the other end of the line, then our friend said, "Why don't you come over and let me fix dinner for you this evening? No one's here and you can spend the night." I shook my head in disbelief at what she had said. It was as if a fire alarm had gone off in my stomach. I was floored and didn't know what to say. Finally I mumbled something about the divorce not being final yet but I appreciated her thoughtfulness.

Good gosh, what kind of world had I stepped into? I called my twenty-four-year-old single daughter, told her what had happened and asked what she said to men who wanted to be more intimate than she did but whom she didn't want to hurt. She said, "Well, daddy, I just tell them something like, 'I think you're a neat person (if I do) but that's just not where I am with you.'"

I thanked my daughter and hung up. And thinking about the woman who had called me, I realized how little I knew about what my identity might be outside a traditional marriage situation. And although I was uncertain about my competence in several areas of my life, I did get some pleasant surprises.

Hidden talents

In order to meet the financial commitments I had agreed to regarding the divorce, I had to sell the house on the beach. But I had a small office in the garage. In order to have a place to live, I decided to keep the garage and make an apartment out of it.

All my life people have told me that I didn't know anything about decorating a house, and the feeling I got was that I had neither taste nor talent in those areas. But inside I'd always been hurt when I'd felt my opinions had been rejected and secretly thought I had some good ideas about design.

So one day I sat down with a pen and paper and listed what I would need in an apartment. I drew a scale drawing of the garage and figured a way to get everything I wanted in the plan, including all the plumbing fixtures and electrical outlets. Then I got a good carpenter who could contract for the other workmen we needed, and we began to build the apartment/house.

I called my dear friends Lynn and Jo Leta Gavit. "Hello, I'm designing a house to put in my garage and need some advice." Silence. "Well, you know what I mean." They came over and we went from there, as I asked about the best and most economical kinds of household appliances and we went over my drawings looking for omissions and/or improvements. But I did the basic planning and design myself. We put in Mexican tile floors, a small fireplace, butcher board counter top in the kitchen and all kinds of built-ins.

When we were finished, I furnished the apartment with furniture I already had and over the next few months added some new things. I put up the pictures and mirrors. And when it was completed it seemed delightful to me! I couldn't believe how warm and welcoming it felt. And everyone who came seemed to have good feelings about the way it was decorated. My daughters didn't hide their surprised and positive reactions. And I realized that when I sit down and dream and then plan, I may have pretty good taste about fixing up a home. I can't tell you how good that little apartment looked to me, because I had done something that I wasn't supposed to be able to do.

As I realized that I could do some things on my own, I felt a much stronger sense of identity as a person and not as dependent on women to tell me what to do about my living surroundings.

After the experience of "building" the garage apartment, it began to dawn on me that maybe being single might be a great time to learn who I really was at last, and to learn about my self-defeating habits and fears, and to enjoy living with myself. Then if I ever decided to get married again maybe I could bring a more whole person to the wedding—me.

I had felt at loose ends emotionally since the divorce. Maybe God was giving me an agenda—to find out about myself—who I am and what He wants me to do and be. At least by examining my life and goals I would be *doing something* and getting out of the holding pattern I seemed to be in. And if I didn't marry again I wouldn't have lost anything, because I'd be a lot more comfortable and at home with myself as a person. I felt like I was on a secret adventure to learn how to live as a single Christian.

The Christian single at church

I hadn't realized until that time that Christian society in the church has seemed to operate on the basis that singleness is all right for the very young. But for people beyond college age, singleness is often regarded as a second-rate state which is at best only temporary—until the right woman or man comes along. Almost no one in the church, it seemed, knew quite what to do about divorced single Christians, so they generally did nothing. I hadn't thought much about this when I was married. But the apparent lack of awareness of the existence of single adults felt like rejection when I was on the receiving end of it.

And I realized that married people in churches evidently don't realize that there is an enormous amount of unconscious prejudice in communications within their congregations. Bulletins and church announcements often say, "Come to the meeting and bring your family," or announce recreational weekends called "Family Retreats." This title often has a double meaning—the earthly family unit and the Family of God. But to sensitive single people with no mate or children, such titles can seem exclusive.

For instance, I never really knew if I was invited to church family gatherings, particularly retreats. When I heard that the activities included Bible study times when "each family will go off by itself, read a biblical passage and then discuss it as a family," I had to assume that singles weren't invited. (Even though common sense told me they might make a place for me somehow if I made an issue of it—which of course I did not.) So I felt excluded.

I found that it can be very difficult for a single adult Christian, after high school and college classes are over, to feel a strong sense of having an acceptable identity, an emotional "place" in the Christian community.

Self-worth—Am I really okay?

But for me the prior question to "Where is my place in the church?" was, "Down inside behind all my friendliness and outgoing personality, who am I, anyway?" "Why was it," I wondered, "that I have always been afraid to tell people my real thoughts, feelings and opinions about things important to me—particularly if they were different from the commonly accepted opinions of 'our group'? For instance, why was it so hard to tell the minister I felt rejected?"

It's difficult for me to understand why I have this fear of revealing my vulnerable feelings since I've apparently been "popular" and "accepted" all my life. But even when I had received hundreds of affirming letters and calls as a writer, down inside, the affirmation was never enough to make me feel I was really okay. And I would drive myself to another project, doing risky or difficult things, believing that in this way I could feel all right—like a "good and acceptable" person. Of course, I wasn't conscious at the time of why I was working so hard. But in any case, the compulsive behavior didn't really work. I never felt I was quite acceptable enough. And I began to think I was just a Christian workaholic freak.

As a divorced single person I felt particularly vulnerable at the point of relaxing and letting my life speak for itself. I felt I *had* to work hard in order to gain *anyone's* love or approval.

I'd gone to a counselor for almost three years before getting a divorce. And I had begun to get in touch with needs, dreams, hopes, and feelings, many of which I had not even realized were a central part of me.

I saw that I had repressed a ton of hostile feelings and that I'm really a shy person who doesn't want to live in the midst of strange crowds. I was surprised, since I had been speaking publicly all over the country. I became aware that I have strong physical and emotional drives, and that I have an intense need to express my deepest feelings, including the negative or hostile ones, with the people closest to me. And I also discovered I had some unfinished business with people in my past— including my own parents—before I could claim my own separate identity. And that was scary for me.

NOTES

Dear Andrea,

I remember your telling me about the identity crisis you faced near the end of your first marriage when it occurred to you that you didn't really know what to do or be, except in response to other people's expectations. Would you describe how that felt and how you began to become aware of your programming to be a nice wife and mother doing traditional female things? What did you discover about your real identity and the personal inclinations you had repressed all your life?

Also, I think it would be interesting if you'd talk a little about the problems you faced in trying to change your personal and vocational "name tag" after the divorce and how you reassessed your vocational life as a single woman. Finally, I can really identify with your struggle in feeling you were being several different people in different areas of your life. And I think a lot of other people might too.

K.

It was morning, and I lay in bed, eyes wide open, realizing that I was alone in the house. It was raining outside, and still dark. My husband had left early and would not be back until late that evening. It was a Saturday, and I didn't have to go to work or get out of bed or do anything. So, as I lay there staring at the ceiling, I started imagining what I would do if I didn't have to do what *anybody* else expected me to do—my mother, my husband, my boss. I expanded the fantasy in my mind to include more questions like, "What if I had all the money I needed or could go anywhere I wanted to go, then what would I do?"

There was absolutely no answer. I couldn't even make a list to choose from. My mind went blank, and I panicked. There I was, with a whole long day ahead of me and I couldn't think of anything *I* wanted to do, either on a grand scale or a small scale, like brush my teeth or make a cup of coffee.

I finally got up, automatically got into my robe, and made coffee. I walked around the living room holding a cup of hot coffee and thinking about that blank in my mind. All I could think of doing was to fantasize asking my mother or husband or boss what to do, imagine an answer from one of them and then do it. I was stunned that morning to realize that I'd never dared think of what I was really like and what I might want to do or be as a person apart from my family's expectations.

What does it mean to be me—apart from them?

A few weeks later, after several other frightening incidents, I began to realize I was losing my grip on what little identity I had. I felt that emotionally I was balanced precariously. And the slightest problem, like the lid on a jar being too tight to open, sent me into sobbing rages.

Through the misty fog which was hanging sluggishly over my mind
I remembered the name of a minister whom my mother had mentioned
while she was in Waco on a visit over a year before.

With this slim thread of contact, and prompted by my desperate
feelings, I looked up the minister's name in the phone book. "Oh *good*,
he still lives here!" I said out loud to myself. I pondered the situation
two more weeks before I gathered enough courage to call. One night,
early in the week, I looked up the name again, and with shaking hands
I dialed the number. After a few rings, a man's quiet voice said
"Hello?"

My stomach quivered strangely and I asked, "Is this Mr. Sullivan?"

"Yes, I'm John Sullivan," he responded.

"Well, we've never actually met. But my mother called you over a
year ago to say 'hello' from your roommate. Do you remember?"

After a pause he said, "Oh yes, I remember now! That was a nice
surprise."

"Well, the reason I called is—" I stammered and paused—"uh,
well, I'm not sure but I think I'm having some problems. Could I come
talk to you to see what you think?"

"Of course you can," he answered warmly. "Would this Thursday be
all right?"

I agreed gratefully, but as soon as I hung up I almost called him back
to get out of it. I cried awhile, which wasn't surprising, since I'd been
spending time every day crying.

Shortly after I began counseling with Mr. Sullivan, I started discovering some more things about my identity. One memory that still
seems vivid was of something that happened when I was about twelve
years old.

An early choice of identity

I was a "tomboy" who loved to run and play and climb trees. One
summer Saturday afternoon, I was sitting on a branch halfway up my
favorite tulip poplar tree, daydreaming, and looking up the street in
front of our house.

Just then, a blue car pulled up and stopped. My father got out. He
was trim and tan, wearing a white tennis shirt and shorts and carrying a

covered tennis racket. He had just been to a tennis match, and he must have won, because he came walking down the driveway whistling and looking very happy.

"He'd better be careful," I thought. "Mommy's in the house waxing the floor and she doesn't want anybody to mess up the clean floor." I thought about that morning, and how mother had said to my sister Linda and me, "You girls go on out and play. I have to wax the floors, so be careful when you come back in. Use the back door only!" So we had gone outside, each to our own favorite place to be.

I remember climbing up the tree, and then thinking about finishing junior high school, and then high school and then college, and then getting married and having babies. And one day, if I was a very good girl, and did everything right, I might be waxing a floor somewhere while my husband was out having fun playing tennis. It all seemed very natural, because, at that time I believed there was nothing else for little girls to do. And besides, I thought, if we didn't wax the floors, who would?

I grew up, went to high school, to college, and got married. And although the memory of that Saturday afternoon which I discussed with Mr. Sullivan has remained with me, my little girl conclusions have not. (Also, I have since remembered times when my father was the one who waxed that pink linoleum floor, and also did lots of other things around the house.) But the scene that Saturday morning seems to typify an identity I adopted for myself without really knowing who I was, what I could be, or how to live differently from that lifestyle in a relationship with a man. And then I got divorced and began to shape an identity as a single adult.

How does a divorced woman change her identity?

At the time of my divorce, I decided to take my maiden name back. It meant a lot to me and stood for security and a close family belonging. But I discovered it was harder than I had expected to change my name.

At that time I had a job as an order clerk. In that job, I talked to people on the telephone who wanted to place orders. When they found out about my name change from the switchboard, I would often be greeted with, "Well, I hear your name has changed. What happened? Did you get married?" The tone of voice was usually friendly and full of congratulations.

The first time I heard that on the phone I nearly hung up. Tears rushed to my eyes, my voice shook and I was afraid to talk long because I didn't want this well-meaning person to know how much it hurt. But I finally cleared my head enough to say, "Nope, I got *un*-married." The person on the other end of the line was silent for a couple of seconds and then I heard him clear his throat and say, "Well, I'm sorry. I hope things go well for you." Then we went on with "business as usual." I was relieved and glad when the questions quit coming so often and the newness of the divorce wore off and was not a topic of conversation around the office.

Can a "lady's" identity include being mechanically inclined?

During the next few years I began to try to do some things I thought I might like that didn't fit the old image of who I "should be." I started by learning how to take care of my car, a 1970 Pontiac. I had always wondered how motors worked.

But whenever I had the hood of my car up in the parking lot of my apartment complex, people (guys) would stop and say, "Anything wrong, lady? Can I help you fix your car?" I was usually just poking around observing how things worked, so these frequent interruptions got to be embarrassing.

I finally asked a friend who was a good mechanic to teach me how a car engine works and how to do things like tuning my engine and changing the spark plugs. I was fascinated!

I also wanted to collect a set of tools, and finally went to a hardware store and bought a fishing tackle box and a half dozen basic household tools. I don't want to discount the value of helplessness as a way to get attractive guys to come in to help by fixing things around your apartment. But for those of you who may want such a kit (even for emergencies) it included a claw hammer, a regular screwdriver, a Phillips head screwdriver, a metal tape measure in a case, some needle-nose pliers, an adjustable wrench, and an ice pick (to punch a hole in the wall before putting anything up with screws.)

One time my blender started acting up. Out of curiosity I took it apart, found a loose screw and tightened it, avoiding having to put it in a cabinet until somebody could come over and fix it for me. (I found many other mechanical problems which were easy for me, but I've had plenty of others which needed a fix-it shop too!)

But in my enthusiasm at being free to do all this, I noticed that I began to talk about it all the time, even brag. Men would sometimes smile indulgently and I got so I felt defensive and half expected people to laugh at me or not approve of me for being able to fix things. I had to learn to keep quiet, and just fix the blender without talking about it for three weeks afterward.

Do all women love to cook?

At the same time I was developing skills that were often considered "male" tasks, I also reviewed the traditionally "female" chores I had learned growing up. After thinking it over, I finally felt free to admit that I didn't like to cook. It is something I had tried to make myself learn and I could do well enough not to starve, but I did not enjoy it. I used to tell my dates, "I don't like to cook," which they often interpreted to mean, "I *can't* cook," which was just fine with me. (Later, after I had had a "vacation" from cooking and felt more at home with myself as a person, I discovered that secretly I do like to cook— sometimes.)

Vocational identity as a single woman

My identity at work didn't matter to me much until I had to depend on my own income for my support. When that happened, my progress at work suddenly became very important to me.

Looking back, I wish I had started off with the attitude that I was going to be a career person from the beginning. When I first began to work and was still married, I had felt, "I don't need to invest much creative energy in this because I'm just going to do it for a couple of years and then go on with my marriage." Some of the other girls I knew who had not married felt the same way—counting on the fact that they would soon marry.

I realize now that I could have tried to make as much vocational progress as possible and still been able to leave the job if it became time to move on. But now it seems that (by comparison to the way I worked after my divorce) I had just "treaded water" in my job when I was married.

I began to plan ways to improve my situation. I had to listen, watch, and ask questions related to "How does a person actually get ahead around here?" This meant that I had to look at attitudes and behaviors that were holding me back—mine and other people's—and to force myself to change the self-defeating ones which were mine, even though it was often embarrassing and painful.

For instance, when someone was harsh in rejecting an idea I'd presented, I would find myself breaking into stifled tears. I struggled not to do that when I saw that the tears made most men not want to deal with my idea at all.

One of the techniques I developed for myself was to imagine a businessman whom I respected for being efficient and pleasant. (Imagining a man was necessary for me because where I worked there were no women who were "visible" to me in my part of the company who could serve as role models.) Then I would think back over each business meeting and compare my behavior to my imaginary male figure.

It was painful to realize that so many things I did and said seemed silly and self-defeating when I imagined a man saying or doing them! For example, my presentation of new ideas in a marketing meeting often went unnoticed or unheard. I usually phrased the ideas as questions—"Do you think we could do so and so?" and then giggled or wrinkled my nose as if even I thought my own ideas were dumb.

When my efficient and pleasant imaginary business*man* presented an idea, he stated it, gave one or two reasons why he thought it would work and then waited, poised yet smiling, during the following silence while people thought it over.

Oh, I was appalled! I was aware of how nervous I was, and how much I wanted the people above me to see my abilities and give me promotions. But my overeagerness and giggly, fluttering behaviors must have made me look like a "bird-brained female!" No wonder they didn't hear my ideas!

I started practicing a more poised, direct behavior. But it came across too harshly at first. I tried so hard not to flinch in the silence after my idea was presented that I probably had a pretty grim, almost belligerent look on my face. I was still not making much progress in communicating with businessmen. But I kept trying to find that fine line between being too silly and too harsh. And gradually, with a few months of practice, I began to feel more at ease in my new executive identity, and communication began to improve.

A multi-faced identity

But an interesting thing began to happen. I discovered that I had developed different versions of Andrea which reflected the different personalities or lives I was living. At work I was supposed to be the competent businesswoman from 8:00 to 5:00 weekdays. On the social scene, however, I wanted to be a fun, swinging date, so on evenings and weekends I was a different person with a different look and a different sound.

The third version was the regular-church-attending-Christian on Sundays. And at church my clothes, attitudes and style of relating were very different from those of the businesswoman *or* the swinging single. To my parents I was yet another person as I tried to appear to be the capable, optimistic daughter who was still the same sweet girl but more mature. They were 950 miles away and couldn't really know, so I would write letters that were carefully worded to portray this image, and on my visits home I would try to be that person.

I wasn't consciously dishonest in being these different people. It was just that I had unconsciously developed these personages to help me deal successfully with the various roles I found myself in—in a way that would win approval from the people to whom I was trying to relate.

Down inside was the real me, trying to pull all the strings and remember all the rules—codes of behavior, styles of dress and so on, in each of my lives. In reality I was often scared, hurt and lonely, and I was almost desperate. But somehow these different façades helped me appear to be in control and to cope for a while.

But then the four neatly divided areas of my life started getting fractured and tangled up. I started having trouble remembering where I had met people when I saw them in a different setting. If I had met someone at work and then saw him at church, I couldn't remember where I'd met him. But if I saw him back at work again, I'd know who he was instantly. And I also got caught if one person knew me in more than one setting, because she could see differences. And that made me uneasy. If someone knew me at work and then saw me out at a singles' party, I felt that the differences presented a shocking contrast. The contrast between my church self and social self *really* seemed great!

And the harder I tried to make all these parts of me fit together, the more inadequate, shaky, empty, and incomplete I seemed to be inside. It felt like I was looking at my reflection in a broken mirror with the pieces of my four lives overlapping, but not really presenting one congruent picture.

A longing for wholeness

After I made my beginning commitment to God, I was even more acutely aware of the fragmentation represented by my different lives. I wanted to feel like just *one* person again, to be put back together in such a way that people who knew me in *any* setting would agree that they knew the same woman. The sense that God was calling me to live with integrity gave me the motivation to begin to adjust my behaviors to this end.

As I thought about the fragmented condition my life was in, I began to wonder how in the world I'd developed four ways of being, like four separate combinations of masks and costumes to please the people in my different worlds.

CHAPTER FIVE

How We Get the Way We Are —The Story behind the Identity Search

---

NOTES

Dear Keith,

    I keep remembering our long, late night conversations about our struggles to grow and find out even a little bit about who we really are and why we act the way we do. And I've talked to other people who are also wondering who they are. Since it seems to be so important and so natural to find out who God made us to be if we want to know what He wants us to do, why do we all have to struggle so hard? Why are our own identities seemingly so well hidden from us?

    Would you take a few minutes to explain a little about the psychological processes that affect you and me and everybody concerning our identities?

A.

How did I get this way? and how can I become whole?—these were the questions I desperately wanted answers for when I became single. Over the years I have been helped a great deal by my friend Paul Tournier. And it was to him and his writings that I turned at this time.

No one, it seems, is really sure about how human development takes place. And it is apparent from reading in the field of developmental psychology that crucial experiences can happen to different children at different ages. But in order to get a rough picture of how our identities may develop, imagine with me for a few minutes that it is a simple story (which it is not, of course).

The "person"

From the time it's born a child responds naturally and openly to the people and events in his or her life with tears, contented looks or laughter. Dr. Tournier calls this natural responding self the child's "person." Along with the needs for food, water, air and sleep the child has an inherent need to be loved by its parents or caretakers. And all goes well as long as the natural responses of the child are not in conflict with the desires or beliefs of the parent figures.

For instance, a guest may be entranced with the cooing noises a baby is making in its high chair while waiting for breakfast. And the mother is delighted. But five minutes later when the baby blows a mouthful of warm otameal all over the guest's face and Sunday clothes—a trick very similar to cooing *from the baby's perspective*—the mother is furious, says "NO!" and slaps the baby's hand. And after a few more tries the baby realizes that he or she will not get love from mother by blowing oatmeal on guests. So the child learnes to hide the urge to blow oatmeal.

Personages

But there is a problem. The child has never hidden anything. Remember that the little "person" responds naturally and honestly. How then do we learn to hide our unacceptable feelings?

Tournier says that something happens at this point (at some point) which allows us to hide. We develop what he calls "personages." A personage is like a painted mask with expressions of the thoughts and feelings which I feel will get me love and acceptance from the people around me. All of us develop several of these personages/personalities, each with its own presenting language.

A child develops a "parent" personage—with a language all of its own for dealing with its parents. Andrea mentioned the four personages she developed: businesswoman, churchgoer, swinging single and responsible daughter. Her true person hid behind these four personages and tried to keep them operating separately.

In every major area of our lives, it seems, we develop a personage which is designed to portray to the people in authority in our group the proper images whereby we can gain their love or approval—regardless of what the actual feelings of our inner person may be about that group or activity.

The personage is not like the "mask" we speak of in America. The American mask is opaque. But a personage is partially transparent. That is, I am afraid for you to see through my personage for fear that you'll reject me, but I also *long* for you to see through the personage to the person hiding behind it—hoping that you will love me. But in actual experience we are usually not conscious of the fact that we even have personages. We just vaguely notice occasionally that we talk and act differently in different situations.

How do we develop "several lives"?

The way a child learns to develop personages could be something like this—although it no doubt happens at different times for different children.

Let's say that a little boy is about three or four years old and living in a small town. His mother walks with him to nursery school the first few days. The first time she walks him to school a certain way by the park. The next time she says, "You can also go around another way behind the stores." Finally, when he's learned how to get to and from nursery school well, she sends him off one morning by himself.

At this point in life the little boy thinks his mother knows everything he's thinking, because she says to him things like, "Son, you've got to potty," and she's right every time.

When he comes home from school by himself, his mother says, "How did you go to school?"

He says, "By the way of the park."

"How did you come home?"

"Behind the stores."

"What did the teacher say?"

In a few days the little boy gets very sick of this probing—after all, she knows what he's thinking so why all the questions? And after about a week he longs for a little privacy.

So one day when he gets home from school his mother says, "Which way did you go to school?" Well, he really went behind the stores, but he's decided he's going to do something today he's never done before— he's going to *lie.* So he says, "I went around by the park," and grits his teeth getting ready for the ax to fall, because he still thinks his mother can read his mind.

But his mother says, "What did the teacher say?" All of a sudden he realizes that his mother *doesn't know everything he's thinking!* Look at the possibilities this opens up for his life! Because now he can lead *two* lives. And his mother won't even *know* about one of them. He can think unacceptable thoughts and not be criticized. But he can also dream beautiful and creative dreams about the future without being laughed at. Suddenly he has realized he can *keep a secret!*

The danger of hiding thoughts and feelings

One of the most significant facts in developing an identity is this moment when a child learns that he or she can keep a secret, that the parents do not know what he or she is thinking. That is in fact the first step in gaining a separate identity.

When a child is able to keep a secret, he or she can hide those impulses to do things which are unacceptable to the parents and might lose their love—like the urge to blow warm oatmeal on visitors. But this ability to hide thoughts and feelings can also lead to some frightening misunderstandings which may shape the child's life.

For example, let's say that our little oatmeal-blower, Herkimer, is a few months older. He is out in the backyard playing in the rain. And in the mud near the neighbor's driveway he finds a rubber dolly. And he thinks, "Aha, a treasure!" He doesn't even know what a rubber dolly is. He doesn't have any sisters and has never seen a dolly up close.

So he brings this one in to his daddy and says, "Look, Daddy, look what I've found," hugging the dolly to his face. But the father's reaction is bewildering and strong.

"*Put that dolly down!*" he shouts. "Real boys don't play with dollies!" His neck is very red and his eyes are glowing with a strange look. Not knowing that the father is afraid the child will be gay if he plays with dolls, all the little boy realizes is that he has been rejected for sharing his real feelings. He now knows it's dangerous to show your treasures to your daddy. He'll hate you. Also it's even possible that the child may begin to get the idea that his daddy hates boys who like anything feminine. So he may reject girls and someday becomes the very thing his father feared, gay.

The shaping of identities by the rewards of affirmation

Since the child must have love and approval—or at least attention if he can't get them—he or she is very likely to repeat certain rewarded behaviors, when the price is right.

Let's say, for example, that our little Herkimer is sitting in church one morning between his parents as they are listening to the sermon. The kid is just looking around and trying not to go nuts from boredom while waiting for the sermon to be over. Suddenly the preacher makes a very dramatic point and there is a hush in the room. The little boy says in a clear resonant voice, "A-men."

Several things happen in the next few seconds. All eyes turn and look at the kid. His mother has a look of pleased wonder and surprise on her face (instead of the rejection he feared) as she whispers excitedly to his father, "Did you hear *that?* Little Herkimer said, 'Amen'!" And in that instant, a minister is born. Little Herkimer begins to realize that he can get the love he's starved for by praying and saying religious things. And as he hears his daddy tell a friend how well his boy prays at home, the religious interest is set. He is only three years old, but when he prays, magic takes place: his daddy loves him. And when Herkimer is thirty-five he may be the senior minister of the First Baptist (or Methodist or Presbyterian) Church.

But the danger of these hidden love transactions is that when Herkimer hits midlife he may feel very anxious and go to counseling, only to realize that he wasn't *called* to the ministry by *God*, but *sent* by his *mother* and *father*. They wanted him to be a minister. And he needed the love so much, first from them and then the others in the church, that he never stopped to consider what *he* wanted to do and be in life—apart from their wishes.

And although I assume that most ministers have valid calls from God, *some* people get their vocational identities the way little Herkimer did. Bank presidents sometimes have bank president sons who may wind up thirty years later hating money and banking. And the same thing can happen to business people, lawyers, doctors, or nurses.

Making bad choices to win love

If children do not develop a strong identity of their own, they may make all kinds of bad choices in order to win their parents' or other people's love. For instance, say that little Millie grows up having been trained to be a mommy. Everything is all right until she passes a certain age (e.g., eighteen, twenty-two, twenty-four) when young women in her parents' culture are "supposed to be" married.

A year or so after that age, if young Millie is not married, her mother gets very tense. She is threatened because her own ego is on the line. After all, Millie is her daughter, and if mother has done a good job, Millie should have caught a husband by now—or so the script goes. So the mother may start putting pressure on Millie to get serious about somebody she's dating.

Millie is not thinking about marriage at this time—or wasn't until her mother began telling her things like, "You aren't getting any younger, you know," and, "Look how many of your friends are getting married." And although Millie isn't really sure her boyfriend is who she ought to marry, she accelerates the relationship. And since she does want to get married someday, she falls in love *with the idea* of marrying the boyfriend. And six months later the marriage is consummated.

It's no wonder thousands of women—and men—are having not only marital problems but identity problems in their marriages. Many of them got married to get love from a third party, a parent.

And if the marriage does break up, the son or daughter may come home and be a child again under the loving but crippling rule of concerned parents he or she has never broken with—even though this "child" may be thirty-five and have four babies.

On the other hand, some children who don't make the adolescent break stay single because their mothers or fathers subtly or openly communicate the message that they need the child. Some parents get sick and want the child—often a daughter gets the assignment—to stay single and take care of them. This may happen even though the parent *says,* "No, no, you go on and live your life. Don't worry, I'll get along somehow." But the child receives a very different message at a semi-conscious level. I know that there may be situations in which this is justified. But, except in rare cases, I know of very few instances where the "child" who feels coerced into staying single is able to develop into a whole person with a strong identity. The parent usually says the child made a free choice. But the question of how free the choice was is a crucial issue in the development of the person.

If you have never been married, do not think I am saying "your parents kept you from it." I am only saying that in some cases these behaviors take place and the person who remains single is baffled and wonders how it all happened.

Some of the most serious adjustment problems in adult life spring from the unspoken messages often unconsciously sent or received between parents and children after a child learns to keep secrets.

Choosing to reveal your secrets—The second step

But being able to keep a secret is only the first step in this process toward wholeness or having a stable sense of identity. If you can keep secrets you can become an individual. But to be a whole person with an identity which is relatable to other people and which is capable of intimacy, one must enter a second movement. The secret-keeper must become free to choose to *tell another person* his or her secrets, what is inside the "person." And this sharing can be the doorway to intimacy. I'm not saying that to be a whole person you *must* tell all that is inside. (I agree with those who think that if you can't ever keep a secret, or have no private areas of your own, you may be neurotic.)

But to be whole, a person should *be able to choose* to tell his or her secrets if and when it seems appropriate. A lot of people simply can't tell their true feelings at all—under any circumstances. It's just too scary.

For example, many of our first comments about sex were unacceptable to parents, so even as adults we feel worthless or guilty when we engage in sexual thoughts or sexual behavior of any kind. And dreams about a vocation parents don't approve are often hidden from the world forever, because when we were little our parents said, "No," *or we thought they did,* when we mentioned being a writer, a football player, an evangelist or a ballerina. And so we hid our dreams inside. And those hidden and unacceptable thoughts and dreams become a secret nest of sadness and disappointment in which our God-created persons often hide.

The fear of being known as we really are

Since we only remember the emotional impact (at age two or three) of our parents' rejection of certain *ideas*—accompanied by the fear that they may be *rejecting us* —we tend to grow up with inordinate fears of showing anyone else our true inner person with all of the collected ideas, feelings, secret sins, hopes and dreams we cherish, but which we felt were unacceptable to our parents. And these fears are just as real *whether or not* the feelings expressed were actually unacceptable.

When we became adults, most of us were afraid to check out how our parents actually felt about our childhood feelings. And in any case we have usually forgotten the *content* of the earlier transactions. Only the fears of revealing our person remain.

The tragedy is that this inability to share our true feelings keeps us from the intimacy in which we could verify the fact that our true identity—our true "person"—is actually okay and even lovable.

The "energy crisis" caused by hiding feelings and thoughts

What often happens is that as we grow up, we polish our outer personages until we honestly believe they are the real us. But when the personages, the behaviors we have to show to the world in order to get love and approval, get *very* different from the feelings and values of our inner person, we become worried and afraid of our "deception" being discovered—as Andrea did with her four personalities. And to keep peace within ourselves, we often repress our true feelings, keeping them out of sight in our unconscious. And when we do, we may find ourselves living by strange values, and sometimes we find to our dismay that even *we* can't know what we are really like any more.

But these repressed honest feelings seem to have a great deal of energy connected to them. They are like great beach balls which we have forced "underwater" in the depths of our lives. It takes a lot of energy to hold such feelings down, and the further we push them from consciousness the greater the pressure and psychic energy it takes to keep them out of sight.

Many people who have beachballed their true persons and pushed them further and further from the personages they present to the world become very anxious "for no reason at all" and feel "out of touch" with themselves. Pretty soon the anxiety may become unmanageable and they may experience all kinds of neurotic and unreasonable fears. The feelings which accompany this sort of experience can constitute a real "identity crisis." Andrea described a little about such feelings when she woke up alone one Saturday morning.

How can we recover our repressed identities?

If our true identity, our true person, is denied and even forced into our unconscious lives because it is so threatening to be ourselves, then how can we get in touch with our identities?

We must enter a relationship in which we may begin to feel safe enough for these buried feelings to come to our awareness. There have been times and places in the church's history when Christians went to other Christians for this kind of open dialogue between "persons." But as I have spoken in churches across America and talked to lay people and ordained ministers in many denominations, I have come to believe that today there is apparently so little genuine intimacy in the average congregation that many people feel it is not really safe to reveal one's hostile, aggressive, or sexual thoughts and feelings there.

So what many of us do when the anxiety gets severe enough is to go to a professional counselor, hoping that he or she will not judge us as being too awful if we find we have unacceptable traits and thoughts in our personality.

But unfortunately it's not that simple. In the first place many of the personage behaviors we initially took on to win love have become real for us, and we wouldn't want to shuck them. For example, little Herkimer may have come to love God and want to be a minister for his own reasons.

In the second place, since we don't even *know* what thoughts or feelings are in our unconscious minds, we can't just "tell them" to someone. Even when we think we want to be open, we sometimes just "don't know what to say."

Feelings and emotions are not evil

Besides, there are some presuppositions many Christians have which can be directly destructive to spiritual and emotional wholeness. For example, many Christians believe that pain, anger, and anxiety are evil or signs of sin. But the truth is, it seems to me, that pain and hostility are like "fire alarm systems" for the body and mind. They are *good* things which can save our lives!

Imagine that you were running barefoot on the beach one day and cut your foot on a jagged piece of dirty glass. Without pain you might keep running until you fainted from lack of blood. But pain is like an alarm which goes off in your head saying in effect, "Look at foot; foot bleeding; get help!" And the pain keeps throbbing until you get help. And even with a terminally ill cancer patient, the pain is saying in more and more poignant terms, *"Please* get help or you're going to die!" The disease is evil but the pain is an ally.

And anger and anxiety are like psychological alarm systems. Hostility at a deep level is often simply the other side of the coin of *fear.* When a rage comes over you, it wouldn't be a bad idea to sit down and ask God, "What am I *afraid* of?" Because when you are really angry (or anxious) it may well mean that you are afraid of something you can't face. Someone or something is threatening your happiness.

But when people look at hostility as evil and try to repress it as being unchristian, they never can find out what they are afraid of, what is really causing their anxious condition. The main point about feelings of anger and aggression is not that they are evil but that they can *tell us things about ourselves which can bring us into a more authentic and Christian way of living* and give us a better grasp of our true identity.

The person-dialogue: a passageway to the submerged identity

When the separation of our personages from our person gets great enough that we repress our person's feelings and get terribly anxious, we often go for help. Let's say that I've decided to go to a counselor. As I indicated earlier we usually resist going because we are afraid to invite someone inside to see behind our personages for fear we won't be accepted. And many of us would rather have a miserable condition we're familiar with than the hope of finding a wonderful condition by taking the risk to discover what we have hidden inside ourselves.

But let's assume that the anxiety gets too heavy, so I go to a counselor. Here I may enter what Tournier calls a "person-dialogue." This happens when two people are willing to lay down their personages and talk about their real feelings—their persons. All healing starts when the client or patient quits communicating through his or her personages and begins to talk directly about real feelings.

But the process is long and sometimes fearful. When you are a counselee and you get one honest unflattering feeling out, it feels as if you have found a little thread sticking out of the corner of your mouth. By expressing the feeling you are handing the thread to the therapist.

As he or she responds, it's as if the thread is pulled a little. And you find there is a string tied to the thread—a deeper feeling—and as the string is drawn out, there's a rope tied to it. And there is a chain tied to the rope. But as you feel the chain coming out you can almost hear a "bucket of garbage" coming up tied to the chain.

And there is a feeling of terror at the idea of the counselor seeing the bucket, because you feel somehow like that bucketful is your real person and that its contents are totally unacceptable.

But (if you are fortunate) up it comes. And to you it seems as if it will look dreadful, like smelly garbage. But when it comes out into the light, it may be a bucketful of gems, of authentic feelings—which are often rare and beautiful in their honesty—even if the feelings are hostile or erotic ones which have never been allowed to surface. And that's a great deal of what our lack of self-worth, our lack of identity, is about: our fear that our true person will be seen as worthless, unpleasant garbage.

But the miraculous thing about the person-dialogue is that when a person "comes out" and is honest about who he or she really is—with true feelings attached—and is sort of emotionally naked before us on any significant level, I have found him or her always to have a haunting family resemblance to Jesus Christ. *Real* people being vulnerable are, it seems, beautiful and lovable. It is when we are hiding and defensive that we are ugly and unlovable. I have never seen an ugly real one (although I've heard some ugly statements come out when people have gotten real). And yet that is the very thing we are afraid to do—pull the person, what we really are, the "bucket of garbage," out to be seen by another human being.

But when we can do this with someone who really accepts us, we can begin to get well and whole. And as we get our true feelings and hopes and dreams out, we can begin to discover who we really are and what we want to be and do. We begin to discover our identity as persons.

CHAPTER SIX

Making the Parent Break

NOTES

Dear Keith,

It must be interesting to see from the perspective of both a son and a father the necessity for people to break from their parents. How did you as a son handle the break from your own parents?

In some ways growing into adulthood seems natural. We grow up, get a job, move away from home and parents. But isn't there a need to separate from parents at a deeper, emotional level? How can we, as Christians, whether we have married or not, become self-reliant adults (i.e., not leaning on mothers or fathers) and still maintain a loving relationship with our parents?

Since I have no children, I haven't faced the problem of children breaking from me. Is there anything helpful you can say to parents whose children may be trying to make a break?

Andrea

A few years ago, I was sitting in a discussion group with a group of Americans, mostly medical doctors and counselors. The leader, an outstanding psychotherapist, had just been asked, "What is the most important single psychological transaction in the development of a healthy adult?"

Without hesitation, he replied, "The most important life transaction is how the child negotiates a clear break with its father."

At the time I had been uneasy, realizing that I didn't know if I'd made such a break myself, and I was almost forty at that time.

Whatever else I thought then, I certainly did *not* suspect that my father was invisibly perched on my shoulder all my adult years, running a good bit of my life *in absentia* while I thought I was running it. And yet this was true, although I didn't face it consciously until almost nine years later, when I was trying to sort my life out with a counselor at the end of my first marriage.

It seemed strange to me to have to begin dealing openly with my relationship with my father at age forty-nine—especially since both he and my mother had been dead for almost twenty years. But before I could discover and establish my own identity as a person apart from their interjected demands and control, I had to do just that.

How can we grow up—Do we have to "hate" our parents?

Since I am a Christian son and also a parent, I know how hard this sort of discussion is. If you are a parent you may be angry if I am honest about the way it feels to be the child. And if you are having difficulty with your parents, you may feel guilty or anxious because you are not facing your relationship with them. Making the break with parents is particularly difficult because there is a sense in which a child *must* "hate" his or her parents in order to grow into a free adult, especially as a Christian. Jesus taught us the necessity for this break. "Hatred," in the way Jesus uses it with regard to parents, evidently means to "pull away from" as the controlling force in one's life (see Luke 14:26). But in spite of Jesus' admonition that we must hate our own fathers and mothers in order to be his disciples, we have a double problem as Christians. We are not supposed to "hate" anyone. And yet there is a *natural* resentment which almost all children have for their parents during adolescence.

As an adolescent, experimenting with alternative values and ideas, I deeply resented my father's apparent attempts to brainwash me into maintaining his views. We argued incessantly, it seemed to me. And sometimes I got so angry I felt that I hated him. But I have learned that these strong feelings of irrational hatred and resentment are most damaging *not* when they are expressed openly but when they are repressed and denied, as happens often, *especially* in Christian families. Not only are we Christians taught that we aren't supposed to hate *anyone*, but particularly *not* our parents. So we often "beachball" our feelings of deep resentment for our mothers and/or fathers.

What if parents think we are being sinful?

One thing which keeps many *Christian* singles from breaking with their parents is what I believe to be a misunderstanding of the powerful biblical injunction to "honor thy father and thy mother." Parents even quote this to their adolescent children who are rebelling. But there comes a time in every person's development when it is no longer honoring your parents to let them control your life—even if refusing to let them do so hurts the parents deeply.

Have you ever seen a parent almost completely spoil a child saying, "I just couldn't bear to hurt her. I love her too much to confront her"? The sad truth is that because of the parent's lack of courage the child may suffer the rest of her life.

But if you turn this around, it's possible for grown children to "spoil" their parents in a similar way. Let's say the son or daughter needs desperately to make a clear emotional break with the still-controlling parents. But if the "child" says, "I just couldn't bear to hurt them by confronting them," a sad thing can happen. The child may simply withdraw emotionally or move away to another part of the country. And the relationship deteriorates (with the parents being left angry and bewildered). When children don't make a clear break it sometimes becomes impossible for the parents to pass through the next stage of *their own* growing up as people. Parents *need* to turn loose of their grown children and get on with their own lives. But this parent-break business is often very frightening. I made this sort of break with my mother when I was about twenty-three.

Making a (mother) parent break

My father had died several months before. And since my brother had been killed, I was the only remaining child, and I was newly married.

Mother didn't have to work. She was an intelligent, capable, strong and loving person. But when she came to visit my wife and me, she very subtly tried to run things—from the kitchen to my "weight and general health." She would say, upon entering our front door, "Oh, Keith, you look so *thin!* I'll have to fatten you up!" My wife was furious, but helpless. After all, my mother was a sweet woman and had lost her husband. The conflict was terrible for me—in the middle.

Finally, I realized how wrong all this was. I went to see my mother alone. All the way to her house, I thought, "I can't do this. If I tell her things have to change and that my wife is first with me (ahead of her), she'll feel rejected and I'll feel guilty and like a terrible son." I fantasized her "hurt look," which always made me feel like a dirty dog.

As I pulled in the driveway at her house I knew this was going to be an agonizing encounter, and almost decided to put it off again. But I realized it had to be done. I opened the back door. "Hi mom! Anybody here?"

When we'd had dinner I told her my concern and how hard it was to talk about. Finally I said, "You've always been a wonderful mother, but I'm married now and you're not first in my life anymore." She just looked at me. And I went on. I didn't know much about Christianity at that time, but I reminded her that the Bible said to "leave your father and mother and cling to your wife," and that I was going to do that.

"We want you to visit us often," the words rushed on, "but when you come to our house in the future, you're not in charge of the kitchen or running the house, and I'm going to stand by my wife if you try to control her." She just looked at me in disbelief. I told her that I loved her very much and that I wasn't sure why, but that what I was doing just had to be right.

She wept, and I felt terrible. I thought she would never speak to me. I told her again that I loved her, but I didn't apologize or try to back down as I always had when she'd cried and been hurt. I just sat there. It was an awful time. Finally I left. But a week later she called to tell us happily that she had gotten a position as a hostess in a sorority house. And she got up from her bed of grief over my dad's death and became an effective and productive person the rest of her life, because she needed to make the break too. And I could then relate to her as an adult—at least most of the time.

I realize that singles don't have the problem of a competitive relationship between parents and mates to drive them to make a parent break, but every person who hopes to become a free adult must at least make some kind of emotional separation from the people who raised him or her.

It is healthy and right for singles to begin to make this break even before marriage if they are through with school and in the job market. But often the temptation for singles is to put it off until marriage because they may not believe they are really adults without a mate. And the parent(s) may be unconsciously and even lovingly promoting the feeling of dependency by continuing to offer support and advice, thus treating their single adult son or daughter as if he or she were still a child.

Even Jesus made the break

Even Jesus broke with His mother publicly in what must have been a very painful experience for her. To disobey your parents was a "stoning" offense, just as adultery was, according to the Law. But once when Jesus was in a meeting, His mother and brothers arrived outside and sent word to Him to come out to them. He didn't obey and He replied, "Who are my mother and brothers?" And pointing to His peers and fellow adventurers for God, He said in effect, "Tell my mother I'm not coming out. This is my family." He was making a definite break with His own mother, and did not let her control his actions (see Mark 3:31–35).

Jesus was saying in loud clear words and actions, "I am not primarily my mother's son any more. I have another identity and I must be true to that." We assume that Jesus always honored His father and His mother. But He also clearly broke with His parents when He had to in order to grow up and be the separate person He was made to be.

I am of course *not* saying that we should be cruel to our mothers and fathers. But I do believe that if we do not break the dependent parent-child relation with them, then sooner or later, our lovers, mates, friends, and God will miss a true relationship with us.

What if I missed the break as an adolescent? Is it too late?

Don't think that because you are over twenty-five the necessity to break from the emotional apron strings doesn't apply. I was almost fifty years old when I faced the relationship with my father, even though he had been dead for twenty years. (One's parents do not have to be alive for you to make the break. Also they can be very old or middle-aged—or young—when you cut loose.) This is the way it happened to me with regard to my father.

It was during the last days of my first marriage, and I was in counseling. It was apparent to the counselor that my first wife and I weren't going to make it in our marriage. And he said so. But even though I agreed with him that this was probably true, there was something deep inside saying, "No, even if you die, Keith, you *cannot* get a divorce!" I was unconsciously slowly killing myself psychologically because it seemed better to die than to go against my father's voice inside my head.

In a guided fantasy the counselor had me close my eyes and go back in my imagination to my early childhood. I had pretty well repressed my growing up, especially my relationship with my dad. And when I had thought of him, I hadn't consciously considered our relations as being painful. I'd always felt that he loved me. Of course I always knew he loved my older brother more—everyone said so. But consciously I'd just accepted that fact and gone on. That's the way it had felt at the conscious level.

But in the guided fantasy I got in touch with how much I'd really loved my dad; how much I had wanted him to love me, and how very much his approval had meant to me—and still did. I saw that in some ways I'd played my whole life to him as the audience. He had, without ever knowing it, controlled my life through the giving or withholding of his approval. And for the twenty years following his death I had unconsciously kept him alive in my head, evidently hoping somehow to win his love.

The therapist asked me if I wanted to change the relationship and declare my independence from my father. I opened my eyes and said that I really did. After all, at best it was an impossible game I was playing with my dad. Who can win proof of the love of a dead person? So the counselor asked me to close my eyes again and to picture in my imagination the setting in which I had last seen my father alive.

In my mind I was again in the hospital room in which dad had died. I saw him in the bed, just as he had been, his face twisted in pain. (I had been the only one present when he had died.)

It was a private room, and he was lying there turning in the sheets, his face very flushed. I was frantic and had pushed the call button, but couldn't find anyone to come. I was in the midst of that scene again in a deep part of my mind. And all of a sudden I realized I *had* to tell my dad to get out of my life and stay out, that my own future and health depended on it.

I felt a rising sense of panic with my eyes still closed and actually began to perspire. I remember looking at my dad's contorted face and, knowing how sick he was, being afraid and very sad at the same time.

I shook my head and said to myself, "You *can't* tell him to get out of your life when he's *dying!*" But I remembered that all my life I'd had "good reasons" not to confront him, not to tell him that I am my own person and not his property. I had usually thought my reluctance was because I loved him and didn't want to hurt him. And that was true, but the real reasons were that I was afraid to confront him and that I needed something from him I'd never gotten—his blessing or total approval or something. So I'd never been able to break from him. But now I realized that I had to. Then I felt a surge of anger and frustration which I'd repressed all my life.

In the anger and terror of a young boy I turned to him in the bed in my fantasy and shouted, "Get out of my life, and stay out! You had a chance to live your life, and I've got to live mine regardless of whether I hurt you or not. So get out of my life—and stay!"

I was sweating all over as I sat there. And in the fantasy in my imagination the figure in the bed turned into a genie-like apparition and and started floating head first toward the ceiling. I was terrified. There was a small square window in the ceiling of the hospital room. I remember climbing a stepladder, which had appeared from somewhere, and helping the figure out of the window—which I realized was out of my life.

But the figure just seemed to keep coming. Now it was like a sheet, unfolding, an endless sheet. And I kept poking it out the window, yard after yard after yard, terrified that it would never quit coming, that I'd never be able to stop doing this, or he'd be back where he'd always been—controlling my life. My arms seemed about to fall off when I finally came to the end of the sheet. And with a great effort I pushed it out and closed the window!

I just stood there on the ladder, exhausted. I could not bring myself to turn and look toward the bed. I must have waited five minutes before I dared look, because I knew he was going to be there. And if he was, I knew I'd never be free. Finally I turned and forced myself to look at the bed. And . . . he was gone!!!

I couldn't believe it. A surge of happiness came from deep within me and seemed to fill the room with light. And I took a deep breath—clear back to my eleventh year, a deep breath. And then came the tears. I knew that somehow I was now a man and could be responsible for my own life without having to earn my dad's approval at every turn. (And interestingly, I feel more free to love my dad now.)

After that encounter I began to be able to take responsibility for my own actions and to relate with more freedom in all my close relationships. And I am beginning to try to free my own children to be who they want to be—even when it's not what I would have chosen.

What should you do about cutting the apron strings?

I am *not* saying that you *have to* go and tell your parents to bug off. What I am saying is that I believe God wants each one of us to become the free and creative person He designed. If this is true, then you have a right, even a duty, to stand up and take the freedom *and* the responsibility for your own life when the time comes. And if as adults we let our parents make our decisions for us, we are not being responsible stewards of our lives.

You may be saying, "Boy, are you tough on parents, especially Christian parents who love their children dearly." You bet I'm tough on the parents *who keep trying to control* their children's lives after they are out of the nest. I sometimes *am* such a parent. And when I discover it, I'm tough on myself—every time it happens.

But if you are single and have never broken from your parents, this time of being a single adult may be the best time (regardless of your age) for you to make a loving but clear break from their unhealthy control of your life. Because if you are aware that they are controlling your life (and you are a Christian) you have to bear the responsibility for continuing to be a "slave." Once you know that you are being controlled as a grown person you can either say, "Yes, I'm going to let them control my life," or you can make a break. But don't be naïve. The way you decide about this matter will have an enormous effect on the long-term success of your intimate relationships with the opposite sex.

Of course, this whole chapter may not apply to you. If you feel that it doesn't, don't worry about it. But if you feel you must make some decisions and talk to your parents, pray about it first and then be as gentle as you can (if you can). We parents didn't invent the system, nor in most cases do we understand it. But in our hearts most of us know that God only loaned you to us to raise—though sometimes it's very hard to give you back to Him so He can fulfill His plans for you.

NOTES

Dear Andrea,

Writing my part of this chapter really stirred up some deep feelings in me. And I've been sitting here thinking about my dad and my mother and how grateful I am for them—and how much I love them.

For a Christian girl to make an "emotional break" with her parents sounds almost like heresy. But since it is necessary for each Christian to find his or her identity in Christ, would you tell a little about your struggle to stay in a loving relationship with your mother and father and yet to cut the apron strings and become an adult as a Christian single? What were some of the ways you began to change your communication to an adult-to-adult relating? Was it easy? Was it worth it?

This sure is a touchy area. I know there are no hard and fast rules about this part of growing up. Will you just describe what happened to you, how you felt, as you tried?

K.

After the rainy Saturday morning I had spent wondering what other people would expect me to do with the time I had that day, I realized how much I still depended on my parents' opinions and values, especially mother's. I had molded myself to be like my image of her so much that I seemed to have very little identity of my own.

Right after my divorce was final, my parents, wanting to help me, offered to let me move back home with them or to send me money. These offers were amazing to me because after I got out of college I'd had the (correct) impression that they were nudging me out of the nest, ready for me to move out, get a job or go to graduate school. And I'd unconsciously assumed that meant "forever."

But I also remember feeling after my divorce that for my own sake I had to know if I was *ever* going to be able to support myself alone— without parental help—or anyone's help. The thought of returning to their home seemed to increase the sense of failure I felt at having to get a divorce. To return to the nest, manless and jobless was something I wanted to avoid.

I reacted with anger at their suggestions (because my fear of not making it as an independent person was so great) and vowed that even if I had to live on "tomato soup and crackers," I would survive on my own! I remember using those words and really meaning them. I managed to move into a apartment and pay the rent, car payment, insurance, gas and groceries with my clerk-typist salary—and still have $5.00 a month left over with which I could do whatever I wanted! (like buy magazines, toothpaste, etc.).

Mother was having a difficult time of her own, because three of her four offspring were at crisis points. I was separated, considering divorce, one of my sisters was to have her first child any day, and my other sister was moving away to live independently in another city. All

83

of mom's birds who had left the nest (my brother was still at home) were flying "wobbly."

After the birth of her granddaughter, mother flew to Mississippi, where my sister and her husband lived, to help with the new baby for a week. Then she came on to Texas to check up on me (at least that's how I viewed her coming). I was happy that she cared enough to come, but I felt anxiety about whether I would measure up to her standards—and I doubted that I would.

I had very little furniture, including only one borrowed twin bed in my bedroom. I managed to borrow another one just before mother arrived. When she got off the little commuter plane, she was in a state of fatigue from being a brand-new grandmother for a week. So I had the remarkable experience of taking care of my own mother for the first time. It was so different from what I had imagined!

I had expected to have to stand up to this well-meaning lady who was going to come in and take over my life like a mother hen, but she just arrived—tired and glad that the baby had been fine and my sister was also healthy. She slept late while I went to work. I came home to eat lunch with her and then she read and relaxed while I was at work in the afternoon. Then we talked and visited in the evenings. Everything, I decided, looked like I had my life "under control."

The day she left, I remember calmly taking her to the airport and cheerily waving goodbye as she walked away to get on the plane. I stood around the airport watching until the little plane was *completely* out of sight before I was ready to go to my car to begin to drive home. About 100 yards from the front entrance of the airport a huge wave of sadness washed over me and I pulled off the road, threw my arms onto the top of the steering wheel and let the tears come. I cried so hard my stomach hurt.

Suddenly I heard a knocking sound on the car window. With a start I sat up and peered through my watery red eyes straight into the face of a concerned-looking policeman. I was so embarrassed! I rolled down the window and he said, "Pardon me for disturbing you, but are you all right?"

Gulping to control the sobs, I took a couple of deep breaths and said in a funny, shaky high voice, "Yes, my mother just left and I just realized how much I'm going to miss her." Then I gave my best trying-to-look-okay smile, still blinking back the tears, and felt very childish, sobbing like that about my mommy. When would I ever grow up?

The weeks went on and the decision to file for a divorce had to be made. Finally, I filed. After that, I began to realize that on a certain day in July I would no longer be married. When the day came, I began to feel a need to visit my family. I was suddenly strangely proud of my new independence and sense of responsibility and accomplishment after the months of difficult decisions and scary appointments with lawyers, judges, counselors and so on. And also, I wanted to find out if my family would love me . . . even if I were divorced.

A girlfriend, Charlotte, had never been out of Texas, and the idea of going to the Smokies seemed like fun to her, too. So we decided to drive my car across Texas, Arkansas and Tennessee and into Georgia, spending two weeks visiting various members of my family.

We arrived in Tennessee, and my parents greeted us with hugs and smiles. We spent a few days with them, and I showed Charlotte my home town. A few days later we all drove down to Atlanta where dad's family lives. Mom's family drove up from Florida. The occasion was a gala family gathering for a large group photograph.

My grandfather on mother's side of the family is a Baptist minister. He had performed my wedding ceremony, and I hadn't seen him since the wedding day. As I drove with mom and dad to the motel where he was staying with my grandmother, I kept wondering how this must look to him: his granddaughter, whom he hadn't seen since he performed her wedding, now divorced. I dreaded the meeting.

I remember starting to walk up a long grassy hill to where he stood. He came down the hill toward me, and before I could think of anything "adequate" to say, he hugged me and said with a twinkle of love in his eye, "You know, I've been wondering what I said wrong."

I just melted on his shoulder and cried for a minute, then looked up at his smiling, wet-eyed face. I couldn't think of a thing to say, and he didn't say anything else either. With his arm around my shoulder we just walked together back up the hill to the rest of the family. I realized more fully than ever before what loving forgiveness feels like, and felt easier about facing the other members of the family.

The rest of the time in Atlanta was warm and fun. I felt my roots again. One night the whole family and Charlotte went out to dinner at a well-known restaurant decorated like the movie set from *Gone With the Wind*. I remember we were all waiting to be seated, scattered around on a balcony which resembled a southern veranda, sitting in old rocking chairs or on benches. The maître d' came out and announced, "The Wells party of . . . twenty-three?" and looked amazed. I felt proud to be a Wells and glad I'd taken my maiden name back.

But after Charlotte and I had driven back to Texas and I began to settle into the day-to-day living routine in Waco, I found that in my letters and calls I began to behave toward mom and dad much as I had behaved during mom's earlier visit. I tried to appear to be capable and happy, yet I often wanted to turn into a three-year-old, suck my thumb and have one of them rock me to sleep at night. I was horrified at this feeling—fearing that I might not be capable of growing up after all—fearing that if I let them know these childish feelings they would try to persuade me to move back home so they could "take me over" again. So although I tried not to lie, I edited out lots of the pain and fear in my communication with them. And I felt *driven* to prove to them and to myself that I could manage to live a mature adult life, and overcome the deep dependence I now realized I had.

A symbolic parent break

One afternoon as I was thinking about my relationship with mom and dad, I realized with a shock that if mom needed to find anything in my apartment kitchen, she could probably guess exactly where to look . . . and she'd be right! As soon as I could, I rushed home from work, threw my coat and purse down and went to the kitchen. After standing there with my hands on my hips, looking around, I decided what I had to do.

I took everything out of the cabinets and spread it out on the counter. Then I put everything back—but in completely different places. I put silverware in the bottom drawer, plates in the top drawer, boxed foods and spices where the pots and pans used to be and pots and pans where the food went. I got tickled when I imagined her face if she were to open the cabinet doors, and I started giggling while I worked. Even though I was alone in the apartment, I finally laughed out loud and started feeling happy, excited and free! Although what I'd just done might seem childish (and I later readjusted some drawers for more convenience), that afternoon symbolized for me the beginning of the feeling that I was taking control of my life.

"Returning home"—A first step

About four years after the divorce, I was at my parents' home for another Christmas visit. By then, I had begun to realize some things concerning the way I had been communicating about myself and my feelings. I had been trying to put the four Andreas back together again and to be the same person at work, on dates, at church and at home. And I had been praying that God would help me see my own faults with regard to communicating with my parents.

One afternoon I was with dad in the living room. I had been thinking about something I'd done a few months earlier when he had come to visit me on the way to a business meeting. I ordinarily would never mention anything I considered to be one of my mistakes to my parents, but this time I wanted to talk about it.

Sometimes I felt dad had a way of talking about impersonal subjects, leaving little, if any, time in a visit to talk about our feelings, both his and mine, which I longed to do (but which I didn't do either). On this particular visit it *seemed to me* as if he had been avoiding being personal for the two days we were together. In my frustration and insensitivity, I had "gotten him back," and I thought at the time I was only "being honest." But I realized later that the way I had done it must have hurt him very much, and I wanted to tell him I was sorry.

So I started out by saying, "Dad, when you visited me last fall, all that time we were together I felt kind of frustrated because of the way you talked—"

He surprised me by saying, "Oh, I know I do that when I'm—"

But I stopped him and said, "Wait. I have realized something that I do to retaliate. Right when you are ready to leave, I tell you how miserable I have been; but I wait until it is too late for you to do anything about it. I should tell you sooner, while we still have time to talk and then we can part on good terms."

I had done exactly that the previous fall. I had waited until we were in the car on the way to the airport before I had told him my feelings.

And I had seen when I spoke the words that they had stabbed him. I had gotten even, and I had not even realized it until months later.

I sat shaking in the chair beside the Christmas tree, wondering what would happen now that I had admitted this painful truth. It was new for me to talk about things like this. When I tried to give the impression that I was calm and composed, I began to notice the "nervous" behavior of the rest of the family. In fact, it was so unusual for me to be aware of things like this that I wrote it all down in my journal that night.

Dad was pacing back and forth in front of the Christmas tree. Mom was in the kitchen, putting away the clean dishes from the dishwasher. The dishes seemed to make a lot of noise to me, as if she wanted us to know she was there. My high-school-age brother was in the den, playing the piano. He was playing a nice little Mozart sonatina, but it seemed much too fast to me. It reminded me of an overwound music box.

All their nervous behavior was due, I was certain, to this rare moment of deeply personal communication between dad and me. And I was feeling so proud of myself for being able to do this so calmly. Then I looked down in my lap. And I had to laugh inside, because unknowingly I had created a big pile of shredded wrapping paper which showed me that I was probably more nervous than any of them!

That moment turned out to be the beginning of one of the best visits I had ever had with my parents, because they began to talk with me as if I were another adult. I was thirty years old, but it was the first time I remember ever feeling that level of communication with them. And I think now that my own fear of being personal might have kept this from happening years before.

We talked about the years when I was a child. Mother shared her concern that she had done certain things that might have contributed to the problems I had in my marriage and as a single person. And I was surprised to see that the things which seemed traumatic to her were things I could barely remember. I had a different set of memories about our trouble spots growing up, and hesitantly, I shared some of these.

I slowly began to realize that when I can come to my parents as an adult, not whining about my difficulties, or complaining about the way life is treating me (or the way they are treating me) but rather facing up to my own faults and ways *I* have *hurt them,* then they can get out of their parent role for a while and we can meet as adults on more equal ground. But when I approach them as a little girl, implying, "Mommy and daddy, I need you," that seems to make it harder for them to keep from trying to run my life, give advice and make my decisions for me.

But as I saw the positive value of cutting the unhealthy ties with my parents, I also had to come to grips with some of the "cords" or crutches which parents unconsciously use to keep their children tied to them. I began to worry about how I was going to get along without their involvement. For example, now that I had taken the first step toward breaking from dad by declining his offer of financial help, how *was* I going to manage financially? What sacrifices would I have to make in order to support myself?

CHAPTER SEVEN
The Problem of Money

NOTES

Dear Andrea,

Since the financial world in America still seems to be a male—dominated culture, how does it feel to be a single woman dealing with the problems of money? How did you go about establishing your financial independence? Was it hard to accept gifts? I remember your telling me about some of your strong emotional reactions to problems relating to money.

Would you tell a little about the way you went about trying to sort out your own basic financial needs? How did you work out a budget to live on a smaller income? What were some of the things you hadn't counted on which knocked you for a loop? How did you feel about giving part of your income to God? And finally how did you plan for your own financial future?

This is a hard one to talk about for most people. But lots of singles tell me money problems are some of the hardest they face.

Keith

I walked nervously into the bank lobby and looked around. There was a group of desks in one corner, arranged beside some windows with long drapes, and lots of green plants sitting in graceful attitudes beside each desk. The woman nearest the door smiled at me, so I walked over to her and said, "I'd like to open a Master Charge account, please."

She said, "Certainly. Let me have your name and I'll tell Ms. Chadwell that you're here." After she left, I sat down on the blue vinyl couch opposite her desk and waited.

This was my second visit of this type to the bank. The first one had been nine months earlier when I had opened my own checking account. Now I had decided it was time to have my own Master Charge card. I thought about all the credit cards I had when I graduated from college, the ones that had arrived in the mail with letters saying, "Congratulations on earning your college degree! We want to help you get started in your life as a college graduate!" I had canceled several when I had married, since we only needed one account between us. How I wished I had kept my own accounts now!

My thoughts were interrupted by the smiling woman, who told me that Ms. Chadwell was ready to see me, and showed me where I should go. I thanked her and walked across the hard blue carpet to a chair beside a desk in the far corner. A pretty blond woman who wore her hair in a smooth, neat French twist greeted me by standing and shaking my hand. I felt excited and nervous as I took my seat and told her why I had come.

She said her name was Margie, and that she was in charge of all Master Charge accounts at the bank. She then told me about the application forms. I filled out a long one-page form, and listed my checking account, savings account, Exxon credit card number and two loans which had been in my name (even though I was married)' and which were now completely paid off. I thought it looked like a pretty good credit record, and so did Margie. She thanked me for coming in and told me it would take about ten days to process the form and she'd mail me my new card when everything was approved. I left feeling good about my new life and the way I was taking control of it.

About two weeks later, I got a call at work from Margie. There were some questions she had to ask me, so would I come by to see her after work? I immediately felt apprehensive, but her tone sounded so friendly that I tried not to worry.

When I was once again seated across from her, she said that they could not find any records of my credit history at the Credit Bureau. I told her I had been married and that I was now using my maiden name. Then she told me about how credit files are kept.

"If two people are married," she told me, "both people's records are kept in a folder together. If a divorce happens, the woman had to go in and fill out a form, pay a fee of $5.00 to have her credit records set up in a separate folder."

Suddenly the whole situation seemed like a huge problem! With my budget, I had little room for $5.00 fees to be paid for a Credit Bureau to "straighten out its own files." From my perspective it seemed that if they kept my records in with my ex-husband's, then *their* files would be inaccurate. And if he remarried, then they would have two women's records in that folder. That would *really* be inaccurate!

"Why don't they require *men* to fill out forms and pay fees?" The thought screamed at me in my mind as the angry tears jumped to my eyes and I fought to stay calm.

Then finally I said, "Thank you for trying, Margie. I guess I'll just try to establish some credit with my maiden name and then come back and apply again. I am not going to go down there and pay that fee. I don't think it's fair."

I left, feeling sad and very invisible. Where could I begin to establish credit if everyone thought I didn't exist because the Credit Bureau didn't have a file on me as a single? I brooded about it for over a week. One day I got another call at the office from Margie Chadwell at the bank. She told me that she had personally verified all the loans I had listed on my application, something which she doesn't normally have time to do.

She said, "I had to go through that same trouble with the Credit Bureau once before, and I knew how you felt." She never told me why she had gone through it, but I assumed she, also, had been divorced.

Within three days I had a Master Charge account, and a new feeling toward the bank and toward Margie who had cared about my feelings and gone to that extra trouble.

Running my own financial life

The beginning of handling my own money was quite a project for me. The biggest surprises, I think, were the feelings that welled up in me from time to time when I was trying to deal with this area. It was very hard for me to hear a wealthy person talk casually about vacations, a new car or some expensive jewelry found at a bargain. And I know it must have seemed strange to people I knew who had more money to hear me say that a gift to me, say, of a $50 dress bothered me. But I was often disturbed when people wanted to buy me such gifts.

Sorting out my personal "basics"

When I first moved, I chose an apartment that would have certain basic features, because I knew I would not have the money to travel and do things that would be fun and entertaining. One of the basics was a swimming pool, so I could go there and lie in the sun and look like I'd been somewhere fantastic because I was tan. I was very thankful to have the money to afford such an apartment.

I finally found one in my price range. But when I got through making a list of all my expenses, and realized that I literally had only $5.00 a month left over, I began studying ways to carefully conserve money in every way. When I bought a package of frozen broccoli, that usually meant three meals' worth of broccoli. I counted the spears and divided by three. The amount of food I fixed for supper wasn't based on how hungry I was, but on how much food there was.

I also conserved gas in my car by lining up my errands and doing them along the shortest route. I wouldn't do one if there weren't at least three to do. So if I ran out of butter or something, it might have to wait two or three days until there were other errands to run.

I felt very pleased with my apartment. Even though it was a small one-bedroom place with garage-sale furniture and a card table for a dining room table, it seemed like a palace to me because I had put it together myself. I tried to have an attitude that these next few years were going to be an adventure to see if I could make the money I was earning stretch to cover my needs, either by careful planning or changing my needs. And my outer façade toward other people was one of great confidence. I tried to behave as if I had $200 a month extra, but wasn't spending anything because I preferred to save it.

Competitive feelings about money

While I was thankful about being able to afford the basics I had, and felt good about the accomplishments I made in putting together an apartment, I also still felt anger inside toward people who had better incomes than I did.

What I'm about to say may sound terrible to those of you with children, because I know money can be a very touchy issue when you have someone other than yourself to be responsible for. But my friend, Charlotte, had a son and a daughter. She was a schoolteacher, and made more money than I. And her ex-husband paid child support to her for the children. She wanted to create a home for them, so she had a bigger apartment with real furniture in it—not garage sale junk like I had. And I didn't really know what she was going through as a single mother, I just knew how nice her apartment looked to me when I compared it to mine. And I felt jealous sometimes, and resentful.

Another strong emotion that seemed to be around almost daily was depression. Apparently the energy required to "not need" things I wanted but couldn't afford really kept me down. I had been raised in a nice home where we could afford a lot more luxuries than I could afford now. And I'd gone to a private college where I had everything I needed plus some nice extras. I had the opportunity in college to earn additional money which was mine to blow on anything I wanted. And now I found myself hoping that a package of broccoli would last three days.

But at the same time, I didn't want my family to know how tight things were for fear they would want to send money to bail me out. I had an intense drive to be really "on my own," both financially and emotionally. I was twenty-six years old and I felt I was supposed to be able to support myself.*

I remember one year, when my car was inspected for its annual inspection sticker, I was told that all four tires were bald and I would have to buy new ones before I could pass the inspection. It was almost the last day of the month, and I didn't have the money to go out and buy four new tires. I had a bicycle, and I lived less than a mile from my office. It was spring, warm weather, so I decided to leave the car in the parking lot to avoid getting a ticket (which I also couldn't afford), and ride the bicycle to work for a while. Then I would have a week or so to plan how I would go about paying $400 for some new tires.

While I was going through that week, actually enjoying the exercise and the novelty of riding my bicycle to work, I accepted a blind date with a friend of someone I worked with. This man was from out of town and was an executive with a large company.

We went out to dinner that night, and it was one of those situations in which I knew immediately that I was in no way compatible with this person. But in the interest of getting through the evening I began chatting about my new adventure of riding my bicycle to work every day, telling my date how much I was enjoying the exercise.

"You can't be serious!" he said. "What will you do if it rains? Why would you want to get exercise that way?"

Before I could stop myself, I let it slip. "Well, I'm really just doing that until I can get some new tires and get an inspection sticker for my car. I can't drive it right now because it didn't pass inspection."

As quickly as blinking an eye, this man said, "Well, if you need new tires, I'll buy them for you!" It didn't seem to be any amount of money at all to him!

Two things raced through my mind. First, an intense feeling of panic and anger. I couldn't accept such a large gift from someone I already knew I would probably never see again. And even if I had wanted to date him more, I had only just met him and this didn't seem

---

*I realize that different people are at different places with regard to their needs for independence, etc., when they are single, and I am *not* saying that it is *bad* to receive help. I'm merely telling my own experience as a person who was trying to grow up and make the parent break while establishing my own separate identity.

right. Of course, I realized later that $400 to some executives may not
be a very sizable sum. But to me it represented about a year's worth of
payments on a small loan.

The second thing that happened was that I suddenly realized I had a
Master Charge account with a $500 credit limit, and I could get the
tires and charge them. Even at 18 percent interest, paying them off
would be better than accepting this offer from a stranger.

"Thank you, but I'm planning to get the tires this weekend," I
declined. "Everything's fine." I was amazed again at the strength of my
anger toward him. I felt as if he were trying to "buy" my friendship
and continued dates with that offer. If I accepted, I would surely feel I
should date him more often. I realize now this may not have been in his
thinking. He could have been genuinely offering to help. But my
feelings at that time did not allow me to see it that way at all. I just felt
hostile and somewhat offended and realized there was a lot about
money I'd never considered. I also saw now how intensely angry and
hurt I was at the apparent unfairness of life in favor of men.

Breaking the holding pattern

A few years went by, and I had several promotions at work and some
raises to go along with them. I began to look around at my little
apartment and at the furniture. And even though I could now afford to
get nicer furniture, I felt that I should wait. If I were going to meet
someone and get married, then we should choose furniture together to
accommodate both our preferences. (I have heard many men say that
they live in unsatisfactorily furnished apartments, because they believe
they don't know how to choose furniture and are waiting until the right
woman comes into their lives.) I lived in this "holding pattern" for a
while, and yet I was really getting tired of my $25 slanted-over
garage-sale couch. I had moved to a larger one-bedroom apartment in a
bigger complex. But my old furniture looked even worse in the new
apartment, which had good carpet, wood paneling and modern kitchen
appliances.

One weekend I finally made the decision that it was time for me to
create my own home with furniture I really liked. I wanted to feel
comfortable and at peace about being single, and I thought having a
real "home" would help.

"And besides," I told myself, "if I fall in love with someone who hates my furniture, we'll sell it and start over!"

That Saturday I went shopping in furniture stores. The first thing I wanted was a dining room table to replace the card table. I decided what I wanted to buy—a solid wood table with one or two leaves, and four chairs that were really comfortable, with arms and padded backs. I had not been shopping in a furniture store in a long time, and I was not aware of what furniture costs.

When I finally found the table I wanted, I looked at the price tag and turned pale. It was $1,500! I was so upset I could hardly be polite to the saleslady. She must have wondered what was wrong with me. The strong emotions started again and I had thoughts like, "$1,500! It would take me five years to pay off a loan that size! But it's not this lady's fault. Try not to be rude to her. Oh my gosh, how am I ever going to create a home at this rate?"

After standing there with the tears brimming in my eyes again, I finally mumbled something like "Oh, I just remembered an appointment," and fairly ran out the door! I drove straight home and tried to calm down.

As I began to think more clearly, I tried to plan more realistically. I did two things. One was to change my standard for the kind of table I wanted. I went out and found another one that had a vinyl top with a parquet wood-grain pattern in it, and four padded vinyl-covered chairs that swiveled. It was quite a nice-looking find. And it was priced at around $650. I didn't have $650 either, but I had become a member of my company's brand-new Credit Union.

So the second thing I did was to go to the loan officer of the Credit Union and get a twelve-month loan. Since my car loan had just been paid off, I could now shift some of the money to this project. I also realized I was building a credit rating—my very own credit rating. So far, the only credit I had was an Exxon card and a Master Charge account. Now I had my first loan in my own name. (The car loan had been transferred to me after the divorce. It "didn't count" because it had been in my ex-husband's name.)

During the year I spent paying off the loan, I enjoyed using the table and also had time to plan and shop for the next large item of furniture—a sofa. I got quite an emotional lift from buying the table and shopping for a couch, and I felt like inviting friends over for dinner. . . now that I had a real table at which we could sit. And my girlfriends who came over to play bridge really enjoyed the four comfortable chairs, which I had chosen with them in mind.

Returning to God what is His

About this time I began reflecting on how much the people in my church had helped me during some really tough times, and how they still continued to mean a lot to me as various friendships deepened. I also thought about how little I was doing for the church or for God in terms of time and money. I knew that even though I was on a tight budget, and my money would not make a large difference at the church, I still felt that I wanted to show God my thanks for the way things had happened in my life through His people. I couldn't afford a real 10 percent tithe, but I started with the figure of $10 a month. As I planned this, I realized that just three short years earlier, I had only half that amount of money left each month for "luxuries." I was thankful again that things had improved for me financially.

I listed the $10 amount in my budget book just as if it were a loan payment, and I wrote out and mailed a check when I paid my monthly bills. After a year I received a statement from the church, and I saw with a shock that I had contributed $120 that year. I never realized I would be able to contribute $120 to my church! That amount seemed like a fortune to me, and I felt really good about having done it. So I raised my monthly contribution to $12.50 for the next year.

Some months I used the money allotted for the church to pay a little extra on my Master Charge or some other bill, but then I would pay $25 the next month, or $18.75 for two months to make it come out even at the end of the year.

A financial future

As I progressed in learning not to charge more than I could pay for on my charge accounts, and how to balance a budget and a checkbook, I began to plan for my "financial future." This was very exciting to me.

I reactivated my dormant savings account, and began to plan for learning about "investments" for my future. I even began to think about finding out how to buy a house. I wanted to develop the material part of my life for the security and sense of accomplishment it gave me. But I think another one of the important reasons for doing this was that taking care of my money needs myself would take the pressure of needing financial security off of a potential relationship. If I ever met anyone to whom I wanted to relate and with whom I might even fall in love, my feelings wouldn't be colored by the fact that I needed new tires or money for anything else. I would want the relationship to develop because that person's personality and mine made something together that was better than either one of us were when apart.

Feelings of confidence and self-worth

Learning to manage money, live within my means and yet still have some of the "extra" things I enjoyed taught me a lot about myself and about life in general. I grew more confident every time I finished a loan payment book. I felt proud whenever I took out my Exxon charge card at the gas station.

I began to feel confident that I could survive if I just paid attention to basic procedures of banking, saving, and credit. And I gained a new appreciation for what my parents had provided for me when I was growing up. I also realized that the ability to earn money and manage it well gave me a sense of freedom—the freedom to relate to men on a healthier basis, to choose my own environment in terms of furniture, vacations and so on, and to give to the church and to other people who might need my help. And I also found the freedom to decide for myself, "What is really important for my life?"

NOTES

Dear Keith,

You and I have both talked to a lot of single people in varying financial conditions. I think it would be helpful to tell a little about what they said. Also, what does the Bible say about money and our relationship to God?

I really struggled with some painful competitive feelings in relating to people who had more money than I did. How do you believe we can take care of our needs financially and still keep the need for money in perspective with God's will for us?

It must be difficult and painful for men to face the loss of "buying power" that comes with a divorce settlement. I know it is a delicate and very personal subject because many people who have never had a lot of money react with sarcasm and resentment when someone tries to explain the feelings that go along with "going backward" financially. But would you tell a little about how you felt and how you're handling those feelings?

And also, if someone should want to try to improve his or her financial situation, can you talk about how that might be done?

Andrea

At the time of my divorce I had been making a good living for many years. And because I had enough money, it didn't seem to be important to me. But due to some drastic changes in property values, I found myself very short of funds after the divorce settlement.

For the first time in years, I had to be very careful about spending money. And a great insecurity came over me. I discovered that although money can't buy happiness, it can sure keep some lumps out of your throat when the bills come due.

And as I talked to other singles, particularly divorced people, I discovered a great deal of bitterness about money—or the lack of it. Some women with small children reported that their ex-husbands don't help out as they have committed to do. And the fact that many divorced women are not trained to make a living means often that they must not only cut their living standards drastically but must take menial, low-paying jobs in order to survive. And if they have lived on a much higher standard of living in their marriages, the frustrations and bitterness may be accentuated.

On the other hand, a few men have told me that they feel reluctant to pay child support money, although they do so, because they are uncertain how the money will be used. They want to help with the bills for the children's clothes, dental and medical care, school supplies and food. But they feel they have reasons to suspect that the money is being used to support a "swinging single" lifestyle of beauty shop visits, manicures, disco shoes and entertainment for the children's mother. How many of these suspicions are true and how many may be imagined rationalizations, I have no way of knowing. But the *feelings* seem genuine—and painful.

And while most single parents appear to be responsible about the welfare of their children, the actions of those who are irresponsible regarding *spending* or *sending* child support money can cause great pain to the responsible parent.

In one sense it begins to sound as if money is the security for all of life. And there are times (when one doesn't have money) when that seems to be true. But as I found myself thinking more about money—and the lack of it—I decided to take a look at the biblical writers' view of money.

Money and God

The Bible is not against money. Jesus didn't say money was evil. It was, in fact, something to be desired. For instance, in the story of the ten talents (Matt. 25:14–30), the guy who had ten talents went out, invested them and made ten more. And *he* was the one who got the reward, not the man who protected what he'd been given. Money couldn't have been evil, or Jesus wouldn't have talked about it like that, even in an illustration.

As I see it, the problem with money is that it *does* provide certain securities. It will help us avoid certain calamities. But the difficulties come when we look to money as our *ultimate* security, so that it becomes a substitute for God who can provide the only security that really does transcend our problems. And if we put our confidence in God and His kingdom, Jesus said, then the material things will be taken care of. But in our panic and insecurity, we forget about God and drive for money with all we're worth. And when we do, money becomes like a totally demanding master which takes God's place as the hope for the meaning of our lives.

Jesus said no one can serve two masters because when we try we'll always wind up loving one and hating the other. "You cannot serve God and mammon (money)," he said (Matt. 6:24, RSV).

The subtle strength of money as a competing security to God is so great that the author of First Timothy says that the "love of money is the root of all evil" (6:10, KJV). It's not *money* that's evil but the *love of it*. Gertrude Behanna used to say, "Money is like bricks. You can either build hospitals with it or slug people." Money *in itself* is not evil, then, for a Christian. But it becomes bad when one attempts to use it as an ultimate security instead of depending on the living God.

When I start going after money as the most important thing in my life, something very bad happens to me. I start calculating all the time about how I'm going to make more money or get more power or control. And all of a sudden all my relationships suffer. I trample over the people close to me to get out and make things happen financially. And the things I believe God considers of value: peace, longsuffering, patience, the kind of love that Christ had, I don't have time for. I seal them off because of a love for material things which I feel I must have beyond basic needs (i.e., luxuries, investments, etc.).

Early attitudes about money

I was raised in Tulsa, Oklahoma, in the oil community. My father made a lot of money. He had an oil company which he had put together just before the Great Depression, and then he lost everything. "Lost everything" is a euphemism for "lost control." He still had more than a lot of people.

Looking back, I think now that we would probably have been considered middle class or upper middle class financially. I felt secretly insecure about not having as much money as some of the other kids, but I was taught by a Christian mother that money didn't really matter as much as other things like integrity and love. But my mother was also very interested in my knowing the "right people" and being accepted in the crowds whose parents had lots of money.

So I got a double message as a child and I had two agendas. One was to "make sure you have enough money" and the other was to "be a fine man and don't care about material things."

God's money vs. paying the bills

I became a more dedicated Christian in my late twenties. I became committed to finding and doing God's will, but I didn't know what to do about money. I had never really been around anybody who tithed and yet I began to hear people talk seriously about tithing. I was just barely getting along financially, supporting a wife and two young daughters. And I really struggled against the idea of tithing. I felt I just "couldn't afford it."

Finally I realized that any money I have really belongs to God. And I'm to take care of it and use it for His purposes in the world of responsibilities He's put me in. I'd heard this for years, but it finally struck home.

So in great agony I started pledging 2 percent of my income. That may sound like a cheap deal to those of you who have always been heavy tithers, but to me 2 percent seemed like *a lot!* From then on, when I'd get a pay raise, I'd give most of the raise to the church or to help someone in need until I got the part that I gave up to 10 percent over the next few years.

During this time I remember hearing ministers and laypeople say that "if you tithe, God will bless you." And I'd always cringe a little when I heard that. I know that God may well bless anyone who tithes, *but not* necessarily in *material ways.* You might tithe and go broke, but God would bless you with a sense of peace and security and the will to go on as His person.

But for me there was a paradox. As I began to tithe, money began to *mean* something different to me. I had enough to pay my bills, but I wasn't concerned about accumulating a lot of money. I just didn't have the same kind of ambition for it. God did bless me through tithing, but not by making me wealthy. Instead He made me more comfortable with what I had. And I have varied the amount and recipients of my giving over the years.

After a few years, when I was about thirty-one years old, I left my job as an executive in an oil company and went back to school, to seminary. And at that time I said, "I'm free. I don't have to worry about the material rat race any more!" (In seminary no one had any money, so one didn't have to worry about making a lot of it.)

But several years later I made some money from the sale of my books. Suddenly I had enough again, and so I still didn't have to worry about money. Then as my books continued to sell, I had money to invest. So I got busy investing it and spending it. Finally I got so preoccupied with material things that I quit facing my personal problems. And that's when things began to fall apart in my life. It was so subtle that I didn't even see it coming.

I'm not blaming my marital failure on money. My own sin was and is my problem. But the money enabled me to buy separation, to get away and not face the growing difficulties in my life.

Beginning again, financially

Then came a divorce. And I wound up in bad shape financially. I owed a bunch of money and I had to set out in earnest to acquire enough cash to pay my debts.

Although it was hard to start again without a surplus to draw on, I suppose in some ways it was the best thing that could have happened to me. I had to decide whether I was going to trust in God or trust in the success of my work. I had to ask myself if I could risk writing, whether or not the writing would make money.

I'm always scared to turn loose of any controls, but I have found myself needing to do this again and again in my Christian life, and I'm always glad when I do. Some people seem to risk easily. But when I have to give up something that's really important to me, I just sweat blood, struggle against it and say, "I don't want to risk it, God!" But finally if I do risk it for Him and for the truth, life looks good again, and I feel much safer and ironically much more at home in the world.

Money represents a strange paradox. If you have a lot of it, it can get in the way of your growth and faith. But if you don't have enough, life can be an absolute terror. The only approach I've found is to go to God with the problem.

I just say, "God, will you become my security? Because I can't seem to turn loose of the idea of how much money I need." And then I begin to face the question of what I need to take care of my obligations and basic retirement planning and form an action plan to take care of it, believing that God will handle the ultimate results of my life as I try to keep Him as my center and ultimate security.

An Approach to Getting the Money You Need

If you're interested in getting your financial life in order, here is a simple approach.*

First, dream for a few minutes. Decide how much money would allow you to live comfortably. This would include some money in the bank

---

*For a more complete description of this approach see *With No Fear of Failure: Recapturing Your Dreams Through Creative Enterprise,* by Tom Fatjo, Jr., and Keith Miller (Waco, TX: Word Books, 1981).

and an annual income figure. Just to have some figures to deal with, let's say you came up with the figures $12,000 in savings and an annual income of $15,000. If these seem large or small, change them.

How much is enough?

Next, in order to find out your *essential needs,* go back through your last year's checkbook and list everything you spent for essentials: housing, food, clothing, car, medical, income taxes, giving to Church, etc. (Every item you consider to be essential.) If you have any debts or "payments" which have to be made, list them.

Then total each column, so that you have a yearly total for housing, food, etc. Next add the column totals to arrive at the total amount you spent on essentials last year. Add 10 percent for inflation, and you will know how much you *must* have to live comfortably. (Don't panic if it looks huge. We're going to work on it.)

Next, by looking at your bank deposits, add any kind of income you received *which will still be coming in next year:* salary, interest income, investments, alimony or child support payments, etc. When you have made lists of each type of income and totaled the columns, then add the totals and see how much income you made for the whole year which you can count on coming in again next year.

Next, subtract the two figures. For example, if your total estimated income for the next year is $10,000 and the expenses you can count on are $9,000, you would show:

$10,000   Estimated income
  9,000   Estimated expenses

$ 1,000   Amount of extra income you will have to begin planning for the future.

Dreaming for a better future

If your first goal after meeting your essential needs is eventually to have $12,000 in the bank you will also need to figure how much you want to save per month so you can know when you will reach your goal.

So let's say that you decide you want to save $200 a month to acquire your $12,000 nest egg in five years. This would mean that next year you will need to earn $11,400 ($2400 more than your $9000 expenses). This will allow you to pay for essentials plus begin saving $200 per month for your future. Now you have a rough picture of "how much is enough" for you to make (plus tax adjustment).

But let's say that you want to eventually make an annual income of $15,000. You will have to look at your present job and see if that salary is potentially reachable where you are now working. Let's say that you do not believe that in five years, even if you work hard, you can be making a salary of $15,000 where you are now working.

Take a clean sheet of paper and list the things you like to do or would like to investigate in order to earn a living. Don't allow yourself to say something won't work at this stage... or even "I don't know how." Just list it. I realize that some of you may feel that there is nothing you can do except what you are already doing, but for the purpose of this exercise, try to let yourself dream about what it would take to build a new life.

When you have listed everything you think you would like to do or can already do to earn money, then rearrange the list in priority order, putting the one most interesting to you first. Let's say that the top thing on your list turned out to be: "To Sell Life Insurance."

Pouring concrete to a dream

The next step is to make an action plan to see if you can become an insurance salesperson. Put "To Sell Life Insurance" at the top of a clean sheet of paper. Then list everything you can think of which you'd have to know before you could become a life insurance salesperson. Your list might look something like this:

To Sell Life Insurance

1. How much do sales people make?
   a. Beginning amount
   b. Potential salary (is it over $15,000?)
2. What company would be best to work for?

3. How much education or training will I need?
4. Does the company pay during training period?
   a. How long is training period?
   b. How much is training salary?
5. Whom should I go see to ask these questions?
6. Do they accept people like me (age, sex, education, etc.)?
7. What is a description of the nature and place of the work (in an office? calling on local people? traveling out of town? etc.)?

Keep listing until you can't think of anything else you'd like to know.

When you have finished your list, then recopy it in the order in which you are going to use it. Your revised list might be something like the following (although each person's order may be different and each person's list may be different).

To Sell Life Insurance

1. Whom should I go see to ask these questions?
2. What company would be best to work for?
3. Do they accept people like me (age, sex, education, etc.)?
4. How much education or training will I need?
5. Does the company pay during training period?
   a. How long is training period?
   b. How much is training salary?
6. What is a description of the nature and place of the work (in an office? calling on local people? traveling out of town, etc.)?
7. How much do sales people make?
   a. Beginning amount
   b. Potential salary (is it over $15,000?)

When you have your revised list, decide whom you could contact to answer the first question, then the next and the next. You might call on several companies before you are able to decide that you really want to pay the price to be an insurance salesperson. If after getting the answers to your questions you realize you *don't* want to be an insurance salesperson or it is not possible, then go to the second item on your list of things you would like to do to earn money and make an action plan to investigate it in the same way you did for the insurance sales job.

God can't guide a stationary object

Many times just getting out and *doing something* about your material destiny is a great help psychologically, emotionally and spiritually. A friend used to remind people when they got stuck emotionally, to *do something*. "Even God," he said smiling, "can't guide a stationary object." Also, as you begin to investigate one job you may get hired for another or get new ideas about what you would like to do.

Actually this discussion is only an attempt to suggest a possible way of thinking about your material future. You may find much better ways to plan. Here I'm only indicating that you *can* plan for your future and become much more likely to reach your goals.

As I said earlier, I realize that this sort of aggressively doing something about your own vocational future is not for everyone. But you may feel so "put down" and insecure that you don't realize how much more potential you have than you would imagine. It may take some time and a lot of courage to begin to take responsibility for your own vocational life under God. But my experience has been that when I try to get out and do something, the results are much better than those I've obtained while sitting around feeling sorry for myself.

I realize that it is really difficult for some people to even think about being aggressive concerning their financial futures. And the problems seem to be multiplied for people who are single parents. But it seems to me that God has a lot of help for all singles.

CHAPTER EIGHT

Parenting Alone

NOTES

Dear Keith,

Even though I don't have any children I have known single parents—both mothers and fathers—and have seen them struggling to maintain or redevelop good relationships with their kids.

What kinds of emotional stress happened to you in your role as a parent? And what kinds of destructive behaviors resulted from this stress? Also, what did you find, if anything, to do about these destructive behaviors? All three of your daughters are committed Christians, as you are. Yet you've said that there have still been some painful times regarding your "parent–child" relationships.

A.

There are several ways of being a single parent which are so different from each other as to constitute almost totally separate experiences. For example, a mother alone with several very young kids has a different universe of problems from that of a middle-aged father with grown children already away from home. But there seem to be a few common elements that all singles who are parents may face.

Experiences That Can Hamper Parenting Abilities

During the process of losing a mate due to divorce or death, some pretty heavy things can happen to us emotionally concerning our self-confidence and perception. And these experiences can definitely affect our parenting methods. As I emerged from the debris of my divorce, I began to recognize some of these, and as I talked to other single fathers and mothers, I discovered that many of us face similar emotional traumas. I'll try to describe a few of them here.

Emotional blindness

During the last months and weeks of a marriage that eventually ends in divorce, the pain and fear in the lives of the husband and wife are often so intense and absorbing that as parents they can't really hear or feel their children's pain.* I know this was true of me. It was as if I had emotional blinders on and could only see that which was directly in my path.

---

*For an excellent book on the experiences of children of high school age or older, see *Which Way Is Home?* by Leslie Williams (Nashville, TN: Thomas Nelson, 1981).

I was trying to hold myself together when I was with my daughters and trying to listen to them and keep a confident face. But inside I was a mass of bad feelings and confusion. And I was going through the awful experience of feeling a lot of self-worth shifting out from under me, like a house with a sand foundation on a mountainside.

Divorce was such an unthinkable thing for me to be involved in that I couldn't see the devastating *but different* experience it was for the children. Their home was being blown away as surely as if a tornado had picked it up and smashed it to the ground. I think they wanted to help me because I was still their daddy, but they were also evidently filled with anger and frustration and grief of their own. I could understand this with my head, but inside I was full to the brim with my own pain and bad feelings. Looking back, I can see that I was, at times, a very insensitive father as a result of this blindness.

Losing perspective

One of the discouraging things I discovered about being a single parent is that without an adult sounding board I lost perspective very easily and began having very unreal expectations about my children. I expected them to understand my faults, forgive my mistakes and reassure me that I was really a great daddy in spite of the divorce and all that had happened.

These expectations were very unrealistic. My kids were having their own problems with themselves, (I assumed with their mother also) and with me. They were very kind and loving, especially under the circumstances of their own pain. But in my skewed perspective, I must have expected them to behave as if everything were the same as it had been.

Another thing I experienced right after I was divorced was that, without a sounding board, I tended to believe all the angry criticism thrown at me. There are two kinds of people, it seems. If you tell some people that there is something wrong with them, they will say "to heck with you!" and walk off. The other kind will look worried and say with great curiosity, "What is it?" I was one of the second kind. I had decided that I must have been a horrible father and husband, and I felt very depressed about these feelings.

About a year after the divorce I remember being amazed when one of my children said to me, "Daddy, one thing I remember about you is that you sure were a good daddy to us when we were growing up." I almost fainted in surprise, because I had gotten so far out of perspective I couldn't see much good about me anywhere.

The need to be loved and understood

Regardless of the circumstances, if a marriage ends in bitterness, there is often a strong tendency for both husband and wife to want to wind up being the one most loved by the kids. Even though I felt ashamed of these feelings, I had them.

I wanted their love very much and I also found myself wishing they could have "stood in my moccasins" enough to understand what I'd been through during the past few years so that they could say, "Oh, yeah, I can understand why you were the way you were and did what you did."

But I realized to my horror that there was no way they were all going to understand me in that way. After all, I hadn't been able to understand myself a good bit of the time. I didn't know what they saw me as. But by the looks on their faces when they were with me, I didn't feel that they saw me as being very much. (It is possible that this was not the case, but these were my fears and feelings, and they were excruciating.)

Some unreal expectations

Depending on how the divorce happened and the ages of the children, many people emerge with unreal fantasies about the future. For instance, Andrea and I have a single parent friend named Jenny who had very young children when she was divorced.

"When I was first divorced," she said, "I didn't think I was going to have the responsibility of raising my children. They were young, and I was young. And I had the feeling that some Prince Charming was going to come by in about two or three years and help me." But gradually it dawned on Jenny that it was very likely that she was going to have to raise her children alone. She said that when that idea hit her, it took her six to eight months of total readjustment to begin living realistically.

"I had to stop and rethink my role as the mother of two children," she said. "If Prince Charming did come by, I realized that my kids might be grown by that time and *I* was probably going to have to be the family who raised them."

I think the sooner one can accept the facts of the divorce and the single parenting situation, the sooner unreal expectations can be dispelled. There can be some harsh blows as one faces this reality, of course. One woman friend said she was stunned when her husband was not regular with the child support check.

"I thought that would be the first and foremost thing he would do each month and that he'd never fail to send it," she commented. But when the check didn't come, she was really surprised and disappointed that her ex-husband's kids didn't come first with him. There are all kinds of ways you assume your ex-mate will be charitable, loving, and patient to your kids—as he or she may have been in the marriage. And when he or she is not or is downright cruel or selfish, it can be devastating.

Dating

Other unreal expectations as a single parent may have to do with your children's opinions about your relationships with the opposite sex. Some single parents feel that it's not good to expose their children to people they are dating. If strong attachments develop between date and kids, and the relationship terminates, the children can be hurt. Other people want their kids to have the exposure to adults who can serve as father figures or mother figures so they introduce all their dates to their children.

But the surprise may come from the kids themselves. They may have some definite ideas about your "dates" or may not want you to date at all. At best they may have some fears and bad feelings about anyone they perceive as a threat to their relationship to you. And by their very presence they can at least color your dating life significantly.

We have one friend who wrote a little booklet for divorced women called "Hints for Hesitant Hustlers" in which she pointed out some of the unforeseen difficulties in trying to be a good mother and operate in what appeared to be the swinging singles' world. She told about the first time she offered a man a beer out of her refrigerator. Since she didn't drink beer, the can had been sitting there for six months. When the man took it out, it had old grape jelly spilled all over the top. She felt anything but sophisticated.

"Dating, as a single parent," she reflected, "has some unforeseen problems." But many of the problems are similar to those we'll look at in the chapter on dating.

Destructive Parenting

While going through the rigors of emotional blindness, losing my perspective, needing to be loved and understood, and beginning to date, I began to realize that some pretty destructive behaviors had started to emerge in my parental habits. As I looked around among my friends, I saw others struggling in these areas as well.

Guilt and self-pity: Holidays

Guilt and self-pity regarding my children were like two malevolent black monkeys which I found could leap on me from out of nowhere, ruining a wonderful hour, day, or week.

Holidays were especially bad. I remember the first couple of Christmases after the divorce. We had agreed that the children would be with one parent on Christmas Eve and the other on Christmas Day. All I can remember was trying to be jolly while seeing all those long sad faces trying to look happy for me and for each other. When the Christmas music or anything about "family" came on TV our faces all fell.

I was miserable and felt like all their pain about everything was my responsibility. "Now I'd deprived my kids of a home for Christmas for the rest of their lives," I thought. In my imagination I could see a white-haired old guy (me) sitting around waiting for Christmas Eve night, getting ready for this ordeal of guilt and misery that he had caused fifty years before.

Besides the guilt, I felt waves of self-pity. I imagined saying, "Well, I might as well go in and flush myself right down the john because everyone would be happier."

But as I was having all this guilt and self-pity I remembered something. For the previous three or four years, Christmas, Thanksgiving and sometimes Easter were about the only times the kids had come home anyway. And the previous few Christmases had not been good experiences either. And I had to face the fact that trying to hold a dead marriage together for 363 days so that the children could gather and verify its death for the other 2 days was probably not very sound thinking.

I realized again that divorce is a terrible and painful experience for everyone in a family. And when it comes, there may be some agonizing holidays and other family occasions. But the tendency is to forget that as the children grow up and leave home, there are some painful times of guilt and self-pity in *every* family, whether there has been a divorce or not. And in either case parents and children must learn to grow up and help each other through the bad times into the future God has for each member of the family. And guilt and self-pity, however tempting they are to wallow in, only block the healing and growth processes and aggravate everyone's frustration and pain.

Overdoing it as a daddy

Feeling insecure about my role as a parent, I was hesitant to do anything which might drive my kids away from me. Although I knew it wasn't logical, I felt that if I confronted them strongly in areas where we really disagreed they would reject me and walk away. So I was often a real patsy for them, and my relationship was not natural. I was being too nice.

For instance, I would find myself trying to meet all their wants and needs, even if I was in a financial bind. Since the problem was inside me and had to do with my not putting realistic limits on what I could now do, the solution had to come from me.

It took me almost two years to get enough confidence to face this self-defeating behavior. And I finally had an honest confrontation with one of them in which I really got mad and said in effect, "Look, I don't want to put up with all this financial pressure any more. I love you, but I can't make you love me. And kissing your feet or making bad financial decisions is not the way to do it in any case. So from now on I'm going to try to be realistic in stating frankly when and how much I can help you." Since previously I had had a great deal more money than I now had, this new policy may have been difficult for them to adjust to and understand. But since they had never been demanding in this area, they have done much better with it than I have.

I have talked to fathers and mothers who have very small children who report the same problem: because of guilt for not having been able to preserve a two-parent home, they have tried to keep their kids' approval by playing Santa every weekend or "slave" during the week—depending on when they have the children. And some kids work their parents' guilt and fear of rejection like crazy to get what they want. But the truth seems to be that children need the reality of having parents who give them some structure by saying "no" at appropriate times and not letting the children have all their wishes met. Since the rest of the world is not going to meet every whim, the spoiled child of divorced parents will have a rude awakening when he or she has to live away from the parents, or gets married.

Condemning the other parent

When a parent is divorced, it is difficult to know how he or she can talk to the children about the other parent.

Since there is no way you can control what your ex-spouse says to your children, it can be infuriating to discover that he or she has been saying bad, damaging or even untrue things about you. The temptation is evidently almost universal to want to "get even" and to look righteous by tearing down one's ex-mate to the children. When you find yourself doing this all I know to do is confess to them what you've been doing and try to stop.

Using the children as weapons

In the warfare of a divorce the children are often used as weapons, as tragic as this may sound. Knowing how much the other spouse loves the children, one parent may try to discredit the other totally in the eyes of the children, with the goal of hurting the ex-spouse.

But this kind of warfare can have serious repercussions on the children themselves. If a young boy is trying to discover his identity as a man and his mother says horrible things about the daddy he has been identifying with, it can cause even more conflict than the boy will naturally have in the face of a divorce. And if the mother, for instance, ever says, "You're just like your daddy!" that may mean to the son, "You're absolutely worthless!" And if the boy has his father for a model, when someone says he's just like his father, the boy may say to himself, "I must not be dependable. I must not be lovable." He feels he must be all the derogatory things he's heard the mother say about his father.

Of course it can just as easily be a father berating the mother. Whichever parent is doing the damage, this behavior can teach the child to hate himself or herself, because of the awareness of the hate the berating parent has for the other.

Although I haven't always been able to do it, I think it's possible to speak the truth as you see it about what's happening without saying the other parent is no good.

Acknowledging the pain of the children

A friend whose husband left her told us that one of her young children asked in tears why the daddy left him. The mother thought a moment and then said, "Honey, it wasn't *you* he wanted to leave, it was *me*. He and I were the ones who couldn't get along."

I told her I understood her feelings, but that from the little boy's perspective the daddy *did* leave him. The mother might have added, "Your daddy is going through some things I don't understand right now. Maybe he'll be able to tell you about them later." But when a child says "It's terrible," I think it is good to agree and say something like, "Yes, it *is* terrible, and it *does* hurt *a lot*. But God will help you get through the hard times and so will I."

Constructive Things to Put into Practice

I found myself in the midst of many of these destructive parenting behaviors. I began to search for better ways to relate to my kids—to begin to communicate with them on a more open level.

Perhaps the most difficult but constructive thing is to try to deal realistically with your children, without trying to overprotect them from reality.

How honest can you be with your kids?

This is a hard question because it depends a lot on how honest you've been with them (and yourself) all their lives.

If you've always lied a little to "protect" your children and suddenly you decide to "get honest with them," you might do well to prepare them for your new approach. Many single parents, particularly mothers with adolescent children, feel that they must now be direct with their children. And many times, even when this causes open conflicts, the relationships are improved.

An example

We have a single parent friend who was having a lot of conflict with her teenaged girl. Knowing that the girl was going through a hard time, our friend, Samantha, always tried to be loving, supportive and encouraging when her teenager got home from school. But the girl, whom I'll call Jane, hadn't had all her mother's psychological training, and didn't realize that the mother also needed love, support and encouragement. So Jane seemed to just scowl when she came home from school and would not talk about how she felt.

The mother found herself with frustrating and hostile feelings and wanted to run away. She heard people say to single parent mothers things like, "Well, *thank goodness* you have the child." But she was thinking, "To heck with that, I'm angry about being stuck with a child." Many women love their children but are furious because the ex-husband is floating around apparently scot-free from responsibility.

But what could Samantha do with her negative hostile feelings about her daughter's insensitivity? She decided she was going to tell her daughter just how she honestly felt, not having any idea how the girl would react. And although the confrontation was very painful, the relationship improved a lot over the next few weeks as the mother and daughter began describing their own feelings when certain situations came up.

Family night

They found it helpful to know each other's honest thoughts, but it was so scary to reveal such feelings that they seldom could talk at that level. So they decided to have "family night" one night a week at which time they could talk out how they were feeling about each other and how things were going—good and bad. And Samatha said, "It's amazing, Jane *likes* it! Even though I get out a lot of negative feelings and complaints, we feel closer and she's getting my full attention." And they've realized some things which have been very helpful. For instance, one time Samantha told her daughter, "You know, it really depresses me when I come in after a hard day. And even if I'm tired and in a bad mood I try to muster up a pleasant 'Hi!' and you just give me your angriest face."

Jane said, "I'm not *mad*, Mom. That's my *sad* look. I've been sitting here for two hours waiting for you to get home from work. I'm feeling depressed and want you to come hug me, so I put on my sad look. But then you ask me what I'm *mad* about and why I can't be cheerful. So then I *get* mad."

So Samantha and Jane decided they would try to tell each other how they were feeling since their sad and mad *looks* were confusing. They decided that they'd try to say a pleasant "hello" and then something like, "It's been a cruddy day, but I'm not mad at you."

All in all my own experience and the reports I get in counseling situations indicate that a direct, honest approach in which both children and parents are allowed to express honest feelings *without being judged, condemned,* or *straightened out* for expressing them can lead to much better relationships between single parents and children.

As I read over the last few paragraphs I remember how frightening and painful it has been to try to be honest about my own feelings *and* hear the honest feelings of my children without being defensive and justifying myself. But as I keep trying (and even when I fail) I feel better about myself and them.

Giving them back to God

There is no question in my mind that in many cases divorce is a destructive and agonizing trauma for the children. But having said that, I have come to believe that some very beneficial things *can happen* through single parents as a result of a divorce. It can become the occasion for everyone in a family, parents and children, to grow up and take responsibility for their own actions. People can learn to do things for themselves. And there may be less conflict. For instance, a mother raising kids alone doesn't have to argue with anyone else concerning each of her child-rearing decisions. She can make a decision on her own and stick to it. In that sense some children have more emotional structure.

But I guess the most important thing I have had to learn has to do with what I now believe to be the true end of being a Christian parent.

As I've said, my own insecurity and need for affection led me to try to manipulate my kids into loving me but also into living as I would have lived in their shoes. And although I didn't consciously intend to manipulate them, I can see now that I did.

But as the months went by and I prayed about the divorce and what to do with my life in the future, I began to feel that God was saying some things to me about my relationships with my children. As I would pray for them after some hot disagreement or other about their lives, I began to realize that I really don't know what's best for them in most instances.

Finally I began to pray a different prayer each morning. Instead of talking to God about each child's needs, I started imagining that I was placing each one, one at a time, in my cupped hands. I would imagine being before God. He also had His hands cupped. I would place my hands inside His and gently take my hands apart, leaving each daughter in God's hands. I didn't *say* anything but just released them to Him. And just this one act seemed to take the pressure off me to run the girls' lives. And within days *they* felt the change. It may take a long time for me to turn them all loose, but I have begun.

Finally I realized what I'd said for years: that God had only *loaned* me these three children to raise for Him. They aren't really *my* kids *or their mother's.* They really belong to God. And I saw that my job was not to control their steps, but to love them and release them to become the people God had in mind for them to be.

So I called each one and told her I loved her but that I'd unconsciously tried to shape her life as I thought best. I didn't know how long it would take me to work it out, but that I wanted to quit trying to control the way they are.

And I now wish I had realized *years* ago with the clarity I now see it, that we parents are not supposed to be responsible for "the way our kids turn out." We are to love them for God and share with them our faith and hope. But I'm convinced that we are really supposed to be "working ourselves out of a job" so that when our children are grown we can release them to fly off on their own. Then, when and if they come back to us, it will be as family friends in Christ who love us, and not as obedient children who come to see us out of a sense of grim duty.

NOTES

Dear Andrea,

Can you share with single parents some
insights about your attempts as a single without
children to relate to single parents and their
kids? Also, what about the arguments singles
sometimes get into about who has the best life,
single parents or singles alone?

K.

The problems of divorced or widowed parents with children seem so vast and complex to me that I can't even imagine all the hardships endured by responsible single parents and by their children.

I have seen evidence that having children affects one's life in many areas—loneliness, identity, money, dating—in fact, almost every area covered by a chapter in this book. I believe it is less *complex* to live a single life without children. But I also believe that it is less rewarding and emptier. Sometimes the idea of a goodnight hug from a child or an "I love you, mommy," sure sounded as if it would be nice. Also, to have someone else in the house to talk to and perhaps share the chores, or laugh at a television program with—all these seemed attractive— even though I realized that the care and responsibility for these children must be enormous. As a woman alone it's often easier to become cynical, bitter and selfish because there is no one else in the house one has to consider or care for.

I had several single girlfriends who were raising children. And in my experience of trying to develop friendships with them, I learned some painful lessons.

Whether it is because I have never had any babies of my own or whether it is for some other reason, I have often felt uneasy around children. I didn't know what to say to them.

For example, one Saturday afternoon while I was visiting with Charlotte, her six-year-old son, Roger, came into the living room. Charlotte was telling me an interesting story about her Friday night date, and I looked up and past her just as Roger came in. I noticed he had on a Mighty Mouse T shirt, so I smiled as he hesitantly approached us. I took a deep breath and said, "Say, Roger, that's a pretty neat T-shirt you have. Do you like Mighty Mouse?"

No response. Roger dropped his head, looked at the floor and froze. I kept my smile to my face, but I had a dizzying sinking feeling that I had said something wrong, inane or offensive.

Charlotte said gently, "Roger, can you answer Ms. Wells?" Then she reached out her arms and said, "Come here, honey. What did you want?" Avoiding my eyes, Roger went hastily to his mother and whispered in her ear. Charlotte winked at me over his shoulder and I tried to keep smiling, sipping my Fresca.

"Sure you can go play at Chuckie's house. But you tell his mother you have to come home by 5:00. Okay?"

Roger nodded, smiling now, and skipped his way back across the living room and out the front door.

Charlotte's eyes followed him out the door and she said, "He's always shy around strangers. Don't worry about it," and then went on with the story she had been telling me.

I was full of questions like, "Charlotte, I've been around your apartment fairly often for a whole year. Am I still a stranger to Roger? What was wrong with what I said? What could I have said that wouldn't have intimidated him so much? Was he intimidated? Was he upset with me or just afraid to interrupt us?" But instead of asking, I just went along with Charlotte, and we talked about other things.

Those brief encounters with my friends' children were always short, awkward and painful for me. I wanted kids to like me, but I didn't know what to do or say and I couldn't tell if they liked me or not.

I think many people who have children may take it for granted that all adults know how to relate to young people. Maybe relating to kids has become natural for them because they are around their own and their friends' children so much. And yet I have no inkling what a six-year-old wants to talk about as opposed to what a ten-year-old wants to talk about. I just know it would probably be different.

I often wished that I could find out how to get along with kids. But I was just as often relieved when Charlotte sent her kids out to play or into their rooms to watch television when I was there. And usually, when I was talking to a friend and her child came into the room, I would become silent. I was afraid I would say something too "adult" or "R-rated" about a relationship or a problem I was having, and that maybe my friend wouldn't want her children to hear it. It never occurred to me to ask. I just assumed this was true. I thought I was doing a good thing for my friend and her children.

One day I was having lunch with a formerly single friend who had remarried. Sylvia and I had not seen each other but once since her marriage about a year before. At first we caught up on small talk, but later in the lunch Sylvia told me, "I actually had to decide to terminate our friendship, Andrea. You and I did not 'drift apart,' as you keep saying. I terminated it because you hurt my daughter's feelings so badly one day that she went to her room in tears."

That was the first idea I had had that thirteen-year-old Susanna had been hurt by me. And now it was two years later! Sylvia described the day it had happened, and it had been one of those times when I had changed the subject when Susanna came into the room, had gotten silent and awkward, until Susanna had finally left. I was so insensitive and unaware that I had had no idea that she had gone upstairs in tears. I thought I was being careful not to offend my friend by talking about personal things in front of her daughter.

When Sylvia finished talking, I was so crushed that I burst into tears and could hardly speak. I suddenly saw how self-centered and insensitive I had been toward Susanna. I had thought that all this time Sylvia and I had an "open" relationship where we could talk about anything. And yet I realized I had never asked her about getting along with Susanna. Sylvia apparently felt that she could not talk to me about it, but that the termination of our friendship was the best solution.

If I had it to do over, knowing what I now know about the feelings of children, I would try to do things differently. I would have brought up the subject with Sylvia and made more of an effort—any kind—to reach her children. I believe it would have shown her in more ways than words could ever say that I cared for her.

But the fact is, I was not very sensitive and did not try very hard to relate to Susanna. And I caused a lot of hurt to two people whom I care about—and to myself.

Many people who have no kids of their own have told me they feel the same awkwardness I am describing. And children can apparently sense this uneasiness very easily, even though they may not know the cause of it. Now I make an effort to include children in my conversations with their parents. Instead of abruptly being silent, I try to find subjects to talk about that children can participate in. This has been difficult, and I have felt awkward and even stupid at times. But I am beginning to see a few good responses from some young people, and that is helping. And now that I've had a few positive experiences, I'm feeling more at home with children. And I hope that single parents can begin to help their single friends who have no children to know what to do to relate to their kids.

Who has the worst life?

I was a part of a group discussion one time about identity. I talked about my exploring various aspects of my identity by learning that I liked to repair things and do other mechanical projects. One woman, who had three teenage boys, said that she was so busy keeping up with her three boys that she didn't have time to "explore her identity." She said, "When I fix the hinge on the front door it's because the door fell off, not because I *wanted* to fix it. I feel like a full-time parent and a part-time woman."

There developed an argument in the group about which was the more difficult: living alone with no children, or facing the fact that you are solely responsible for the welfare of one or more children. I think both can be frightening.

I remember thinking several times that if I got sick and died in the middle of the night, no one would know for hours, or maybe even days, because no one would miss me right away since I lived alone. I remember spending long lonely weekends where—even with my awkwardness with children—I would have welcomed a child to talk to, or even fight with. As I'm saying this I can already hear my friends with children say they have often longed for a long, lonely weekend with some peace and quiet.

Sometimes when I've been terribly alone I have been overcome by a strong urge to just "give up" and not do anything anymore. But the responsibility of having other "mouths to feed" I think would have given me more incentive to keep on struggling. I also believe this responsibility can often be a motivation to achieve at one's job, whereas having no one but one's self may provide less urgent motivation.

I don't know whose life is the most difficult. Since I've never had the responsibility for kids, I have never experienced that kind of pressure. But I do know that living totally alone—with no kids or no room-mate . . . no one at all—a long way from family and people who knew me as a child can be frightening in ways I couldn't have imagined. I think the end result may be that most of us tend to be so concerned about ourselves that whatever problems *we* have seem to swell and fill up all our worry space so that the bad parts of our own situation get magnified and the good parts get overlooked.

I'm praying that God will make me more sensitive to the pain of the people around me whose problems are different from mine and give me the desire and wisdom to reach out to them in love.

But in any case, arguing about "who has the worst life" seems to me to be a dead-end street, when all that energy could be put into helping each other understand better what we can do to help out at the crisis points.

CHAPTER NINE
Friendships

NOTES

Dear Keith,

As I think about some of my friends, I realize how great a difference having their support has made in my life! Even when I didn't have dates I could still get out of my apartment or cook a company meal, because of girlfriends and married couple friends.

When you found yourself single did your already existing friendships change? What were some of the feelings you had when approaching new friendships? And do you think it's easier to be friends with other single people or with married ones? How does being a Christian flavor friendships for you?

                                        A.

I have a friend who is a lovely woman and a very good cook and who has more dinner parties than anyone I've ever known. When JoAnne got divorced, she had brunches, lunches, and dinner parties for all her single friends.

I heard another friend ask her, "Why do you have all these parties where you feed everyone?" JoAnne answered very honestly, "Well, it never occurred to me that anybody would want to come to my house just to come. I always had to have something to offer them." She smiled, shaking her head, and continued, "I probably should have been a waitress so somebody could leave me a tip. That would be tangible evidence that I did good, right? And then I wouldn't have to keep asking for these other strokes."

As I heard this conversation I realized that I'd never thought much about making friends but that I had always depended on "institutional settings" to provide them (e.g., school, clubs, marriage, church, etc.). I've always felt I had to have a project to offer or to be on a committee or team together before people would want to be my friend. But the problem with this approach is that when I always *do* something to *earn* friendship, I'm never confident that I have a real friend.

Reaching out as a single

I've realized that I am a loner and don't feel secure about my ability to make friends. But I've always stayed too busy to have to face this. When I got divorced, though, and was alone, I decided that I wanted to change my loner pattern.

There were two men I had always liked but had never taken the time to get to know. I called them both and set up things to do with each.

Both had always been friendly and had, it seemed to me, given clear indications that they would like to be friends.

Both men responded favorably and I enjoyed being with each one on several occasions, though we all three lived in different cities. Here, I thought, are two possible new friends. And they both seemed to be expressing similar kinds of feelings. But the subsequent relationships have been very different.

One man, whom I'll call Robert, loves to hunt and goes hunting a lot. I invited Robert to come for a visit, and we set up a time when he'd be coming to Texas to a business meeting we were both involved in.

About two months later when the meeting time arrived, Robert called. "I've just heard from an old friend who now lives in Wyoming. He and I have been talking about getting together for years, and this weekend is the only chance he has. So I wanted to let you know that I'm coming to the meeting, but I'll have to leave from there to go hunting. I really hope we can reschedule our visit some time soon."

"That's fine, Robert. I understand," I said cheerfully, but my stomach tightened. I waited until I heard the dial tone on the line, then I slammed the phone down and jammed my fist into my open palm. I had really been looking forward to our visit. In my paranoia I thought, "This just goes to show that people only want to be with me as friends when I can do something for them!"

But as I paced around the living room, I managed to talk myself out of that feeling. I remembered that Robert had told me how much he loves to hunt, and I knew the trip was a marvelous opportunity. Why couldn't I be happy for him? After I thought it through, I felt better.

But about eight months later, as I was planning a business trip, I realized my itinerary would take me right by where Robert lived. He had said he really wanted me to come see his town and where his work was, etc. He seemed to be elated that I was coming when I called to arrange it.

So, although it really squeezed my time, I arranged my trip so I could stop off for a day and two nights with him. Then about a couple of weeks before time to leave I called and told Robert's wife the exact time I'd arrive (he was out of town).

A few days later the phone rang and it was Robert again. "Hello, Keith? I've got a problem."

It seems that he had found this super place to hunt and had gotten some guys together to go. But the weekend I was coming to see him was the only weekend they could all arrange their schedules to go. He had known about the schedule conflict before I'd ever mentioned that I might be coming by, but he hadn't mentioned it until now.

"Come on and go with us," he had said. But since I was en route to a speaking engagement, I couldn't. Even though he really sounded sorry that things had worked out that way, my heart sank. Since he hadn't mentioned the hunting trip on my first call, I didn't know what to think.

I couldn't sleep that night, trying to figure out if Robert and I were friends or not. But after a few bad hours, I realized that this man had an agenda for his life in which some key priorities are higher than a friendship with me. And in my head I realized that this doesn't mean I'm no good. By my stomach gave me a fit at the time. I still like Robert very much and want to be his friend. And we've straightened out the hunting trip incident between us. But I have a real hesitancy to *instigate* getting together now.

The other man I had called also loves to hunt. But when we set a date to do something I have the feeling he would turn down almost any kind of social offer or try to reschedule it if we have agreed to get together.

Both are good men and if you asked them, I feel sure both consider me to be a good friend. But they have taught me that being a friend takes not only time together but a certain *giving of priority* to the friend in ways that create a security base for deeper commitments.

Friends in the Bible

It has been some comfort to me to realize that many of the leaders of the Hebrews were loners who had few close friends. There are a few great friendships like that of David and Jonathan in the Old Testament, and Ruth and Naomi. But can you name a lot of others? And even Jesus, though he worked with the Twelve, seemed to have only three friends he shared with closely—Peter, James and John.

I don't think it is really possible to have very many deep lifelong friendships. But we can have good friends along the way who are having similar life situations to ours. Singles are often not as tied up with social obligations and responsibilities as married people, and *ad hoc* friendships can spring up and flourish on short notice. Such friendships were a real source of comfort and enjoyment to me.

And the people I found it easiest to relate to were other Christian singles who were on the same inner journey I was to try to be God's person. These were Christians who also had (and could admit) the frustrations, needs and lonely-guilts about the single life.

Another neat deal about a bunch of Christians is that in that kind of fellowship it's possible to express and receive love for someone in a way you can't (without being misunderstood) in the non-Christian singles jungle. In a small group we found we could speak frankly about the resentments, loneliness, sexual temptations and our prayer life without feeling weird because our feelings weren't the same as those expressed in the other parts of the church building.

In these groups I began to recognize that I wasn't the only Christian single struggling with doubts and fears in trying to live my Christian values. We talked about how hard it is sometimes to make friends and how scary any personal commitment is because of the fear of being hurt. And just being able to talk openly about these things was a great help.*

I've run across some single Christians who think that there should not be "singles groups" in the church, that part of the problem in the church is that it tries to segregate singles into a safe corner so the marrieds don't have to deal with them directly. These "non-segregationist" people want the church to have "person groups" where married *and* single people get together to talk about the problems of life. Ideally I think this would be the best way. But unfortunately many married Christians are so out of touch with what's going on among singles that an honest interchange in such mixed groups is often virtually impossible. There would have to be some patient explaining and witnessing about the truth of the singles' jungle before much reality could emerge.

---

*One of these groups was recorded as a twelve-week course for singles called *Faith, Intimacy and Risk in the Single Life* (Waco, TX: Word, Inc., Educational Products Division, 1980).

That brings up another set of problems a single Christian faces in trying to make friends; how do you have a *married* friend of the same sex without being a threat to him or her with regard to the mate (of the opposite sex)?

Friendships with married people

For a while after my divorce I didn't have any single friends, except a few I'd known for years who moved in the "married society." At first I went out to dinner a few times at the homes of married friends. They were nice and we all tried to talk as we always had. But my ex-wife was missing and we were all painfully aware of this. We couldn't talk about the usual things and there was a lot of silence and a lot of polite and shallow chit-chat.

Also, I felt a new kind of self-consciousness. For instance, for years I've been a hugger when I greet people I haven't seen, men or women. But when I was first divorced and would go to a couple's house, I'd hug the wife and sometimes feel paranoid, as if the husband were jealous or suspicious.

Or if I'd arrive at the house before the husband got home from work I felt uneasy.

John and Jenny were two of the first to invite me over for dinner after the divorce. This couple had known my ex-wife and me, and now the three of us were attempting to maintain our friendship, even though I was now single.

I drove up the familiar driveway, parked the car and went to the door. Before I rang the bell I glanced back at the driveway and noticed that the garage door was open and John's car was missing. I glanced at my watch. "No, I'm not early," I thought. "It's 6:30, just like John said. Maybe his car is in the shop." I rang the bell.

Jenny came to the door with a cheerful smile, and said "Hi! Right on time, come in. John must be running late. He's not here yet. Come on in and we'll have a drink and wait for him."

An uneasy feeling passed through me, which I dismissed with irritation. "Nothing's going to happen," I told myself. "Jenny is a good Christian wife who loves John very much and I'm certainly not going to do anything." But just the fact that I was now a divorcé made me feel uneasy. I went in and followed Jenny to the kitchen.

The smell of dinner cooking brought waves of feelings—a mixture of sadness and pain along with enjoyment. Jenny fixed our drinks and handed them to me and I went into the living room with them.

By the time she followed, I was sitting on the front edge of a recliner chair, and had set Jenny's drink on the coffee table in front of the sofa. Somehow I wanted some space between us when John came in.

We talked for about fifteen minutes about superficial subjects—the weather, my new remodeling "garage apartment" project, their kids, my kids. The time dragged by and I kept resisting the urge to look at my watch.

At last I heard the sound of tires in the driveway and John's step on the front porch. I stood when he entered the room, and Jenny went to greet him with a kiss. As he hugged her, he looked at me over her shoulder and I saw a strange look on his face—of suspicion or shock, I didn't know which. It was as if he had forgotten I was coming. And although Jenny and I were just sitting in chairs in the living room visiting, I suddenly felt guilty—as if I'd done something wrong. And it was hard to be normal that evening.

It was as if I'd turned into some sort of dangerous monster because I no longer had a wife of my own to go home to. Whether there was any basis in the guy's mind for my feeling of paranoia I don't know, but I do know that being single and trying to have married friends has some complicating factors.

Possible complicating factors

In counseling couples about marriage problems, I'd learned that in spite of all the protestations Christian married people may make, often there *is*—or there can be—an uneasiness about having an attractive single friend hanging around a lot. It seems to depend on two factors, one or both of which is often invisible to the single person. As a counselor (and as a person who has been married) I know that many times there are serious strains in a marriage relationship *which don't show on the surface*. For example, the husband or wife may be going through a period of insecurity which can make him or her much more susceptible to jealousy than would normally be the case. If the single person doesn't realize this, he or she may come sailing in to dinner kidding and laughing and innocently flirting with the other partner. This can be very painful to the insecure husband or wife and add to the problems after the dinner party is over and the couple is alone.

There are all kinds of things which can lead to this same result. One member of the couple may have had an affair twenty years ago, and no one around knows, except the other member. Or the symptoms of aging or being overweight have hit one or the other of the partners and lead to vulnerable feelings. And I think it's a good idea for single people to be sensitive to the couple's possible problems when going out with them.

Besides the *couple's* problems, the other often unexamined factor is the *behavior of the single* when with a married couple.

When a single person comes to dinner at the home of married friends, he or she may seem to be unusually bright and cheerful. From the single's point of view the cheeriness may be caused by the fact that survival is taking place or to show the world that he or she is really a neat person in spite of having failed to make a marriage work. Or there may just be a lot of relief to be out of a bad marriage situation. But the behavior is exaggerated, overdone.

Whatever the reason behind the exaggerated cheerfulness, this behavior can be easily misunderstood by one or both of the married people. Being confronted by a "singing" happy person who has gotten out of his or her marriage can be very unnerving if the couple is not happy. Therefore I think it's helpful to be as open and direct as possible about where you are—if you are dealing with close friends.

Unconscious flirting

There is another type of unconscious behavior which I want to emphasize, however. Most us of want to be considered attractive. And many of us have learned to flirt or be cute or kid in ways that affirm the sexual nature of friends of the opposite sex. This kind of innocent gamesmanship is so natural for some people that it becomes unconscious. It was unconscious for me for years. And when one is single and feeling insecure about his or her masculinity or femininity, the unconscious emotional flirting-kidding behaviors can be heightened. And what can happen is that the single can be having a great time playing the flirting game with his friend's wife—even while the husband is in the room—feeling at a conscious level that it's just innocent play. But for the husband witnessing this game (who is of course not included) the feelings are quite different.

Since this flirting behavior is often not conscious; and even if it is, is not considered serious (by the flirter), he or she is amazed and hurt when the couple never calls again. The false conclusion drawn may be that "all married couples are 'against' singles."

I'm not suggesting that singles should be long-faced zombies around their married friends. But I am saying that sometimes a single person does not realize the extent of the threat when he or she relates to a married couple—either because of the couple's invisible problems or the single's unconscious needs for love and affirmation. I learned this both by experience after I'd been single awhile, and by watching other singles being insensitive. I could see the effect of the flirting clearly in others. It was much harder to spot in my own "innocent behavior."

There is also the situation in which your friend's wife or husband starts flirting with you. The only way I know to deal with this and still keep the friendship is to politely and goodnaturedly *not* get in the game. This is tricky, but to have integrity in the situation I know of no other way. And if *not* flirting gets you rejected by the couple, you may have saved a real tragedy by refusing to get involved at that level.

Having said all this, I realize that some singles have wonderful relationships with married couples with none of the problems I've been discussing.

But there is so much fear and paranoia afoot that married people often get stereotypes of all singles being irresponsible and lecherous (all the time) and singles get the picture of marrieds as being closed, exclusive and happily isolated in the coziness of their marriages. One single lady I know—it was JoAnne—got so tired of being misunderstood by her long-time married friends that she finally told one of them, "I'll tell you what. We won't think all of you are Marabel Morgans if you won't think all of us are Happy Hookers."

Two societies in the Church

For most singles it seems that there are really two societies in the church: married and single. And although married Christians may imagine that this is not true, the facts are that in social situations the marrieds do not often include singles. This may be neither good nor bad, but I think it is a realistic appraisal of the way things are in many Christian communities.

The best way I found to deal with this as a single was to try to carve out a life for myself with my work. I tried to be with other singles when possible socially, because I felt more at ease and we had common problems and experiences. Christian friendships were the best for me generally because being friends is easier when the friends are on a common and absorbing adventure. Also being able to bring our common problems to God was, and is, a very strengthening thing.

When going to a couples' gathering I usually tried to get a date to go with me so as to have a better time and to put people more at ease. I realize that it's not always convenient or possible to get someone to go with you. And when I didn't have a date, I tried to go and participate in as natural a way as possible without making flirtatious moves toward people's wives.

During the period following my divorce several of my old friends kept calling and maintaining contact. I could share my feelings and counsel with them. And in different ways they gave me hope and the courage to go on. But being single in a new world, I had to face the problem of making friends in a way I never had to before.

I don't have any "answers" to the problem of making and maintaining friendships. I think it's hard. But as a single I tended to forget that it was also not easy for me to make friends when I was married.

NOTES

Dear Andrea,

I've come to realize that several friends really saved my life. How about talking about some friendships which meant a lot to you?

What did you do about things like the competition for men? How did you relate to married couple friends? How about "friends" who were single men? Did that ever get complicated?

K.

One day about three months after my new friends from church had helped me move into my first single apartment, my friend Charlotte knocked on the door. She was nervously pacing outside my door and she stammered a little as she asked if I would come for a ride with her in her car. She wanted to talk to me. So we drove around town and finally stopped in the parking lot of a big discount store. She looked at me, took a deep breath and said, "Steve just told me he wants a divorce." A few tears leaked out of the inner corners of her tightly closed eyes and rolled down her cheeks. Her hands covered her face and her shoulders were tense and raised.

"Oh, Charlotte!" I breathed, not knowing what to say. I wanted to hug her or beat on the dashboard or express myself somehow, but it all seemed inadequate. Everything about everybody seemed to be falling apart.

A friendship deepens

A little while later we drove back to my apartment, talking about what she would do. A few weeks later, she told me she had decided to move out of her house and sell it. So I went with my car to her house and we loaded things onto a pickup truck and into my car trunk and moved them to her newly rented apartment. About two months later when we realized that our divorces would be final within three weeks of each other, we decided to plan a party for just the two of us.

On the evening of the day her divorce was final, I ordered a pizza, Charlotte brought a bottle of wine and we went to the drive-in movie and ate pizza and drank some of the wine.

When we came back to my apartment, we played records and talked.

I had a new Helen Reddy album, and we played "I Am Woman" several times, marching around the living room singing along, laughing until we cried. I felt brave and strong like the song said, and I wanted Charlotte to feel that way, too. But my day in court was still three weeks away and hers had been that day. She had a six-year-old son and a ten-year-old daughter. The extra responsibility for the two children was frightening.

We both managed to laugh a lot somehow, and the evening helped get some of the fearful feelings out of the way so we could think about the days ahead with calmer minds.

Sharing the crisis points of life: what friends can do for each other

Another woman friend who came to mean a great deal was introduced to me by people at my church. This church has a procedure of matching people up who are at similar crisis points, so that they can help each other. In this case, shortly after I joined the church, I was introduced to Jean, a woman who had been divorced almost a year earlier. She invited me to her apartment one Sunday night, and we became friends almost at once.

It was such a relief to find someone else to whom I could talk about all of the things I was having to handle, and the feelings and events that had led up to my present situation. She talked to me a lot about her own situation and how she had gotten to be single. By hearing her story, I could really believe that she could understand mine, even though a lot of the specific details were different.

Through this process I came to feel that we had a lot in common, and I had someone new who cared about me. She would call me up in the evenings just to say "Hi! How are you doing?" and she would tell me what her day had been like.

And I now had a new place to go—to her apartment. We also went to church events together, which was a relief, since I hated to go alone. Most of the time it was hard for me to get dressed, get in my car and drive somewhere alone, even though I knew there would be friendly people there when I arrived.

Another good thing was that I now had someone I could invite into my apartment, a reason to clean up and cook a dinner, or just spend an evening drinking coffee and talking.

And yet at the same time there was safety in the relationship because of all the things we *didn't* have in common. She had four children, I had none. We were in two different social worlds, and liked different types of men, so we had few feelings of competition in that area. Having Jean as a friend made me feel needed by someone, and I enjoyed doing things for her. I often felt free to call on her if I needed someone to do something for me.

A chance to "reciprocate"

Then a year later I was asked by the minister to go meet a girl whose divorce would be final in a few weeks. When it became my turn to be the helper, I saw how difficult it must have been for Jean. But even though I was afraid, I called the new girl, and drove over to her apartment.

I sat in the car for a few seconds looking at her door and trying to decide what I would say when she opened it. Finally I walked up the sidewalk, still not knowing what I would say, rang the doorbell and stood there listening to my heart pounding. She opened the door. We both had on bright smiles and said at the same time "Hi!" "Hello!" Then we laughed and I said, "I'm Andrea Wells."

Jennifer was only two years younger than I, had no children (like me), and had been married only a few years (like me). We became friends eventually, but we were both so shy it wasn't easy. Remembering how good I felt in my friendships with Charlotte and Jean, and how much I had begun to depend on them had gotten me to Jennifer's door the first time. After that it was easier, and fun!

Even though Jennifer and I had a lot more in common than Jean and I, this friendship seemed more threatening to me. Fortunately she was a person who wanted to communicate honestly about problems, so we really could talk about the threatening things. To me, the most threatening area between us was that of dating.

The threat of competition over men

One night we were having dinner together at a restaurant. We met a guy who then sat down to talk with us for a while. When he left, he had both of our phone numbers! Jennifer and I drove back to my apartment, sat down at my dining room table and stared at each other. We both had really liked this guy. Finally I broke the silence and said, "Well . . ." then I took a deep breath. "What do we do now?"

Neither of us said much that night. I remember we mumbled some things about not letting a guy come between us, but I was aware of the feeling that it could really happen. I remember also being torn by the hope that he would choose me—and the hope that he would call her. I knew it was a particularly lonely time in her life.

The worst possibility, I thought, was that he might call each of us! This situation presented an almost insurmountable strain on our relationship. I never really felt as comfortable with her about the subject of dating after that, even though the guy chose me. And, I felt *guilty* about going out with him.

The power of the male call

But eventually, sooner than I could imagine, Charlotte remarried. Both Jean and I were part of the wedding. About six months later, Jean remarried. I took part in her wedding too, bursting into tears at the worst possible moment—when the groom kissed her! And we drifted apart . . . they into the world of establishing new relationships with new husbands and I into a renewed career effort and search for a new female friend. I felt I was a "veteran" single after four years, and I still felt no desire to remarry.

Two special married couples

There were two married couples with whom I became friends. These two couples presented different kinds of friendships to me. One couple was about my age and had no children. I met Dick in the sharing group I had joined at the church. One night he invited the whole sharing group over to his house. That night I met Cathy, and the three of us slowly became friends.

I think that what I got most out of that relationship was a chance to see a marriage that was working. They didn't try to hide bad things from me. They didn't have actual fights and arguments when I was there, but they never pretended (as I was doing) that their life together was the "high life." They were simply saying, in effect, "We love each other and we have a commitment."

The other couple was twenty years older than I, with children in college and high school. They were both in the sharing group. They often invited me over for dinner on Sunday after church (which had been a hard time for me since my divorce). As a child I had been accustomed to big traditional family sit-down dinners after church. And after the divorce there were only solitary Sunday lunches at my apartment. This couple treated me like a member of the family, expecting my help with setting the table, opening cans, whatever needed doing.

I almost never felt that I was taking up too much of their time. Suddenly it would dawn on me that I might be staying too long, and I would leave. I had the feeling about Frank and Evelyn that if I woke up at 4:00 in the morning, really sick, I could call them and they would come and take me to the hospital in the middle of the night. I never needed anyone to do that, thank goodness, but it was a good feeling to know they were there.

"Friendships" with men—a moving target

I have heard women say that they have some very good friends who are men. In the past I have referred to some relationships I have had with men as "friendships." Yet, I always had a hard time distinguishing a "friend" from a potential "date" when it came to men.

There is a different dynamic when I talk to single men around the swimming pool, at work, or anywhere else, that draws out my feminine flirting characteristics and goes beyond what I call "friendship." There's a different way that I laugh at a friend's joke, if the friend is male. I noticed that I dressed a little more carefully when I was going to see a male friend. I checked my makeup more often when I was in the bathroom, wore perfume, paid close attention to everything he said, and tried to appear intelligent and feminine all at the same time. It's mostly unconscious, but it's not like a friendship with a woman or with a married couple.

At one time I developed a friendly relationship with a single man who was almost my father's age and a good friend of my father's. I just *knew* this one was only a friendship. But since I later met and married a man only a few years younger than my father—even that one looks "suspicious" to me now!

Every relationship with a man is not "romantic"—at least not on the surface

And yet, most of the time I preferred to label some relationships with men as friendships, because at some level it really bothered me to call them anything else. I've often wondered why.

Now, I think that most of the time I would not admit the relationship was anything other than a friendship because of my fear that if the relationship were to end, I would be disappointed in a deeper way. If I considered the relationship a friendship, then it was more understandable and less devastating to have it end, especially if it ended because the man became involved with another woman. But if I considered it a romantic involvement—or at least a *potential* one, then my attractiveness as a woman was on the line at another level, and I "lost out" if the relationship ended.

So to protect my own feminine pride, I referred to certain relationships with men as friendships and felt more comfortable about them. Yet I think that being aware of the potential these relationships have to blossom into romantic involvements can help avoid many misunderstandings in the singles' jungle.

I went out to dinner with a man I'll call Bob, supposedly a male friend. He was someone I could call when I was "down" or when I wanted to talk. Sometimes he would come over to my apartment and sit and talk with me, or take me out for a cup of coffee or a drink.

This particular night, I was really down. He took me out for dinner, then we went to a place for an after-dinner drink. We kept right on talking the whole time, just as we always did. Only something was different this time. I ignored this intuitive feeling, telling myself that this was Bob, and we were "just friends."

But when he brought me home, he followed me in the door of my apartment and made a proposition which I consider beyond the limits of "just friends." I was surprised, angry, and confused. I thought he knew we were "just friends" and would never assume more than that! But looking back on the evening, I realized I had assumed it was "safe" to go to a club, have a glass of wine, look into his eyes, tell him all my deep woes, because he would not misunderstand . . . we were, after all, "just friends." I was wrong. He did misunderstand because the potential for escalating such a relationship was lurking behind the façade of friendship all the time.

I want to repeat that I think it is perfectly all right and healthy for singles to have friends of the opposite sex. And I know many people have such friends without having encountered any complications. But I have learned that it's good not to be naïve enough to think that the goal can't change for one party or the other . . . without prior notice. And when that change happens, you are then into the whole question of dating.

CHAPTER TEN

Dating

NOTES

Dear Keith,

When you "hit the dating scene" you told me
you were pretty confused for a while about the
rules (or lack of rules) concerning permissible
behavior. From a man's point of view, how did you
cope with both your own expectations and those of
the women you met? What various attitudes did you
encounter?

A lot of people, women especially, seem to see
dating as one thing only—the way to find a
husband. How does this affect the men they date
from your point of view? And how can women who
deeply want to be married stop putting so much
intense pressure on their dates?

What was your reaction to the "no—commitment" attitude that is so prevalent in
the dating world? Do you think it helps or hinders
the search for intimacy through dating? And
finally, how can a relationship with God help
someone find a relationship with a person of the
opposite sex?

One more question: How about going out with me
on Friday night (my treat)?

A.

"Dating" sounds like a simple and straightforward subject. But when I came out of twenty-seven years of marriage to one woman, I was not prepared for the emotional reactions I had regarding dating relationships. I was afraid of looking foolish, of being intimate, of *not* being intimate, of being misunderstood, and sometimes of being understood. Everyone else in the singles' world seemed to be so busy smiling and looking confident that I hesitated to discuss my own fears, feelings of insecurity and questions about what was going on. But after almost four years in the singles' world I am convinced that most single people, and certainly most Christians, have some real uncertainties and frustrations about their dating relationships—or lack of them.

In the chapter on sexual choices we will talk about the specifically sexual aspects of the relationship between a man and a woman. But here we want to deal with the particular sort of friendship with a member of the opposite sex, the goal of which is to blossom into genuine intimacy of the romantic kind. Sexual intercourse may result from an intimate relationship, but they are not the same thing. (I am convinced that much of the sexual activity among singles includes very little vulnerable emotional intimacy.) But how can a dating relationship develop into that genuine sustaining closeness which many of us have longed for?

As I mentioned, when I first became single I was floored by the modern version of what had been called "dating" when I was growing up. I remember within days after the divorce being invited to dinner at a bachelor friend's house with two divorced women. My "blind date" arrived a few minutes after I did. And she was a very attractive person. After dinner the host and his date disappeared, and my blind date and I were left in the living room obviously expected to figure out our own intimate entertainment—and we had only known each other for two hours. My reaction may seem very backward to you, but, although we made it through the evening, I was very ill at ease at first and had no idea of the woman's expectations. We had just met. And that was my first experience with a date since being on my own.

Three perspectives regarding "what is appropriate"

As the months went by I had some revealing conversations with several single friends, men and women. I began to realize that although all single people (including Christians) may look alike on the outside, on the inside, where the world cannot see, they are operating under several very different views concerning what is appropriate behavior for singles on dates.

One group believes that dating is a way to get to know people and that the dating relationship should be kept on a friendly but superficial level. Being personal is permissible and eventually kissing and perhaps some further physical intimacy—but definitely no sexual intercourse before marriage.

In the second group are those who believe that sex is a very special thing, but that after a long courtship and a good deal of trust, commitment and closeness, then personalness of a deep nature and sexual intercourse are permissible.

The third group of singles believe that overt sex is such a natural and integral part of dating that there is something wrong with anyone who is not willing to go to bed on the first date. And if sex is not included by the second or third date, many people in this group do not care to continue the relationship. They simply disappear with no explanation, or are not available for dates any longer. One woman told me that if a man doesn't try to get her in bed after three dates, she suspects that he's gay or that he isn't attracted to her. Another said she was devastated that several men had, after one "sexless" date with her, indicated that they had enjoyed being with her and would call soon, only to disappear forever.

Of course there are all kinds of variations of the three perspectives just described. But it's easy to see that if a man in group one meets a woman in group three (or vice versa), there is very little chance for genuine intimacy to develop. And the existence of such widely divergent attitudes means that there can be an enormous amount of extra loneliness and sense of being unattractive which may be the lot of the Christian man or woman who believes that sexual relations should wait until marriage.

Intimate verbal sharing as a goal of dating—but what about commitment?

It seems to me that regardless of which group a person falls in, the goal of most dating is to get to know another person personally with the hope that a special relationship may evolve. And most people I've talked to consider that a successful dating relationship would move toward intimacy and vulnerability. In other words, as you get to know someone better in a dating relationship you want to share at deeper and more intimate levels.

But it is frightening to share your intimate thoughts and feelings, because the other person may run away, *or* share what you are saying with another date. So most people will not be vulnerable (and wisely so) without some sort of commitment from the other party. A commitment which gives some structure to the relationship can lead to the feeling that it is safe to be vulnerable and to move ahead with relating more personally. And a commitment can be anything from an agreement to date the other party exclusively to an agreement to have dates every Friday night.

The catch is that one of the cardinal rules in the singles' world is "no commitment at all." There are many people who will talk personally with their dates and be totally physically intimate, but want no commitment to the relationship beyond one day or night at a time. They say in effect, "I'll talk to you, go out with you, even sleep with you. But don't try to put any strings on me about tomorrow or about my other relationships when we are out of sight from each other."

And if someone starts being vulnerable and intimate with such a "no-commitment" person, moving the relationship toward a place where commitment would be natural, the risk is that the "non-committer" will pull a disappearing act, leaving the vulnerable person bitter and determined never to be open again.

This code of behavior makes it very difficult for a person to get to know another well enough to see if the relationship has the potential for a lifetime commitment. Many people seem to choose a "no-commitment" position as a protection against getting involved, but many others who live the "no-commitment" lifestyle are confused and depressed because they can't seem to find a way to be vulnerable or to have a relationship that has any depth or meaning. But in a world of "no commitments," how does one ever get secure enough in a relationship to find out if this is the right person to keep going with?

Finding "the right one"

It seems to me that one of the greatest sources of frustration and loneliness among singles is the fear that "I'll never find the right person to marry." Somehow many of us—and especially many women—got brainwashed with the idea that marriage is the only good life and that the primary goal of a single person is to find the right mate. It seems that this is especially true for Christians. When this is the way a single person feels, then all energies are focused on finding what one of my daughters calls the KSA, the "Knight in Shining Armor." And when this is true of someone—either man or woman—dating can be a nightmare of unreal pressure and anxiety.

For instance, let's say you are a woman and a cousin has arranged a blind date for you with a friend of her husband's who is supposed to look like Robert Redford. Consider what may happen. The guy has taken a bath and put on clean clothes. He thinks this is a casual evening in which he is going to take a nice girl (you) to the movies (or whatever). But you are thinking all week, "Maybe this is THE ONE, the KSA!" So when he walks in the front door you are so intense you start "examining his teeth" by checking his credentials and cross-examining him about his biographical information and vocational aspirations. Right away he's scared and very cautious, because he senses your anxiousness and intensity. And your behavior makes it difficult to get acquainted on a normal basis.

Another thing which can happen to people whose whole focus is on finding the KSA (or "Princess in Shimmering White") is that they tend to have impossibly high standards for seriously dating someone. That is, if a woman on the husband hunt sees that a new date is balding, keeps a messy apartment or drives a junky car, her tendency is to dismiss the guy by saying, "Obviously he would not make a good husband" (or "She would not make a good wife")—without ever getting to know *the person*. Such a seeker can bypass a lot of wonderful people who don't have the outer appearance of being the knight in shining armor, but who at least might be fine friends.

I am *not* saying that one should get rid of the vision of getting married. But the paradox is that as long as you have that vision in the forefront of every relationship, your perception will often not be natural, and your life can become nothing but an anxious holding pattern in which you are wasting perfectly good years merely waiting for the "real" action to begin.

Andrea and I were counseling with a young single woman who was apparently living for THE HUNT for the KSA. Dorine was always scheming in her mind about making relationships go. "It was so bad," she remarked one day, "that I could hardly make myself go out to the laundromat in the evenings for fear I would miss a call from a man!" (I remember at the time that Andrea said, "I know! But what you could do is take the phone off the hook while you're gone. If anyone calls they'll assume you're home and your line is just busy, and call back later." They both laughed.) But Dorine concluded that it was not fun being so controlled by a bunch of unknown men that she can't live a healthy, happy life.

As Andrea said in chapter seven, living in a holding pattern can keep people from finding their own identity and from enjoying using their own gifts to make a place for themselves in the world.

But let's say a person has decided to get out of a holding pattern, find his or her own identity and get on with living. How can such a person risk intimacy when an opportunity comes along?

An approach to intimacy

With the widespread fear of any commitment to a regular dating relationship and yet the need for a period of extended closeness before a couple can get to know each other, there are only two approaches to intimacy I've found as a Christian.

One is, after a number of dates, to say something like this to the woman you would like to get to know better: "I'm scared of commitment and I'm not ready for a permanent relationship. But I like you and want to get to know you better. Would you be willing to date only me, and I'll date only you for a certain period so we can kind of go on an adventure to get to know each other?"

If the person says, "no," you may have blown the relationship. But then again you may not have. And if she says, "yes," it's possible that you will have some structure in which genuine intimacy might happen. Unfortunately, if a woman says this to a man who isn't very secure, it might really frighten him. In the male chauvinist society in which many of us live, since many men are afraid of being "trapped" or "dominated" by women, this fear may prevent the man from understanding what the woman is trying to do. And therefore the risk is often greater for a woman who initiates this sort of move toward intimacy. But if she believes the man is secure enough to approach, or that he would be able to talk through his fears, it might be worth the risk for the woman to try it.

What I am talking about here is the idea of being honest and vulnerable in a relationship, of talking about what you really would like to do to learn more about a person you are dating. Although it is scary, often your being honest about your feelings allows the other person to as well. But this is not a manipulative technique to "open him or her up." If you decide to become more open and honest with the other person, she or he does not "owe it" to you to become open and vulnerable with you. You must be open because *you want to and need to* whether or not the other person *ever* is open. The response is up to the other person. That's why it's so frightening. Other people may run away. On the other hand, they may say that they'd love to make a commitment for a certain time and your relationship can move forward.

The second approach to risking an intimate relationship is really connected to the first approach. I felt that the only way I could risk getting emotionally close to a woman without an agreement with her to date exclusively was to commit my future (including the relationship) to God. I had to tell Him, "Look God, I'm afraid of getting hurt. I'm afraid of getting in too deep with this woman and not knowing how to get out. And I'm afraid I'll reveal myself and she'll walk away.

But I'm going to try to risk being vulnerable and loving her, knowing that even if she leaves me, I will have learned a lot and that You will be there to pick me up and give me new hope and direction."

And although it's better to have an exclusive commitment from the other person, you can make the commitment to God and risk getting to know someone without his or her being able to commit as you start out.

It seems to me that each intimate relationship is so unique that it's very difficult to describe in general terms how two people get from a first date into genuine intimacy. But the adventure is an exciting one even though the hurts, failures to communicate, and sudden terrifying "disappearances" can come at any time. The problems are numerous but the rewards are very great for those couples who can stay in there and keep communicating in honesty and love.

Because each person is unique in terms of background, hopes, fears, and expectations, dating will be a different experience for everyone, depending on the premise each one starts out with concerning what dating is. So it might be a good thing to stop and think about what you expect from dating before going out. And it could be crucial to begin finding out what your dates think dating is, too, since she or he may want a lover—and you're only looking for a friend.

NOTES

Dear Andrea,

The experience of dating in the adult singles' world (beyond high school and college) must be a very different experience for a woman from what it is for a man. And I think some of the things you've told me about the way you felt at first might really help here. As a man, I can really identify with the insecurity stage you told me about, of having to prove that you were attractive after your divorce. But the particular problems of not being able to instigate and control relationships just because you were a woman (in a society in which men are "supposed to" call, etc.) must have been very frustrating. What were your feelings about that? You said once that you realized you were hooked on the need for male affirmation and that made you mad. Would you talk about that? How were you able to begin to change your behavior in this area?

I know some of this is hard to talk about, but I think it will help a lot of people at least see the issues.

K.

The apartment complex where I lived had a swimming pool. One of my favorite Saturday afternoon activities was to go to the pool, lie in the sun, sleep, read books and cool off in the water. One Saturday, shortly after my divorce was final, I was there again. I had been there every Saturday that summer, had never spoken to anyone, and no one had spoken to me.

This particular day, I was lying on a towel on the concrete. I woke from a nap and decided to get in the water to cool off before reading a book I had brought with me. I slipped into the water on the opposite side of the pool from two guys who each had floats. One of them said, "Would you like to use this float for a while?"

"No thanks," I said, too quickly. "I'm just going to cool off and then read."

"It's really okay," he said. "I'm through with it and I don't mind."

Something in my head clicked. Why am I being so unfriendly? Or is it that I'm shy? Why not lie on the float for a while? So, with my heart in my throat I said, "Well, in that case, thanks. I will."

After I had climbed awkwardly up on the float and stretched out, I found that the sun was right in my face. All of a sudden I felt awful. I felt like my pot tummy was showing, my wet hair probably looked stupid and the squint caused by the sun made my face look silly. I figured the guy was sorry he'd ever offered me the float! But I just lay there, trying to to keep my balance, not daring to shift my weight or call any attention to myself in any way. I was miserable.

The guy and his friend continued talking and laughing, and pretty soon I found myself listening to what they were saying. Then I made a comment, and I found myself right in the middle of their conversation, having a great time. I forgot about my tummy, my hair, and my squint... and the time. I stayed on the float much longer than I had planned. When I realized how long I had been there, I quickly slipped off and said goodbye. And after gathering up the towel, suntan lotion, glasses, hat, and book, I went down the sidewalk, around the corner and into the cool of my air-conditioned apartment.

"Amazing!" I thought. I felt as excited as a young girl who had just been asked for a first date. It hadn't seemed so difficult to talk after all. Then I remembered those awful minutes at the first when I had felt so ugly, and I realized it wasn't going to be easy getting back into the dating world.

The first two years

I began to get phone calls, and to go out. The most popular place to go was a club called The Shadows. The town I was living in had never had a nice club before, and it seemed that everybody wanted to be seen there, dancing, laughing and having a grand time. I was no exception. As I met more and more people, it seemed that I would have no trouble getting dates. This was certainly a different world for me from my high school social scene. I had been a tall, slightly overweight, bookworm who made As and Bs, played the piano, and loved bridge and symphony concerts. Needless to say, the social crowd wasn't standing in line to take me out! And I was scared of them, anyway. They moved too fast for me, or so I thought.

But now things were different. I had lost weight, and seemed to look like most of the girls in this dating scene. While I was in my middle twenties, however, most of the girls were in their late teens or early twenties. It didn't matter to me. I felt young and really enjoyed the crowd. Besides, most of the guys were nearer my age or a little older.

I quickly adopted the rules of the singles lifestyle . . . no commitment, we're just going to be friends and have a good time . . . you do your thing and I'll do mine . . . there will be no jealousy because we don't have any special relationship to cause jealousy. I adopted this line of thinking so completely that I remember actually feeling *good* about seeing a guy I had dated out with another girl. "That means he won't expect me not to date other guys," I told myself and felt very free and modern inside.

This kind of social life continued for a couple of years, and I had one or two main relationships and a lot of dates that were "just friends," and relationships that didn't last very long . . . maybe just one or two dates. I remember being happy to have the freedom to meet new people and to choose to go out or not, based on my own feelings and thoughts about a person. I liked not having to say "no" to some new possible relationship because of a commitment to someone else. There wasn't anyone I knew for whom I was willing to give up this freedom.

Over the hill

But after two years or so that social setting began to seem repetitious, shallow and sometimes boring. I started spending a lot of time looking around the club to see if people were really as happy as I had thought they were. I noticed a lot of glassy-eyed stares, serious faces, lonely groups of girls, and individual guys leaning on the bar. Others were standing near the walls or clustered around small tables. Their eyes roamed the room, as if trying to make a connection with "Mr. Wonderful" or "Ms. Wonderful." Occasionally a guy would walk over to a table full of girls, ask one to dance, bring her back and disappear again. I had never gone to this club without a date, and I began to notice this kind of hunting game the men and women were playing, and it sent chills down my back.

Sometimes when I went in the ladies lounge I would see a beautiful young girl torn apart by tears, crying in the corner, with two or three of her girlfriends looking miserable and depressed. The friends were trying to comfort her, saying things like, "No man is worth all this pain!" and encouraging her to just "Go out there and act like it doesn't bother you a bit!" and "Show him." This scene now began to look very painful and destructive.

Also, I began to get fewer and fewer phone calls and to go out less often. Two and a half years after my divorce, I had stopped hurting and wondering why my marriage hadn't worked out and had begun to think about questions like "What kind of person am I . . . really?" "What do I want out of life?" "Do I want another husband or not?" "Am I cut out for marriage?"

But at the same time, the lessening of male attention brought a certain degree of panic and depression. I became uncertain, as I was in high school, that any man would want to be around me for anything other than a dancing partner, a cook, a maid or a sexual conquest.

I thought the reason for the lessening of male attention was that I was getting "too old" for the disco scene—after all, I was twenty-eight—and guys were not interested in anyone my age. Or I thought that I had gotten to a professional level that was threatening to most guys my age. Or perhaps my moral standards (which were not "Puritan," but were not very relaxed either) had gotten me a reputation for not being a good date. As the panic increased, I tried to counteract some of these fears.

I kept my hair long. I had let it grow from the time of the divorce, and it was now two inches below my shoulders. I wore it in imitation of the many college-age girls I'd seen—parted down the middle and flipped a little on the ends. Later I even had it cut into long curly layers in imitation of the then-popular "Farrah Fawcett" cut. I even wore clothes like the college girls around me.

One night I was sitting across the table in the disco club from my date—someone new. We were going through all the beginning conversation about who we were, where we worked, where we grew up, etc. Sam said that he was twenty-five and he thought I looked twenty-three or twenty-four and wanted to know which one was right. I hesitated, studying the napkin beside my glass, trying to think of a cute way to tell him my age without sounding awkward. But there was no way around it.

Finally, I took a breath, looked up at him, put my elbows up on the table and said with a smile, "Well, actually, Sam, I'm twenty-eight."

His jaw dropped slightly, although he recovered very quickly. It was his turn to stir his drink, and then he offered me a cigarette, lit it and lit his own. After another long moment he laughed a little and said, "Well, it doesn't bother me if it doesn't bother you."

We talked on, danced a little, then he drove me home. I had realized that it did bother me. The disco club, the smoke, the headaches in the mornings, the noise level, the whole routine of telling my name, what my job is, how long since my divorce and all that other data all bothered me. But the fact that I had succeeded in dressing and acting younger than I was and guys his age were believing it and asking me out disturbed me the most. All these things suddenly seemed flat, meaningless, boring and empty. Just the week before that, dating had been full of glamour, excitement and promise. I had enjoyed it for two and a half years, but that night I recognized that the feelings had all changed. And I was finished with that kind of dating.

Falling in love—breaking up: The continuous cycle

I thought back on the few serious relationships I had had and realized that a pattern was beginning to emerge. When I realized that a relationship was getting to be "serious," I would begin to relax and enjoy the new warm secure feeling. I realized that I didn't have to be "on" all the time or act like "company" was coming over. The two of us shared a wider variety of experiences because of the amount of time we spent together.

But then came the second wave . . . my fear of emotional dependency. There usually was no commitment to dating exclusively, because I believed at that time that going steady was a dead-end street which cut off future options and led to possessiveness.

However, since there were no guarantees that the relationship would last, I knew that to get deeply involved with a man was inviting tragedy if the relationship got snapped off one day. There I'd be, with this deep feeling of love for him, and he'd be gone.

At some point in one particular relationship after this second wave of fear hit me, I noticed that the guy, Barry, started behaving less warmly toward me, and I felt less warm myself. Then one week he didn't call for a couple of nights, after not having missed a night for six weeks in a row. And the next time I talked to him, he pretended nothing was wrong. Perhaps Barry really felt nothing was wrong. *I* definitely felt something was wrong, yet didn't know how to ask about it. After all, we had said we weren't committed and didn't have to answer to each other for our actions.

Then Barry was out of touch for two weeks. When I asked him about it, he declared, "I'm not tied down to you so what's the matter? What's your problem?"

There followed what seemed to be a struggle for control and I started trying to manipulate our conversations to find out what I needed to know. I wanted all the information I could get about him when he wasn't with me. "Where is he?" "Who's he with?" "Is she pretty?" And at the same time I hated myself for needing to know, and put off admitting that I was getting emotionally dependent on the relationship, that it was slipping away from me, and there was nothing I could seem to do about it.

So I'd go around places where I could find out if he was at home or not. Maybe I'd make up reasons to drive down a certain street, just to check on lights in his apartment, or cars in the parking lot. Maybe at the last minute I'd decide not to do it, and wouldn't make the last turn. I'd floorboard the car in anger. And once I got a speeding ticket because I was so mad about the whole situation.

After one particular night like that I had a stern talk with myself. Obviously my behavior was not going to come across very pleasantly to Barry. No wonder he was disappearing. "But why can't I seem to help it?" I asked the mirror. Then I laid out my two options to myself: I could decide I needed to talk with him about the whole situation, which he had usually said was being "clinging," "possessive," and "old-fashioned." Or I could pretend it didn't matter, which would be "modern," "strong," "cool," and independent.

So I tried the approach of being "strong and independent," even though I was full of pain inside. It was like beginning my own personal struggle for independence all over again. "I'm in over my head," I said. Then I'd start staying away from home in the evenings, going to visit girlfriends or working late at the office, just so I wouldn't be there if he should call. Of course, if anyone else should call, I would miss that, too. But at that point in the development of things, *knowing* that he *hadn't* called was worse than sitting there at home alone on the chance that someone else would call. When I was with him, I'd be cool and distant or angry.

By that time, my behavior had probably convinced Barry that I didn't care about him. I was never at home anymore. When he did see me I'd practically ignore him, or my voice was cool, controlled and phony sounding, even when I was cheerful. We both didn't know what was wrong with the other, but since we couldn't talk about it, we were trapped . . . doomed to continue the destruction of a once-fulfilling friendship.

Something like this relationship with Barry happened to me several times during a period of about two years.

Hooked on a feeling

About six months later, one January, I decided to do something different for a while. I was sick of moping around, or trying to attract the attention of every male I met who looked like a potential date. I decided to "forget" about hunting for dates as much as I could and to concentrate on discovering what *I* liked to do. I found books to read, looked at furniture for my apartment, went to movies and concerts with girlfriends, got an attractive haircut, and bought some new clothes that seemed to fit my age and vocation—a soon-to-be-thirty junior executive with a music publishing company.

That change in attitude brought on a year of struggle that surprised me! I thought it would be easy to "forget" about men. But the more I tried reading books and watching television, the more I realized I was "hooked" on male attention. It was hard for me to believe in my own self-worth as a woman if I didn't have some kind of affirmation that I was attractive—from men.

One day I was attending a sales meeting for my company. I sat in the meeting through the long presentation by another division, going over in my mind what I had planned to say when my time came. I was also aware that in the room with about thirty-five men—salesmen and marketing people—I was the only woman executive. A couple of secretaries were sitting in taking notes during the meeting. They were five or six years younger and were new with the company.

When the group took a break, I wandered slowly over to the coffee table. My new policy of flirting less and being more businesslike had begun that morning, and I was wearing a below-the-knee length skirt, a cotton button-down blouse, a blazer and pumps instead of the usual knee-length straight skirt with a slit, sweater and open sandals with heels. Even though I felt uneasy in this new outfit, I knew it was in style.

One of the more flirty guys came up to me and said, "I gotta tell you, that skirt makes you look *old*. You're too pretty to hide your legs that way!"

A lump rose in my throat. This was my old "buddy" who was always friendly and made me feel *great*. He had just criticized me lightly, but the pain was deep. I didn't know what to say, so I laughed and batted my eyes and said, "Well, it's the new style, you know!" Instantly I saw myself back in my old flirty behaviors—responding to a comment about my legs instead of talking about business or at least something neutral like the doughnuts or the weather.

The rest of the day was very hard for me. Hardly anyone spoke to me, and most of the men either clustered around one of the two young secretaries or stood in pairs talking to each other. I felt virtually invisible to the group. They were polite but not warm as they had been at previous sales meetings. I thought, "I'm over the hill. I am definitely not attractive to anyone any more." And I was too devastated to go up to anyone and join a conversation.

I realized later that my change in behavior and dress was perhaps as hard for these salesmen to understand as their reactions had been for me. In my determination not to flirt I must have seemed cool, edgy or hostile. And the message telegraphed by the clothes called for a new reaction from them. It must have seemed that I was almost a stranger, and none of us knew what to say to each other! They were actually responding to me the way I had wanted them to, with little or no flirting, and with businesslike respect. Yet the change felt, to me, like a bucket of cold water. And I wasn't ready for the way it felt, given my need for male affirmation.

The nagging thought that I wasn't attractive because I wasn't getting male attention or invitations to date continued to plague me. At that point I could *really* begin to see how *much* I depended on male affirmation in order to feel pretty. I was angry at myself for needing this, yet I couldn't seem to shake the vague, uneasy feelings, the slight depression that hung around my mind like a cloud.

My girlfriends had all remarried or drifted away. The weekly bridge game had crumbled when one of the girls decided she didn't want to play regularly any more and we never found a replacement. All the people I had dated seemed to have moved away, lost interest or gotten involved in committed relationships with other girls. And my friends at the church, Dick and Cathy, had moved to Phoenix. Frank and Evelyn still listened on Sundays, but I felt myself withdrawing even from them.

I started working later and later at night to avoid going home and facing that transition time from work to whatever book I was reading. I kept asking the question, "How can I feel assured that I am somebody and I am worth something when I am all alone like this?"

Kicking the habit

While I was struggling with these feelings, I almost got into a relationship with a married man at the office. He seemed to think I was attractive and he listened to my ideas about the job. But he apparently thought I was open to the idea of a relationship with him. My lack of confidence in myself and my sending signals to find out if I was attractive must have given him the idea that I would be interested in a sexual relationship with him.

When he made the suggestion openly to me, I was not totally surprised, but I was disappointed in myself. I knew I had subconsciously led him on, yet I hadn't been able to stop myself. I guess I had kept hoping that he would never actually try to begin a physically intimate relationship with me.

I declined the invitation, and also ended our "friendship." I felt ashamed of my part in the escalation of the relationship and angry at him for trying to "take advantage" of me. The knowledge that I was attractive to him was ruined by all the negative feelings that went with it. I wanted to "kick the habit" of flirting and being "misunderstood," but couldn't seem to stop sending those signals. I resolved to try harder to tone them down. This experience left me feeling very lonely and depressed.

On the outside I tried to appear to be coping well. I tried not to be so sensitive in meetings, keeping tears strictly out of sight. But I often felt close to tears when my ideas weren't accepted, or when they were even questioned. I felt defensive most of the time, as if "they" were trying to prove I was incompetent. But I kept all that inside, or so I thought, and tried to do the best job I could.

On the one hand it was a painful time. Yet I enjoyed the satisfaction of getting things done in a situation where relatively few women had made it as far as I, of dreaming up new marketing schemes or a more efficient way to do something. I learned new office procedures that fascinated me, and I loved having a "family" of people to be with at work each day. When praise did come, it would lift my spirits for a whole week. And I began to feel that in my job I was good at what I did.

I also saw that my efforts to be more businesslike were paying off, and that I was being trusted with more and more responsibility. While I was getting less and less flirty, teasing attention, I was receiving more and more businesslike responses, job responsibility and respect. It was hard to give up one kind of affirmation in order to get another. But in the process my job became a career, a vocation—and not just a place to meet men and something to do until "Mr. Wonderful" came along and took me away from it all, or somewhere to spend the hours until it was time to go out on a date.

But it was during this period that I began to wonder what a really intimate relationship would be like. How would it start out? Would it be different from the kind of dating I'd known? Or would an ordinary relationship suddenly change at some point and become close and vulnerable? I wanted to be sure to recognize genuine intimacy if I got close to it.

CHAPTER ELEVEN

The Anatomy of an Intimate Relationship

NOTES

Dear Keith,

    With the lack of consistent "rules" to go by in the dating world, it's hard to know if you're dating someone who has the potential to be a lifelong partner or who is really only a temporary relationship until you find the right person. Or, if a person has decided not to marry, dating may be just a social activity—a way to spend a few evenings relaxing and being with people.

    But how can we know what a really good relationship is like when it happens? Would you take some time to describe how a relationship might develop into intimacy? And please don't leave out the rough spots! What happens when two people get too close or when jealousy strikes or when things are blah?

    We've talked about this so much, and I like what you've told me from your own experience and studies.

                          A.

*I have sought intimacy all my life and have felt as if I were in some track-*less jungle without any reliable native guides. I have been frightened when it looked as if I were getting close to someone, and have found myself doing things which seemed to destroy the very relationship I was consciously trying to build. It was baffling, and I couldn't find anyone who could or would tell me anything much about what it is like to participate in an authentic experience of growing intimacy in a dating context.

I don't believe a lot of dating relationships include much genuine intimacy. Perhaps many should not. But I would like to describe a hypothetical meeting between two people of the opposite sex and how it might develop from a casual social encounter into a deep, intimate relationship—falling in love. There are many paths which can lead to intimacy and this description pictures only one way such a relationship might develop. Though it may seem very specific, I believe many of the elements are common experiences in many cases, no matter what the particular setting may be.

The meeting

Let's say that you meet someone of the opposite sex who seems to be pleasant. You are in a social situation, perhaps at a party or a meeting of a singles' group. For the purpose of describing this development, I am going to assume that you, the reader, and I are meeting. (If you are a man, imagine that I am an attractive woman.)

After meeting we would probably begin at a surface level, "What's your name?" (if we haven't been told it), "Where do you work?" and perhaps, "Do you live here?" This is a part of the awkward beginning singles have to go through again and again.

But if we like what we hear and see, as the other person is fielding the front-doorstep questions, we may feel drawn to each other ever so slightly. And if so, the conversation moves imperceptibly to a deeper level. I could ask you if you have any brothers or sisters. And as we talk I might drop some little personal comments like, "You know, when I was a kid, I used to be a movie addict," and you might say, "Me too, but I could go only on Saturday afternoons."

Exchanging personal histories

As the conversation goes on and we begin to reveal ourselves to each other, primarily concerning safe aspects of the past, we may find ourselves speaking of our childhoods or hometowns.

This exchanging of personal histories is one of the neatest ways to begin to get to know people intimately. It's not just the *content* that is meaningful. But the *way* I talk about my family or past experiences tells you a lot about me that I am not even aware I'm communicating. For instance, the way I talk about my father or the death of my dog, or the nostalgia when I speak about walking through the woods alone as a boy—these things give you clues to my real "person." The progression I'm describing may take place in a few hours, on several dates or even over several weeks or months.

But as our involvement deepens I may find myself suddenly revealing something about my past I have never told to another person, like a personal fear which bothered me as a child. And when you seem to understand, I am deeply touched. When this happens, a feeling of warmth and emotional closeness can envelop us both.

Refocusing on details

As things like this begin to take place, we may start to notice each other's features in detail. I start to wonder what's behind your eyes. Instead of just "seeing a face," I begin to imagine silently what is going on inside you: "Are you as interested in me as I am in you? Do you think I'm attractive, too?"

And even if we are in a crowded room, it is as if the two of us had stepped into an emotional glass bubble where we can only see and hear each other. The surroundings simply disappear and we are the only two people of importance in the world. This exclusive preoccupation is one of the approach signs of intimacy.

Wading in

When a relationship reaches this threshold, some things may begin to take place which seem like magic for people who have never experienced them. You may find yourself expressing thoughts or feelings which you would normally never reveal, because as a child you may have been rejected for having them, or felt that you would be. And as you tell me such things, you are excited and you are watching me to see if I will accept you, almost knowing that I will. And when I do, you may laugh with relief and wonder.

Then one of us may drop the sophisticated personage and plunge into the feelings we are having at *this time* in our life—which feel much more dangerous. For instance, I might blurt out something like, "You know, I'm really shy at parties. But I've learned to joke a lot to cover my shyness, so no one will get too close to me." (And this is true of me, but it would be threatening to tell you, for fear you would laugh or think I am emotionally unbalanced.)

But instead of laughing or looking shocked, you might say, "Hey, that's the way *I* feel!" (if you do) or you might just nod to let me know you understand. And then, even if you don't feel that way yourself, we share a secret about my life and the way I relate to people. I have been vulnerable enough to trust you with that part of me. And in doing so, I have indicated that I would like to go further in this relationship.

Trust and freedom

Of course the subject matter might be totally different but this kind of exchange without criticism or judgment breeds a growing trust in the relationship and an increasing freedom to begin to express true feelings and goals. And at some point we may feel that we could tell each other almost anything.

But strangely, every time one of us starts to relate something that might threaten the relationship, there is a fear of "Oh, oh, now I'm going too far. She'll never be able to accept me with *this* feeling or experience in my life!" But if I go ahead, and am accepted, then I know a happiness and wonder that's hard to express. This experience of freedom and acceptance is the beginning stage of genuine intimacy.

We may find defensive walls of a lifetime crumbling. And we can hear each other better because we hear the echo of our own experiences as they hit the sounding board of the other's heart with nothing in between. It's a feeling of quiet wonder.

Because we don't have to hide our feelings, we can begin to state preferences. So many couples waste endless time saying, "What do *you* want to do?"

"Oh, I don't care, what do *you* want to do?"

But in an intimate relationship, we can each say, "This is what I'd like to do," and negotiate differences.

Of course, some of the things I reveal about my feelings or my past may hurt or shock you and you find yourself recoiling in fear. But if you find the courage to tell me your feelings and I can understand your hurt or fear and give you time to assimilate this new information about me, we can go forward. This can be very difficult, but as we make it through some hurts and fears together we feel even closer.

And we begin to feel sorry for the rest of the world. "It's a shame every couple can't have the closeness we have and tell each other their real feelings, the way we do." We have the feeling of being uniquely favored by God in finding each other.

As we begin to let our *current* feelings show and get through some of the hurts and fears together, we may move into confessing our sins against each other and being forgiven. And if this happens, we may begin to be amazed at how well we understand each other in some important area or areas. We may have times of knowing what the other is thinking and about to say. As a matter of fact, this is a common experience of an intimate relationship, because when we don't have to hide our feelings to avoid rejection, someone who loves us can "see" what we mean before we say it. Being understood in this way is what people search for everywhere.

We Christians believe the root of this search for intimacy is a part of our search for a personal relationship with God. And the point at which the Gospel meets our personal need is when we realize that we are known and accepted as we are, without having to earn that acceptance. That's the free gift of God: Grace. And genuine intimacy is a human experience of this kind of grace. Both people feel accepted, just as they are.

Reexperiencing the magic

One of the delightful habits couples get into in order to re-enjoy cherished feelings is that of remembering and retelling the first glorious, scary moments when they met. And as we begin to laugh and retell our story, the first magic comes back. And again and again we can enter that first glow of love which brought us together.*

Enter sex, exit vulnerable sharing and calm reason

But about the time we really begin to get open with each other and find that we have warm, loving responses of security and trust, then a bunch of physiological feelings are triggered. The touch of your hand may become sexual—electric. We both want to kiss and hold and touch all the time. And sooner or later we are both wild to consummate the relationship in sexual intercourse. And whether we act out these feelings or not, they send out a magical atmosphere like a powerful perfume over the whole situation.

This tingling sexual aura changes the relationship so much that it often becomes very difficult to work out personality problems and express threatening confessions regarding the intimate relationship.

Sex becomes so important that the risk of sharing something which might break the romantic aura is too great. And unfortunately, many people stop the progress toward personal openness in dealing with the relationship when the physical aspect of the relationship becomes dom-

---

*In a sense this is a microcosm of our Hebrew-Christian practice. The Jews recall the first deliverance by God of Moses and his people from Egypt over and over (e.g., Passover), and in the Christian communion service, we drink the blood and eat the bread "for the remembrance of Him." (The liturgical scholar, Dom Gregory Dix, said that should be translated, for the "re-calling" of Him. We re*call* Him to the present moment so we can express our love now and experience His.)

inant too soon. Also, a threatening moment of honesty can be a real sexual "turn-off" which many people feel will destroy the relationship, when in fact the turn-off is usually only a passing experience caused by the fear of facing the issue at hand. And those couples who have the courage to stop and deal honestly with their feelings often find that they feel even more drawn to each other after having done so.

Intimate sharing: powerful, but harder than sharing with a stranger

It may take weeks or months for two people to reach the place where personal sharing is deep and very important to both. Sometimes a kind of depth sharing happens faster with strangers than between people who have known each other for some time. This is one of the secrets of the success of singles' bars and the disco scene. It's safer to share with someone you will never see again.

But it is difficult for *genuine* intimacy to take place quickly because there must be a sense in which the other person is *not* anonymous but is a person you *will* see again—or would like to. The risk in telling a stranger about your hopes, dreams and sins is nothing compared to sharing these things with someone you hope will love you and care about you in the future. There is a sense in which true and lasting intimacy requires continuity in the relationship. Without the assurance of continuity, the other's vulnerability cannot be trusted (since either party can walk off unscathed). And unless one is open about his or her inner feelings, the inner *person* is not really exposed to either rejection *or* love.

This experience of trust and the freedom to express true feelings is so rare and so powerful that many young people get engaged or even married on the strength of one brief experience of this sort of beginning intimacy, because they think it is LOVE. They have exposed some of their true feelings and not only were they not rejected, but this "angel" they have met says, "Hey, I think that's terrific!" And this acceptance where one has always been braced for rejection is so exciting and promising that people are ready to commit their lives. But this trust and freedom are only steps into the entry hall to a lasting intimate relationship.

The freedom to say "I was wrong"

Still another seemingly impossible change which can come about in an intimate relationship has to do with pride and the admitting of mistakes. One of the bad by-products of being put down and rejected as a child for having certain natural feelings is a highly developed defense against being wrong. Kids learn to hide mistakes, rationalize them and otherwise avoid "being wrong" since "wrong" has been translated to the person inside as "evil" and "not lovable." So it is very hard to say "I'm sorry" and admit that our behavior is less than perfect. This defensiveness and the dishonesty it breeds are especially hard to live with in close relationships.

But in genuine intimacy, when two people have fallen in love, an amazing change can take place. When I make a mistake or am wrong and hurt you, I may find myself admitting I've been wrong and trying to make things right for you. I can sometimes do this because I feel that *you* (unlike the people in my past) will accept me even with my imperfections. So I don't have to defend myself as being okay—your love tells me that you already think that. It is evidently the fear of not being accepted which keeps me from admitting I have been wrong. So if I have let you know me and you love me anyway, I can begin to be more realistic and honest in confessing my sins and errors.

And when a person hears his woman (or her man) say sincerely, "I was wrong," with no excuses or manipulative games, the experience is a little bit of heaven. And forgiveness is much more natural—though not without pain.

The importance of honesty

I believe that a commitment to try to be honest about our own feelings is essential to continuing intimacy. I'm *not* talking about being obligated to express every thought that enters your mind. To "not have an unexpressed thought" would be neurotic in my opinion and could hurt the other person desperately.

For instance, if the thought crossed my mind that your eyes are too close together, to express such a thought could help no one and might do a lot of damage—since this is a subjective opinion and nothing could be done about the observation in any case. Or if one of us sees a person of the opposite sex who is very attractive to us, pointing out how we are attracted (in the name of honesty) would hardly be helpful. And that's not what I'm suggesting.

But when one of us has fears, angry feelings or bad past experiences which color our reactions to each other, I think it is helpful to risk talking openly about such things, and listening nonjudgmentally to each other. I know how difficult being honest about certain feelings is.

There are, of course, some areas which need to be approached very slowly, and it may be that one or both parties cannot handle talking about certain subjects. It is good to face that together and not insist. For instance, the subject of past relationships in which sex has been involved is a very loaded and threatening subject for many people. But whenever the partners agree, it can be very therapeutic to learn to be open in as many areas of life as possible in maintaining an intimate relationship.

Ideally, if we are both committed to being open, then I think a habit of hiding significant thoughts and feelings destroys more than it protects in the long run.

The arrival of blindness

Sooner or later I may get a sudden shock as I come to realize that I *really care for you*! In fact, I care for you a *great deal more than I had planned to*. And the love and acceptance you are giving is *very important* to me. I realize that when I express an honest feeling, I *expect* acceptance from you, instead of the rejection I always feared and expected before. And suddenly your love and approval mean so much to me that I hesitate to be honest about my real feelings for fear of your rejection.

There is some mechanism in the human psyche that performs what looks like a trick at this point. There is an invisible and wonderful experience of *self-deception* we experience which seems necessary in order for the relationship to continue.

First we begin to change our standards when the loved one doesn't measure up. And we begin to see each other through different eyes. My big nose gets smaller. Warts, varicose veins, height differences and opposite personal preferences seem to disappear. Habits which have always seemed obnoxious to me in other people become almost attractive in you.

For instance, let's say that I talk too much (which is true), and that incessant talking has always been a very irritating trait to you. But in the aura of love *my* conversation may sound so interesting that you listen intently and even encourage me to talk more. The sound of my voice may be soothing or stimulating. And you laugh at yourself, as your realize what a miraculous change has taken place in your life. Here is proof that you have found true love, because you have changed the reaction of a lifetime!

But all such changes may be part of an unconscious decision to put aside anything that may interfere with the magic of love which is taking place in your life. And since such decisions are not conscious to the people to whom they are happening, you do not see that you are suffering from at least a temporary blindness. (This experience may be where the expression "love is blind" comes from.)

But parents and friends can see what is happening with more "objectivity" and are often appalled at what is taking place. They may say to you, "You are *not* like this person! Don't marry him (her)! You're crazy!" because they can see that you are blocking out information about me that is obviously against your nature.

Hiding the truth

Many people make a sad mistake at this point. Let's say that I do become consciously aware of some things about you which irritate me, and of values which are different from mine. Since I don't want to risk the wonderful relationship we are developing, I decide *not* to be open about the problems—because I am confident that we can "work it out later." (Meaning that I can manipulate you into changing because you'll love all that I am going to do and be for you.) So we "don't talk about it" now. But the truth is that if we should get married and you come to realize that I am trying to *change* you (so you'll be acceptable to me), you may get *very* angry. Because all during this intimate period, we have *said* we were being open about our problems with each other. And it turns out that I was not open. And you may feel deceived.

But where did that beautiful free spirit go that you liked so much in me? Suddenly *maintaining the relationship* has become more important to me than *being open*. The fear of losing you changes something, and before long we don't know what has happened to us. The intimacy, trust, and freedom have dissolved, and the hiding behavior turns out to be the beginning of the deterioration of the intimate relationship it was supposed to save. As long as I didn't care about our having a permanent union and had no commitment to making the relationship a lasting one, I could be free to risk being myself. So the magic of my being open and your natural acceptance of my real person was possible.

But the minute I care more about maintaining peace in the relationship than being myself, I start hiding feelings and insights which I think might threaten you or "hurt you." And as I do that, I begin to rationalize and deceive you, destroying the intimacy and trust the relationship was built on.

At first glance, honesty in a close relationship is almost too painful to risk. In fact, even a relationship which becomes intimate and in which both parties *keep* being open can have some stormy, painful times. Many people believe that when disagreements and painful truths are handled openly, the resulting hurt and discomfort mean that the relationship is no longer intimate. But intimacy is not sweetness, happiness and joy all the time. In fact, I have found that for me the *deepest* joy comes *only* after a painful time of examining the truth.

The power of love

The need for love and acceptance is so great and the intimate exchange so powerful that it is difficult to analyze the effects and value of an intimate relationship on the persons involved.

The experience of being loved in an intimate relationship is sometimes so freeing and so strong that it is like a kind of salvation from the emotional chains of the past. I may *become* the strong, courageous man *you see* me to be. And sometimes the experience of love is so strong that I may *continue* to look and act like the beautiful person your love-filled lenses see from this time forward. The person I was inside, but didn't dare show the world, has been freed to come out and live. This could be why some apparently mismatched couples have very compatible lives.

When someone has been transformed or freed by being loved, apparently insurmountable differences can be resolved or accepted. The power of love is very great.

When a relationship gets "too close"

Up to this point I have been describing the development of an intimate relationship during the initial stages: the beginning excitement, and even some of the psychological changes (like repressing irritating factors) that occur as the relationship becomes more and more meaningful.

At a certain stage (and it can happen soon, or after a year or more), surprising dangers can arise from out of nowhere. After we have been moving toward each other steadily, at some point one of us may feel that our freedom and identity as a person are threatened. You may experience a sense of being smothered by my almost constant presence—as if an emotional cage is being built around our lives. The urge rises to run away. And it seems irrational, because we are still in love.

But if you do not face these valid needs for an *independent* identity *within* the intimate relationship, then the fears of losing your freedom can cause you (consciously or unconsciously) to do something to *bring about* the *breakup* of our intimate relationship.

And strangely, this "something" is usually an action unrelated to the real problem of feeling smothered. So your "attack" may seem irrational. I've come to think of this kind of irrational attack on the relationship as "sabotaging." As a matter of fact, sabotaging is almost a characteristic method of getting out of a relationship which is becoming intimate. I am sabotaging when I start *causing* the breakup rather than facing the difficulties.

For example, let's say that I want more freedom in our relationship, but am afraid to tell you for fear that you will think that I want *all* of my freedom—that I want to go away and leave you. So instead of facing my need for some privacy, I begin to pick at you about being late or messy. I may start a fight over these little things, and destroy the relationship, when in fact, I love you and want you very much. And if I'd just face the problem with you and talk it out, maybe you'd feel fine about my having some time alone, because you may want some space too, but are afraid to say so (which is often the case). Or at least you could tolerate my having a little privacy, simply because when I have had time alone I am usually more fun to be with.

The only way I have found to deal with this problem directly, rather than by sabotaging, is to confess my feelings, even at the risk of your thinking I am rejecting you. It is very frightening. But I can say something like, "I've got a problem. I need to tell you that I get scared when I feel I can't get my work done (or ever play golf with the boys, etc.) because we are together so much. I want to be with you *a lot,* but I'm finding that I'm getting behind in my work (or stale from no exercise)." When I have been honest like this, the woman has understood and we have set certain times apart when each of us can make plans separately. At first this was very threatening to me, but now it seems freeing and brings a sense of freshness and newness into our relationship. But I've found it's good to *say* "this is scary" if it is for either party.

I've come to realize that intimacy usually thrives when there is some space for a man to be with his men friends occasionally and for a woman to be with her women friends—that is, for each one to have "identity things" he or she does without the other. So I believe it's necessary to get the "space" problem straightened out between the parties if intimacy is going to have a long and healthy life.

Building a case

When one of us wants to *get out* of a close relationship, a strange thing can happen to our perception which helps to justify a breakup. At first, when we were getting to know each other, I noticed all the good things about you and none of the bad. But later, when I am building a case to get *out,* I unconsciously start reversing this, seeing all the *bad* things you do and none of the good things. I "build a case" by making a mental list of your "bad behaviors" in order to justify my desire to leave the relationship.

When a person finds himself or herself doing this, I believe it is helpful to stop and think "What is the *fear* behind all this? What difficult subject am I afraid to bring up?" It may be something like the issue of being too close, the fear of permanent commitment, or the problem of jealousy. Because often, building a case so that I can justify leaving you is much less threatening than facing some deeper fear or threat—which could actually be worked out if I had the courage to bring it out in the open.

The green-eyed monster

Jealousy and the fear of being deserted are two of the most common causes for ending intimate relationships. These feelings can cause endless haggling, accusations, and exquisite pain.

If we don't discuss the nature of our commitment or the ground rules concerning exclusiveness, I may assume that we have an exclusive relationship. This is especially true if we have been dating a lot and taking up large segments of each other's time. In many people's minds, this implies a commitment of some sort. And if I am living as if we are dating exclusively, then I'm likely to become very angry and jealous if I learn you've had a date with someone else, because I will think you have broken a serious commitment. But if we haven't talked about the terms of our relationship, how can I be mad at you? Because "exclusiveness" was just something I had assumed, but which had never been mentioned.

The only successful way I've found to deal with jealousy is for both parties to talk openly and specifically with each other about what their commitment to each other includes. And regardless of what you decide about dating exclusively, you can ask some direct questions: "Under what conditions can we tolerate each other seeing other people of the opposite sex? When you are out of town, could you tolerate my going out dancing? To church? For coffee at the drugstore?" There are all different ranges of toleration. And you are less likely to be jealous if it is clear that I am not sneaking around seeing someone else. Also, talking openly about feelings often helps to relieve the pain of jealousy.

Let's say, though, that we have an agreement, but I am jealous anyway. You have two basic courses that you can follow with me. You can say, "There's nothing to be jealous about!" and add something like, "You are the most unreasonable, narrow-minded man I have ever met!" (which will just drive me up the wall and make me defensive!)

Or you can try to understand the irrational nature of jealousy. And you can help me by trying not to incite jealousy through flirting behaviors (like emotional "flashing," which I'll discuss later), through being secretive about what you feel about other men, or by hinting subtly or openly how attractive men find you. (All that I'm saying goes for women as well as men, if you are the one who becomes jealous.) Many people just try to tough it out in silence when they are jealous. That may be all you can do. Since it is often considered a sign of insecurity to feel jealous in today's single world, it may be embarrassing to admit having these feelings. But apparently a certain amount of jealousy is almost universal and feelings like this are not reasons to feel guilty. But burying these feelings can lead to years of unnecessary misery. And in a truly intimate relationship where two people really love each other, I believe a way to peace can often be found without cramping either person's life too much.

Jealousy-inciting behaviors: An unconscious trap

This brings up another related problem. I've talked to a number of people who have the conscious intention of being totally faithful to their partners or to their principles, only to be horrified when somebody makes a pass at them or tries to seduce them. I believe that in many cases these advances can be the result of an unconscious psychological game. This game is very common, and I understand it well because I have played it. It is a social game, a "harmless" habit of flashing your beauty or handsomeness *and not consciously being aware of the extent to which you're doing it.* I was trained that that's the way to behave in order to be nice to people, to affirm them with your eyes. Being "nice to people" is one thing, but hooking them into thinking you are sexy and desirable is another.

Let's say that a fine Christian woman (and it could be either a man or a woman, but let's say it's a woman for this example) may have as her conscious intention to engage in casual social relations with men, limited to dinners or movies, or just talking to the men she encounters. Although her conscious intention is not to seduce the man she's with, she unconsciously gives him encouraging glances or laughs and kids in such a way that he feels increasingly that she wants him to move closer and closer.

And finally, when he feels her encouragement is very real, he moves in physically, or tries to. But since the woman is not *conscious* that she has sent any "come hither" signals, she is offended with his approach and stiff-arms him.

Many women often don't understand that the average man is every bit as afraid of true intimacy and rejection as she is. These women think that a little "harmless flirting" is acceptable—almost necessary if she is to be considered attractive and friendly at all. And she feels safe, since it is not her conscious intention to get the man she is with into bed.

But what she may not realize is that if the man is sensitive at all, he will not risk being rejected unless he has seen or heard what he believes to be some pretty clear signs of encouragement. And if he is very lonely, the effect on him of "harmless flirting" could be quite strong. And he may move toward her suddenly and with little warning if he senses that she really wants him. So, if you are a man or a woman who keeps getting approached by people who want to be more intimate than you feel they should, it might be good to really check out how your "friendliness" might look to the other person.

If a man or a woman is not aware of sending out "come hither" signals, then enormous jealousy can be triggered in his or her partner. What if the accused says, "Listen, can I help it if women are attracted to me?" *Can* he help it? The real answer is "*Yes*." He can help a great deal of it by not playing flirting games. But the tragedy is that many people need attention from the opposite sex so much that they cannot even dare to risk looking at the effect of their flirting behavior on their most important relationship. Consequently, as a result of these kinds of "look at me" games, many intimate relationships and even marriages are destroyed by jealousy.*

---

*There is a kind of jealousy which is almost unrelated to the behavior of the beloved. But if both parties go together to a good counselor they may find help and clarification as to the cause of the jealous feelings.

Talking about the blahs

And finally, I have found that maintaining intimacy isn't just a matter of dealing with problems. When there is no crisis, sometimes it is good to say, "Hey, I really love you" or "I really like you." Assuming that the other person "knows" you love him or her and so does not need to hear you say it is a sad error. The more often you can express your love and affection verbally (without being ridiculous), the more the other person's level of assurance can grow. People who feel they are logical often miss this very important truth. But if a couple have honestly expressed their love verbally when things are peaceful, a crisis is not as likely to blow them apart.

It is important to realize that intimacy is always an ebb-and-flow matter. Don't panic if the romantic feelings are not receiving high voltage expression at any particular time. Sometimes people panic when the feelings are gone. I have done this a hundred times. But there are times when things are just plain vanilla in a very intimate relationship.

It's even normal to want to run away sometimes. And it is often very helpful to express this feeling. You can say something like, "I am scared to death. I have this strong urge to run away. This thing is going 'blah' for me. I really care for you, but I have these scared feelings." I realize it will probably frighten the stew out of us both if you say it. But it might also free me to say, "I want to run away too. I wanted to run away yesterday or last Tuesday." Once I have expressed it, there is often no need to run—especially if we both realize the urge to do so at times is almost universal. But remember that this kind of communication is *very* threatening to some people. And it's good to discuss with your partner whether you both want to be open about such threatening feelings.

As a person who has always sought intimacy, I am happy to be finding some of it in my life now. It is the hardest and most exciting way of relating I've ever found. But in order to have the courage to keep being open about the problems which must be faced, I've had to commit the whole relationship to God—again and again. If I didn't have a relationship with Him which was beneath and beyond any intimate human relationship, I don't think I could risk the threats of genuine intimacy. Because where would I go if a really deep relationship were broken?

CHAPTER TWELVE

Broken Relationships

NOTES

Re: The pain of endings

Dear Andrea,

I recently saw that I have often thought about broken relationships from a very limited male perspective. What does a woman do about handling the feelings that come when a close relationship is broken? How about dealing with the need to <u>break</u> a relationship? When should you consider it? How did your relation to God figure in the process of dealing with broken relationships? How does a woman feel when the man instigates the break? How do you get over a broken relationship?

I know these are agonizing questions. Last night I couldn't sleep as I relived some of the agony I felt when we broke up.

K.

Dealing with relationships that were broken was one of the most difficult parts of being single for me. It was hard to know when to stop trying to fix up a relationship and to quit hoping that things would work out. I kept wondering when I was supposed to accept the fact that it was over, begin the long healing process, and start looking forward to a future relationship.

When to break a relationship

For me, one of the purposes of dating was to get to know different kinds of men and to find out who might be compatible with the "me" I was discovering. Unfortunately, I often found myself in my old "people-pleasing" habits of trying to be what the man wanted me to be so we could "get along." Again and again I found myself bending my preferences around my date's preferences. For example, I might cook for him much more often than I wanted to, or watch much more television than I enjoyed (his favorite programs), or not discuss my favorite books. I was not fully conscious that I was doing these things. But after a while I would start to feel stifled, and realize what was happening. I would have to actually tell myself that I have as much right to prefer books as the guy does to prefer television.

My preferences and identity as a person and as a woman are important to me. I know that if I have to smother too many preferences, or overlook irritating things all the time, the relationship will be too much of a strain. It seemed better to end it and try to find a relationship with a person who has preferences more similar to mine.

Although I knew that to be true, the bleak possibility of not having *any* relationships at all was so hard for me to face that I often let a semi-compatible relationship drag on for months because of my fear of not having *anyone* around. I realize that there will always be differences and that to make any relationship thrive one must sometimes (or even often) do things which are not always her (or his) first choice. But the kind of relationship where differences are never out in the open is, I feel, somehow dishonest. It's using a man to satisfy my need for company or protect me from loneliness, and it is not being honest or fair with him if he is hoping for a permanent commitment. My goal was to try to live up to this. But sometimes, just having someone around, irritations and all, felt better than being alone.

For example, Chuck was a garage mechanic. He talked about carburetors and engines and pistons all the time. While, as a rule, I was interested because I was learning to tune up my own car and needed the information badly, I found that I couldn't get romantically involved with him. I felt awkward because I was at home in a white-collar world, while he was definitely "blue-collar." While I didn't like some of my feelings, they were real and came between us. Something just didn't click.

But Chuck was a nice person, and he treated me with respect and was fun to be with, so we dated, and from my perspective were just friends. There was lots of laughter, and there were dinners at my apartment, trips to the country to picnic, my hanging around the gas station until he got off, his phone calls to my office and jokes about my having a secretary.

After a while I began to notice that people at the gas station considered me Chuck's girl. At first I thought this was amusing and put it out of my mind. But then I realized that Chuck was beginning to act differently . . . there was something more serious in his eyes when he looked at me and something more tender in the way he held my hand.

"Oh, no," I thought. "Chuck is getting serious." I liked him as a friend. I thought he was a pleasant, nice-looking man. But I was not in love with him, and I knew I probably never would be. "It's time for us to have a talk," I told myself and began to plan my opening line.

We talked, and Chuck said he understood. He said there was no rush, and he was patient. And I realized that he thought that eventually, if he was patient enough, I would fall in love with him.

I suddenly felt awkward and jumpy around Chuck in my attempt to make sure that everything I said and did conveyed the idea that we were just friends. But I could see that he didn't buy it . . . sooner or later he felt I'd change my mind. I knew deep down inside that I wouldn't, and I felt frustrated because I couldn't convince him of that. I didn't want to lose his friendship, but I didn't want to lead him on, either. And I certainly didn't want to hurt him by rejecting him in a cruel way. As the weeks went on, I felt worse and worse about this relationship. And, finally, I just had to tell Chuck goodbye.

Truth and consequences

As I began to face my real feelings about my relationships, my worst fears began to come true. I found myself with fewer and fewer people to date, until finally there was no one left with whom I felt I could have an honest romantic relationship. This was the beginning of a period of time in which I dated no one at all.

Withdrawing from an active dating life into a relatively passive single life alone was an excruciating experience. My energy was so consumed with anxiety, depression, frustration, and hostility that I didn't feel like doing anything but "moping around and suffering."

Looking back on that period of time with my 20/20 hindsight, I believe now that this was the beginning of my learning to depend on God rather than on dates. I couldn't control "having dates" anymore. It seemed that no one wanted to be with me. I felt ugly and awkward. And I feared I would never find anyone to date. I felt like a misfit in the singles' world—perhaps in the *entire* world, since my marriage had failed too.

For a while I didn't care if I gained weight or if my hair needed cutting. I just trudged through each day and night in sluggish apathy.

Praying for God's help

I believe now that if I had depended more on a relationship with God, I might have spent my time in a more profitable way. By praying about this problem and asking God what to do with my fears and the empty time, I might have come up with some exciting new ventures. I might have spent the time learning more about myself. I could have done some of the things I kept wishing one of my dates would do with me, like going to a symphony in another town or driving through the countryside to smaller towns nearby and browsing in antique shops or having a picnic with a girlfriend or alone.

When I finally did begin to learn to pray, I found some very positive changes taking place in my attitudes and feelings. But at first I approached a prayer time with my mind full of doubts, feeling silly, and just said, "God, today I am sick and tired of feeling depressed and sitting around stewing about men all the time. I don't know what You can do about this problem; but I want Your help. I am asking You to come into my mind and soul and help me do something constructive. Help me see some of my own fears and my pride that contribute to men not wanting to be with me." Then I added whatever I could think of to be thankful for (some days I couldn't feel thankful for very much), such as my job, my apartment, my car, and the realization that things could be a lot worse in my life. And then I would go on with my day.

But I was so cynical at first that I didn't want *anybody* to know I was praying. And the more I undermined my prayer time by telling myself that it wouldn't help—which is in effect saying that "not even God can help me when I am this miserable"—the less good I felt from the experience. But the more I believed that "this will really help me get over some bad feelings (maybe not this hour or this day, but eventually)," the better I would seem to feel about myself, my situation and what I was doing. My energy level perked up little by little until I was sometimes whizzing through a day, surprised by how much I was getting done!

This may sound too simple, but I started approaching prayer this way by saying to myself, "I'm going to find out for myself if this will really help or not." Some people say that prayer is just a psychological manipulation and that it's not really God working in me. After thinking about that for a while, I realized that prayer is like a laboratory hypothesis—you have to try it to know if it's true. And my constant doubting seemed to be only a part of the undermining process by which I had closed myself off from God's love for years. I finally said one morning, "I don't care if it is a psychological manipulation. God created our minds, and maybe He has to manipulate me somehow to get me out of the rut I have created for myself. I'm just glad when it helps!" And it did.

When the relationship is broken by the other party

I rushed home from work one day and got into my tennis shorts. As I pulled on my shoes and tied the strings, I felt happy anticipation about this evening. Mark and I were going out to play tennis together for the third time in two weeks. He lived in my apartment complex and I had met him only the Saturday before last at the swimming pool. This was Thursday night, and I was hoping that he would ask me for a date for the weekend. I really hated to spend weekends alone.

Mark came to the door and we started for the courts. As we drove in his convertible down the shaded road, he said, "I don't know what's happening to me. I haven't dated the same girl three times in two weeks since my divorce over a year ago. You really must be something special." He looked over at me with a smile and I felt happy and excited. I had just ended a two-year relationship with someone a little over two months before, and I was ready to be "somebody special" again. And I really liked what I knew about Mark so far.

We played at tennis, then went to grab a bite to eat and he drove me home. We sat in my apartment and talked. After a while, he said he had to go, and as he went out the door he turned and waved and said, "'Bye. I'll call you later!" and he was gone.

I didn't hear anything from him that evening, or on Friday. By Saturday morning I was feeling a little down. I realized he probably wasn't going to ask me out, and I had no other plans.

The next week went by and I was amazed at the number of times I thought about Mark. I remembered his parting comment, "I'll call you later," and I kept hoping that he'd call. I started staying close to my telephone in case he tried to reach me. And I felt irritated with myself for doing it at the same time.

One night about a week later I felt a wave of hostile anger washing over me. I couldn't seem to stop it, so I let it out with a good crying session. After the wave had passed, I stared up at the ceiling from where I lay on the bed, blowing my swollen red nose on a soggy kleenex. I wondered why this huge amount of anger had come out over what seemed to be an event of small importance. Then I remembered something from a book about friendships which said, "One of the main causes of anger is the feeling that this shouldn't be happening to *you*, that you don't *deserve* it."

Now I realized that I felt angry at Mark because I didn't *deserve* to be ignored. I hadn't done anything wrong or said anything rude. And he had "said" he was going to call. In this new light, I began to see why I was feeling all this anger toward him. That he would "treat me that way" was an insult to my dignity.

But then I began to wonder if there might be a reason for his not calling—perhaps something I had said or done had caused him to disappear. So after about two and a half weeks, I decided to ask. I called one evening right after I had gotten home from work, and then went to his apartment.

When I went in, we both sat down on separate chairs in the living room. I said, groping for words, "I was wondering if I have said or done anything to upset you. I'm sure I can understand your feelings whatever they are—I just have trouble not knowing what's going on."

"Well," he said nervously, "I've tried to call you a couple of times, but you didn't answer. Sure, I think it would be fun to date some. I've got a tennis game tonight, but I'll be calling you."

The awkward way he sat with his arms folded across his chest, one ankle propped up on the other knee, and his eyes focused on the ceiling and walls told me that he wasn't being exactly up-front with me. I could also tell that this line of communication wasn't getting me anywhere at all. It only seemed to be making matters worse. So I pretended to believe him, feeling anger again over his obvious lie, and said goodbye.

As soon as his door closed behind me, the wave of anger grew. This time I knew I wasn't mistaken. There wasn't anything I had done or said, yet this was really happening to me and there seemed to be nothing I could do about it but drop it and try to get over it.

I knew then that it would be hard for me to relate to anyone who could not level with me—both about the bad things and the good. I felt so embarrassed about having gone to Mark's apartment in an attempt to clarify matters, and was enraged that it had ended the way it had. It must have taken me weeks to quit feeling a surge of anger and embarrassment every time I thought of him or glanced down the hill at the apartment building where he lived.

That kind of "ending" of relationships had happened to me several times, and each time the uncertainty about when to decide that the man wasn't going to call again and to get over the hope and go on living was difficult.

Dating exclusively—and my problem of control

About a year later, when Keith asked me to date him only, my fears of this kind of ending flared up again. So Keith and I agreed that we would date each other exclusively until a time when one or the other of us saw that he or she needed or wanted to end the relationship. We each promised to come to the other and say that the relationship was over (rather than just disappearing) in the event either of us wanted to end it.

We also promised to be as open and honest with each other as possible, fully aware that this could lead us to some discoveries which would let us know that we were not compatible for a long-term relationship like marriage. This would be the risk we would take. But however it turned out, we believed we could learn some valuable things about ourselves and each other that might help us mature for a marriage, a future relationship with someone else—or a life without marriage.

I felt I could take the risk of cutting off all my other relationships if I knew I would have a definite decision about the ending of this relationship. Even though that would certainly be painful, at least it would be better than having the relationship "drift" into something different from what we each thought it was in the beginning.

After about eighteen months of dating only each other, Keith decided he needed to end our relationship. He had some reasons, which he explained to me, and I fought hard to "help" him overcome his reasons without ending our relationship. Finally, I had to accept that it was his decision, and it was not my place to make such a decision for him. I accepted the end of the relationship, although it was very painful for me.

My first reaction was of fright, hurt, and tears. But as the next few days wore on, and I couldn't seem to lessen the pain at all, I remembered to try something I had been learning about for the previous two years. I began to pray. I wrote long letters to God in my journal as I tried to sort out the jumble of hostile, angry, frightened, loving, and painful feelings I was having.

In these letters, I asked God to help me see what I needed to learn through this experience. I saw, in a way I never had before, my huge need to control everything, to know what is going on and to try to influence people to do things my way. I was shocked to realize the extent of this need to control as I now could see example after example of it in my relationship with Keith and in other dating relationships I'd had before. I recalled examples of this in my relationships with people at work, with my parents and with my sisters and brother.

I wanted to eliminate this controlling habit because now I could see how destructive it had been in all my relationships. I realized that I would not be able to find out how a person would handle various situations if I kept *telling* him or her *how* to handle them. I needed to learn to keep my mouth shut and let people go through their own decision-making processes. If the decision was that they wanted to be with me, then I would know that they *really wanted* to be with me. If the decision was to do something the way I would have done it, then I would know we had a lot more in common. By always giving advice and directions, I was actually depriving myself of valuable information about the people in my life.

So I began to pray that I could learn to give up this control. And I started by giving up my attempts to control Keith. It may sound strange to say I tried to give up control of him after he had broken up with me and was out of my life. But it was amazing how much anger was created in me when he didn't do what I wanted him to—keep dating me.

When I was finally able to say out loud to God, "I no longer exert any control over this man's behavior. He can do anything he wants to do without retribution or punishment or reward from me," then part of the pain began to ease. The angry feelings about his going away seemed easier to handle.

"Who am I," I asked myself, "to tell him he has to date me forever? He is free to do as he chooses. If he chooses not to be with me, that hurts, but it's his right. My responsibility is only to myself and to

God. I'll just have to ask God how to get through the rest of the pain."

So the anger at his leaving healed first. The sorrow, disappointment and hurt lasted longer.

Getting over a broken relationship

After a few weeks, when the anger had lessened, the sad part of the pain became more noticeable: the ache of empty hours that we used to share, the old remembered jokes, the feeling that something really good had died and my life would now be nothing but a long period of grieving.

Praying, listening, and trying to relax and think, gradually began to ease things. I was finally able to go through an entire morning or afternoon at work with no thought of Keith. I began to "boy-watch" again and to laugh and be friendly with other people at the office.

One of the first things I had done when I realized he was really gone was plan to repaint that desk I had painted at Thanksgiving time four years before. I decided to scrape off all the old paint and stain the wood. I wanted the project to last a long time, for more than the half-day it had lasted before.

I remember buying all the materials, moving my dining room furniture aside, laying down plastic and placing the empty desk in the middle of the plastic sheets. There the project sat for several days.

When I finally started the project, it was one of those nights filled with the angry pain, just a week or so after the breakup. It was 11:00 p.m. and, as tired as I was, I just couldn't get to sleep. I got out the paint remover, slapped it all over the top of the desk, put on my old clothes while it soaked, then started scraping. I let all the pent-up anger come out in the long strokes as I removed layer after layer of old paint. I thought about the last time the desk had been painted, and wondered how many more crises it could stand! I worked on removing paint and pain until 4:00 A.M., fell into bed for a nap, and went to work the next day too exhausted to feel anything.

Time and prayer: Two important ingredients

Getting over a broken relationship that I did not end was hard work. And I couldn't seem to hurry the process. Sometimes I just had to go on living in spite of the pain. I struggled just to get through a day at work and an evening at home alone. Even playing tennis with a girl-friend, eating lunch or shopping dragged on forever. Sometimes it seemed that fifteen minutes lasted for hours.

Time and prayer were two important ingredients in the healing process, along with a real desire to go on and *get over* it, and not wallow in the misery. I had to go to God over and over again with my pride, my anger at being "treated that way," my need to control, my feeling of being misunderstood, my desire to be attractive to a man—my weaknesses one after another.

My hatred toward Keith had to be drained away. Living with it was only hurting me—not him or other people. I believed that God loved me and did not intend for me to lead a sad, angry, hostile life. I felt that He could heal my pain if I would bring it to Him and allow Him to do so. To seal myself off from this healing and refuse to get over a painful ending to a relationship was to keep myself from being the person He made me to be.

I knew it was my responsibility to care for myself—my mind, my heart, my body—and allow myself to develop and become what God had in mind for me. But it was so hard to turn loose of my feelings. And I *hated* having to admit my weaknesses, to acknowledge that I had been proud, fearful, manipulative and selfish. I wanted God to see how "wronged" I was and that I "deserved" some kind of revenge or special reward.

But facing my own part in the deterioration of the relationship was also necessary. Trying to learn to be patient and honest with myself about my pain, pride, fears, and working hard to repeatedly bring these to God were all necessary, for me, in getting over a painful broken relationship.

NOTES

Re: Some Possible Reactions to Breaking Up

Dear Keith,

It seems that with every exciting beginning in a relationship, there is always the possibility of a tragic ending. I have endured enough breakups to know that the human responses of fear, anger, hurt, and loneliness are very difficult to handle wisely. It seemed like I'd <u>never</u> get over some of them!

Did you as a man ever feel unattractive or unlovable because of breaking up with someone? I had those feelings a lot! People react differently to breakups, and make choices which seem to lead either to a healthy recovery or to a lengthy, painful time of misery. Could you talk about some of those reactions and the effect they can have on us?

This was one of the most painful areas of the single life, to me. I kept wishing I would discover the magic answer that would eradicate all the pain but leave all the learning and wisdom!

A.

When a close relationship has been broken, my experience has been that the separation, loneliness and sense of loss constitute a taste of hell—which I believe is the ultimate and eternal separation of a person from God. A breakup between two people is, of course, not a broken relationship with God. But what does one do with the emotions which follow the breakup of a significant relationship?

The feelings have been very different for me when I've been the person who has instigated the break rather than the person who has been left. But the hurts inflicted in the breaking-up process often leave some very painful emotional scars on both parties. And there are some strong feelings which must be faced and dealt with before the people involved can recover enough to be able to enter a new relationship with someone else, or to reconcile the relationship with each other.

Fear and distrust

After a very painful breaking up with a woman I had come to care a great deal for, I was surprised at the amount of fear and distrust of the opposite sex which surfaced. I felt devastated and fearful about the future. I thought about this woman night and day. In some ways life was like a dream sequence in a horror movie. My whole universe seemed to be out of focus, and as I looked ahead, the future seemed desolate without her presence.

It was very scary. My mind was filled with all kinds of anxiety and frustration. But there was also a sinking feeling as I became aware that my confidence as a man had simply vanished, leaving a frightened and insecure adolescent boy where only a day before had stood a reasonably secure adult.

My confidence in the ability to know what was happening in a relationship was shaken. I thought, "My gosh, if this relationship was not what I thought it was, what *else* isn't what I think it is? Maybe I've been deluding myself in thinking I'm fairly attractive or fun to be with." And as such doubts hit, my heart sank and I wanted to run away and never come out to face people again.

During the conflict which had taken place as that relationship broke up, I had lashed out in some pretty harsh ways. Of course, *to me* it had felt like I was hitting *back*. That didn't surprise me, because I know my deep need to justify my actions. But there was no question that my pride had been on the line. In the heat of arguing and to bolster my faltering ego, I had said and heard cutting, crippling and devastating things. And when the dust had cleared and I was alone, the haunting memories of insults and cruel shots made the aftermath even more miserable.

At one point I remember looking in the mirror late one night and seeing wrinkles and dark circles around my eyes and wanting to cry. I was shocked as it struck me that the frightened older man looking back from the mirror was I. Suddenly I felt ancient, ugly, and afraid no attractive woman would ever want to be with me. I became depressed and thought perhaps I was through in terms of ever having a good relationship with a woman.

Along with this depression came some guilt and bad feelings about things I had said and done. And later I discovered that there was a great deal of unfaced resentment and hatred backed up inside me, which I couldn't get out and face squarely at the time.

I began to wonder what happens to other Christians when a very important relationship is broken in their lives. What other reactions were likely to hit me as I began to deal with the fact that this relationship was over?

Grief

An almost universal and very natural response to a significant broken relationship is grief. To me the final separation in a breakup has always felt like a "death in the family" in some ways. The same depressed, hollow, lonely feelings, along with emotional guilt and regrets are likely to come flooding over my life. The advantage the widow or widower has over the divorcee or rejected lover is that in the case of the former, the ex-partner is dead and cannot *actively* hurt or cause heartbreak any more.

But grief is a very natural response to a breakup. And it is helpful to remember that getting through grief takes time—as does the whole process of "getting over" a broken relationship. I didn't know this. Well, I knew it and had told dozens of counselees that it took time. But when *I* was divorced or broke up, I evidently expected myself to be able to handle the emotional aftermath faster than other people.

Anyway, when I met Andrea a year after my divorce was final, she asked me how I was doing and I said, "Fine." But when she found out I'd only been divorced a year she shook her head and said, "It took me a couple of years to work through a lot of stuff, and I'm still working on some things." A year later, I knew what she meant.

And now I agree that it often takes two or more years to get through some of the aftermath feelings following the breakup of a serious relationship. And some may take a lifetime.

Playing "Whose fault was it?"

When a relationship is broken I've found that one of the most destructive reactions people can have is to try to establish whose fault it was, the assumption being that either one party or the other is to blame. So we feel (incorrectly) that if we can just *show* other people how wrong they've been, they will see our point of view and the break will be healed. WRONG!

Once my pride is involved by having someone imply I am not a "good," "fair," "right" person, I often quit being able to hear or speak rationally. The game changes from rational dialog to a warfare aimed at winning back my sense of being right. And even though I have had training in dealing with human relationships, I sometimes find myself so angry that I subtly or openly damn the other person. And I may, either consciously or unconsciously, bend or break the facts to fit my need to see what happened in a light favorable to myself.

I have come to realize over the years that it is often not even possible to find out "whose fault it was" when two people break up. One reason is that even when there has been undisputed disloyal or immoral behavior on the part of one partner, no one knows what unseen behaviors by the other partner over a period of time may have driven the offending party beyond his or her limits. And since each person often *feels* justified in his or her behavior, the "who's to blame game" seldom gets clearly won.

Keeping the past alive

When a relationship has been permanently broken it's very tempting to keep talking *about* the other party, how she or he has "done you wrong," and what that person should do now. This is a self-defeating reaction (since your friends will soon get tired of hearing your vicious attacks on your ex-partner and you may drive them away). Also, in running your ex-partner down, you spend valuable energy which could be used for getting on with your own future. And besides, there is usually almost nothing one can do to change someone who has ended a relationship, gone away, and doesn't want to change. When a relationship is over, the only thing I've found helpful as a Christian is to put the other person and the relationship in God's hands and move into the future, trying to keep listening to Him.

NOTES

Re: Facing the Truth

Dear Keith,

It's often infuriating to realize that when I'm in a relationship that's having trouble, <u>other people</u> can usually see my contribution to the problem better than <u>I</u> can! And I've noticed that I seem to be able to see trouble spots in someone else's relationship from a mile away while each person in that relationship is unaware that he or she is causing any problems at all. Why is this true?

I think many people (including me) <u>want</u> to be able to deal with problems by becoming more aware of their true feelings. How can we start to face some of these things and learn to wrestle <u>through</u> rather than <u>around</u> the difficult bad feelings to more peaceful and intimate relationships?

Also, isn't a good Christian supposed to have understanding and compassion for loved ones? What can we do when we don't feel love, but feel anger and hostility instead?

A.

*Although it may sound strange, many people will not let themselves even ac-*knowledge that a relationship is in serious trouble. They blind themselves (repress what has happened) and do not admit that they have done anything which the other person should be bothered about. Or they may be so afraid of risking a broken relationship that the insults and injuries from their partner are ignored.

Some wives or husbands in counseling insist, "We haven't got any problems," when their mate is on the way out the door because the "insister" refuses to face the problem which has broken the relationship. This "repressing the problem" is closely associated with the more basic everyday habit of hiding anger and hostility from ourselves and also refusing to let others express it in our presence.

How do you tell if you're repressing anger?

It seems that I'm saying that many people repress their true feelings and hide their dishonest, manipulative behaviors and their anger and hostility even from themselves. If that's true—and I think it is—how can we tell when we are repressing and hiding feelings from ourselves?

This is a very hard question, because when you are in a relationship that is breaking and you want so much to be justified, then it's very easy to put on psychological blinders and *feel* as if you are being totally honest and open while the other person appears to be hiding the truth about what she or he did.

When this happens to me, I keep trying to make my own point and have a lot of trouble listening to the other person's view. I still have trouble with this because I seem to have such a desperate need to be right.

The thing which has helped me most is that I have a couple of

Christian friends who know me very well. And I ask them what they hear me saying when I present a situation. Bruce Larson and I have done this for each other. I have gone to him and said, "Listen, Bruce, let me tell you about this," and I'd present a situation concerning a broken relationship to him. Then I'd say, "What do you think this is?" And he would tell me exactly what he thought it was.

Sometimes he would see it the way I saw it and I would say, "Bruce, that's right, that's right! Keep talking." And then in a minute he would say, "It seems to me that at *this* point you've kidded yourself totally. You have not really dealt with this part of your relationship at all. You seem to have repressed your real feelings." And I might say, "Now wait a minute!" Or I would start saying, "I don't think you *heard* me, Bruce," or I would try to justify myself somehow. Later, I would think very hard about what he'd said and pray about it. I'd try to see how I might be hiding some feelings from myself because I would realize that Bruce had no reason to say it if it weren't true.

So I think that it is good to get with some Christian friends or a small group in which the kind of relationship exists where you can have this sort of intimate exchange. Within such a group it's possible to find out a great deal about your own repressive and hiding behaviors.

But the process of discovering our repressed feelings is complicated by the fact that we have been *trained not* to feel certain things.

Recognizing anger and hostility

The underlying difficulty in facing our negative feelings when a relationship is threatened is often that many of us were taught as Christians never to hate anyone or even have hostile feelings. So, many Christians who feel that even experiencing hatred is evil, repress their true emotions and smile benevolently, saying that they don't have any bad feelings toward the loved one or mate who clobbered them and/or walked off. And they *really feel* benevolent in their conscious minds.

But I am convinced this is *not* a Christian response. Because of being taught as a child that "good Christians don't have hostile feelings" and good guys didn't feel hate, I was "too fine a person" to hate. I never really hated anyone *until* I became a Christian through committing to a personal relationship with God. Christians can afford to face the truth about life, because we can be forgiven and made clean. And as a counselor I had realized for years that feelings are neither good nor bad *in themselves.* They are simply *automatic responses* to things that happen around us. If a sudden icy wind comes up, we *feel* cold. That feeling is neither good nor bad. But if when we feel the cold, we turn and rip off our neighbor's coat, that *behavior* is bad—but not the *feeling* of being cold. And if I experience feelings of anger, that is not evil. But if when I experience anger, I murder my wife, that's bad. And if feelings of anger and hostility are natural responses to real or imagined threats in anyone's life, then hostile feelings are certainly normal parts of most breakups in which the two parties have been very close.

Another difficulty which arises if we aren't in touch with our hostile feelings is that we can't experience and be healed from our deep fears and hurts either. Because, as I said earlier, hatred and anger are often the *other side of the coins of fear and hurt.* When I'm feeling hatred I often stop and ask myself, "What am I *afraid* of or *hurt* by?" But if I repress the anger then, I may not even feel the hurt enough to ask God for healing and a new start.

So I believe that when hurt or attacked, every human being who is sensitive has at some time feelings of deep hostility at least verging on hatred. As I suggested in another context, these feelings are sort of like a psychological fire alarm system, telling us that we are in danger and should prepare to face the danger. Angry feelings are to the mind in one sense what physical pain is to the body—a warning system. What I think a Christian does is to face the hostility, confess it and ask God's help in dealing with the person or persons involved. Then the inside parts of our lives can be cleaned out through God's love and forgiveness.

Not ever having any hatred or hostile feelings is *not* a Christian virtue. It is a kind of neurotic sickness which keeps us from bringing our real feelings to God. I don't want to make you nervous if you don't have any hostile feelings, but if people whom you care about deeply treat you unfairly or take things you hold dear and you do *not* hurt or have any angry feelings, that does not necessarily mean you are a saint.

I think sometimes people develop enough love and understanding that when somebody hits them they can understand where the other person is coming from enough to diffuse the resulting hostility. But in a large percentage of cases, I am convinced that the "never being hostile" phenomenon is repression, not sainthood. Besides, as Jesus indicated, even God has trouble helping us when we don't know we have a problem (see Mark 2:17).

Now that it's recognized—how do you experience anger without blowing up a relationship?

Sometimes the breakup of a relationship might be avoided if the parties involved could learn to let themselves deal openly with their feelings of anger. But before anger can be dealt with openly, each partner must be willing to let the other *experience* his or her own angry feelings.

One way to keep your partner from experiencing and expressing anger is to apologize "too fast." One person may confess how he or she has hurt the other and ask for forgiveness *before* the other person is ready to give it, just so he or she can "get right" with the injured party. But the injured person is often furious and doesn't know why, only somehow "smelling" that the exchange is too fast and that he or she has been cheated from having a legitimate angry reaction. And the one who says "I'm sorry" may get very indignant and self-righteous if, after the apology, the other party doesn't immediately respond with, "That's okay, you're forgiven."

When I was a child I learned to say "I'm sorry" quickly, and my mother thought that was very good. But when I left home, I was surprised when my Christian-fast-draw "I'm sorry" didn't get a positive response. I felt that the other person just wasn't as good a Christian as I. But people kept being angry with me.

I strongly believe that saying "I'm sorry" and *really meaning* it is part of the process of real repentance and healing. But another important part of the process of being sorry is to *hear the other person's pain and anger* after you have hurt him or her—*before* you expect him or her to forgive you. This agony of hearing the other person's anger is part of the price we pay when we hurt someone.

Have you ever seen two dogs "frozen" after a fight—one lying on its back with its hind legs thrown open revealing its vulnerable underside, and the other dog standing over the first, just bristling with hatred—but not attacking? What sometimes happens is that a small dog will run up, bite a larger dog and run. Then, just as the larger dog is about to catch and kill it, the smaller one quickly rolls over on its back, triggering the built-in-block-against-attack in the big dog.

Students of animal behavior have discovered that when a dog signifies defeat by exposing its underside and being totally vulnerable to the kill, the winning dog often appears to be unable to attack (although it seems apparent that the bristling dog would love to finish off the vulnerable one).

I thought that was only a fascinating bit of information when I heard it—until I realized how it was related to saying "I'm sorry" too fast. Let's say that one partner in a relationship insults or cuts the other deeply with a nasty remark or behavior that calls for strong retribution. Just as the other is feeling the cut and is about to retaliate, the first says, "I'm *really sorry!*" I can almost see the one saying "I'm sorry" rolling over and showing his partner the "Christian" underside. It's no wonder people get angry at such "Christian" behavior. I now call this "playing puppy dog" when I do it or see it being done in a relationship.

Sometimes it's helpful when you have done this to confess that you have said "I'm sorry" too soon (because you really wanted to avoid honestly facing your desire to hurt the other person and get off scot-free). These sorts of motivations are very difficult to admit—even to ourselves.

The boomerang effect of hatred not faced

Many divorced people are still feeding off their hurt feelings, trying to justify themselves to people around them, condemning their ex-mates, and staying miserable and full of hate for years. But unfortunately, hatred often has a way of transmuting itself into serious physical or emotional symptoms. Repressed hatred can eventually express itself in arthritis, ulcers, perhaps even cancer, or other physical symptoms in a vulnerable area of your body. It's as if the repressed anger is seeking a way to become visible to the hater as a warning of its presence and the danger it signifies.

This phenomenon of repressed hatred and pride may be one of the reasons Jesus, as a healer of physical illness, often connected a sick person's cure with the correction of a sin which needed forgiving in his or her life. It seems that because we want to be "right" or to be known as the "injured party," our intense pride can keep us from the beginning of being healed.

In Canada there is a healing center Bruce Larson told me about where people come to try to heal their broken relationships or to get healthy again after having failed in a relationship. Over the fireplace at the center were carved the words, "DO YOU WANT TO BE RIGHT OR WELL?"

It seems amazing that we would cling to our sense of being "the righteous one" or the "nonhater" to the extent that we would ruin our lives, but it is very common for people to do so.

Harboring hatred to punish the other party

Sometimes a person will have a conscious hatred of his or her ex-partner which is very intense. In counseling, when asked if he or she wouldn't like to forgive the person and be free of the hatred, the response is, "No way. I'm not going to let her/him off that easily!" He or she feels that to quit hating the ex-partner will let the other person get away with the offensive behavior too easily. But it's *not* a matter of letting *the other person* off the hook. It is the *hater* who is trapped by the hatred more than the person on whom the feelings are focused.

In several ways I have tried to say that regardless of how much you want to hold on to your bad feelings and make your partner or ex-partner pay, in the long run if you cling to the bad feelings or stuff them out of sight from yourself, it's very likely that *you'll* be the one to pay.

NOTES

Re: Learning to Trust Again

Dear Andrea,

One of the things which helped me have the courage to risk marriage again was the agreement you and I made while dating exclusively to examine together the fears and jealousies we'd hidden inside ourselves.

Would you talk a little about your own experience concerning trying to learn to trust again?

K.

Learning to trust men again—that has been a big obstacle for me in dealing with a past broken relationship so that I can enter into a new one.

I sat across the table at a little Soup 'n' Salad restaurant from Sara, a beautiful woman with a trim figure, shoulder-length curly red hair and blue eyes. We were talking about trust.

Sara is going with a man who means a lot to her, but she is having trouble trusting him.

She said, "I feel so guilty and ashamed, but these nagging thoughts creep into my mind whenever Joe is out of town. He says I have to learn to trust him because, after all, he's never done anything to hurt me."

But she has been hurt, before Joe came along. She's trusted and been deceived so many times that it's just plain hard to trust at all. Sara starts out with good intentions, but then those crazy doubts crash in, and keep circling in her head.

"I wonder what he's doing out there? Is he having dinner with a woman? Why didn't he call every night he was out of town?"

Do these thoughts represent doubts about the basic relationship? And if not, is this kind of doubt being too possessive? Some people say it is. I also felt it was, even though I was plagued by these kinds of questions, especially late into the night. Sometimes they were only mild passing thoughts. But at other times they were so strong that all the angers and rages of past hurts and deceits swept over me like a sea of smoldering ashes, leaving me tossing and turning at 3:00 A.M.

Yet the idea of sharing these fears with the person involved, of asking the questions out loud, seemed ridiculous. When asked, the man almost always became defensive and responded with something like, "What's the matter, don't you *trust* me?" Or perhaps he would say, "You're getting to be a nag, you know." Another familiar response was, "I wouldn't do a thing like that, and it hurts to know you think I would."

How to handle these kinds of doubts is the problem. I don't think it is possible (at least not for me) to have a close, intimate, trusting relationship without dealing with these fears. Just swallowing them and trying to get along somehow didn't seem to help the relationships I was in. But telling these fears to "go away" didn't work for me either.

The method that really worked best for me was to get the help of the person whom I wanted to learn to trust and to "work through" each nagging doubt. When Keith and I started dating seriously, I told him I realized he had never done anything himself to cause me to doubt him. But I still had "nervous reflexes" from past experiences that I needed to talk with him about. He agreed, and told me he had some of his own that needed working on. So we decided to bring up these kinds of doubts and talk them through.

We had agreed that we wanted to date each other exclusively at this point, and I think that really helped the process I'm describing. If we hadn't been dating exclusively and I had wanted to talk about some pretty silly-sounding doubts, I would have hesitated to be as open with him. My fear was that he and other dates would discuss me. Or even if he didn't, I worried that the other women he knew would seem to be more "cool" and "in control," and not appear to have any "hangups" like my doubts. So dating only each other was a reassuring factor.

A few of the doubts we discussed

Even though we had promised not to date other people, I began having doubts about what constitutes a "date." We both traveled and worked with people of the opposite sex. A business dinner could turn into a "datelike" situation . . . or could it? And what about people of the opposite sex who were "just friends" and wanted to go to the show or out for coffee when one of us was out of town? We discussed how we both felt and decided together what would make us both comfortable without putting each other in social straitjackets. Other couples could decide differently, but the point was that *we* had gotten *our* fears and feelings out in the open and we both knew what our agreement was.

To my relief, Keith took me seriously. It was his willingness to hear all my questions, no matter how dumb I was afraid they might sound to him, and answer them with factual data, information and honest feelings that helped me understand. If I asked him where he was one evening when I tried to call from out of town and got no answer, he would explain whatever it was . . . out getting groceries, working late, etc. Gradually, I began to learn this particular man's patterns and that the things he did when he wasn't with me were not harmful to our relationship.

Learning to believe again

I also had to learn to *believe* what he told me. Trusting is a conscious act of will, I discovered. Believing what the man tells you is necessary. And it's also very important to tell the truth, even if it means confessing that you transgressed the agreement. Hiding these transgressions with "little white lies" or evasions creates great difficulty for the person trying to learn to trust.

Learning to believe what Keith told me was a struggle for me. The difficulty was not due to Keith's trustworthiness. I felt he was honest. But I had been lied to frequently by men who apparently didn't like my kind of questions or who didn't care about our relationship enough to face the questions with me. Or perhaps they didn't want to "hurt" me with the truth. Trusting became very difficult after a few years of encountering this.

I don't know why . . . it seems so illogical . . . but I feel *stupid* when I find out someone has lied to me. When I can be rational, I realize that it is the other person's responsibility for the lie, and yet he often seems to feel so smug that he's tricked me (or outsmarted me)! So the way I tried to "protect" myself from being tricked by lies was to not really believe people. I had gotten pretty cynical and doubtful by the time I met Keith. In fact, I'd gotten to the point that I couldn't really believe anyone, and had a kind of paranoid feeling that men (and even some women) were always trying to trick me.

Time, patience and returning the favor

But our taking the time to patiently work out these fears was a turning point for me. I had to accept Keith's words as truth in order to get over the doubts. But at first I needed the data from him, too. I needed more than his saying "Look, just *trust* me!" I had to hear detailed accounts of many little things that crossed my mind. And he patiently answered all my questions. And sometimes, I'd have to ask questions I knew sounded dumb just to get my feelings out.

I tried to do the same for him, but I was surprised to find that I often felt irritated if *he* would doubt *me*. This helped me realize that it is as hard for the person answering questions as it is for the person asking them. When I was *asking* questions, I felt apologetic and silly or nosy. But when I was *answering* them, I felt irritated. I was angry that I should have to explain my every move when not with Keith (exaggeration, of course), and I saw what a price he was paying by answering my many questions to help me through this phase. It made me more willing to patiently try to answer his questions.

Sometimes when I'd ask where Keith had been, I'd get a shock. Once he said he was with someone he had dated before. But when I calmed down inside I could understand the circumstances by which they had met (since I occasionally ran into someone I'd gone with before). And our being able to ask and get straight answers helped in these cases too. These discussions were usually very painful, especially if one of us had just blown it and done a thoughtless, selfish thing.

Two steps forward—one step back

It took me months of asking questions before I could relax. Just as I began to feel I was making progress, something new would happen and trigger a whole new set of doubts and questions in my mind. I had been more deeply scarred than I'd realized. And after he had broken up with me, I felt very little trust when, nearly three months later, he asked me to date him again. Since we had always tried to be as honest as we could with each other, I decided to try our "talking it out" policy to see if I could overcome my fears enough to trust again. And I knew that getting things out and laid to rest could lead toward healing and trust.

Now, after three years of our consciously working through things together, I feel much more trusting. And I am able to transfer that trust to other areas . . . God, friends, co-workers. It's much more relaxing.

But I realize that there are probably more dark areas of doubt hidden in my mind that could be triggered any day by an event. The promise that Keith and I have made to each other is that we'll "talk it through" until we're both satisfied we are understood and that we understand.

We realize that many people may read this chapter and think we're crazy for relating this way. But since we both had always longed to relate this openly but had never met anyone who wanted to try it, we thought we'd provide at least one way here for couples who are interested in discussing the structure of their own relationships, as they're trying to learn to trust again after being hurt.

CHAPTER THIRTEEN

The Question of Sex:
Two Personal Struggles

NOTES

To the Reader,

     In this chapter and the next we are going to discuss some of the issues involved in making sexual choices as a single person who is also a Christian. Although the traditional "rules" are clear, this is not an easy subject to write about. The making of sound choices in the sex–filled subculture of the singles' world is an agonizing experience for most people. It was for us. And there are many bad preconceptions and strong emotional reactions among married people in the church about sex and about single people. If we try to be honest about the real issues here, we are almost sure to be misunderstood and even accused of being unchristian or of leading people astray.

     Since we are both committed to Jesus Christ, the thought of this reaction is very unpleasant. But since we both looked for and could not find good realistic counsel in this area when we were single, we have decided to risk being as realistic and open as we can. We hope that this discussion may provide a little helpful information about some of the sexual choices or options which you may face as a single person—and some of the possible consequences of making these choices.

K. and A.

NOTES

Dear Andrea,

    Would you consider telling what your feelings about this subject were as a single—both before and after making a commitment to Christ? What choices or options did you see open to a single woman when you got divorced 1,000 miles from people you'd known in the past? How did you face the singles' jungle's pressures to be sexually active? What did you discover about contemporary views toward free sex? And finally, how did God affect your life in this area?

    I know this is a big order, and I realize that this is a difficult area to discuss. But I think women particularly have been left alone with some big stereotypes to cope with and a lot of misinformation about how it "really is" for single women in trying to make good decisions regarding their intimate relationships with men.

                               K.

When it came to making sexual choices, the reality of the single life and the ideal of my Christian upbringing didn't match well at all.

I was taught the traditional Christian standard: sex was designed for marriage and should be reserved for my husband and him only. Sex outside of marriage is wrong. And that was the black and white of it. But as I stated earlier, I had gotten away from my Christian background and didn't really make a renewed commitment until four years after my divorce.

In the six years that I was a divorced single, I had some agonizing hours trying to come to grips with the question of how sex should fit into my life. In fact, at times this was one of my most difficult struggles as I tried to live my own life and relate to friends.

I remember a six-hour drive to a secluded beach house which I took with a single girlfriend from another town, who was one weekend away from an abortion. She was a sensitive girl, had a good job and had been divorced only two years earlier. When she had learned she was pregnant, she had realized that there was no room in her life or her reputation for an illegitimate child, and no possibility of marrying the father.

I was stunned by her situation, because I knew it could have been mine. I felt a deep sense of comradeship with her because we were both trying to figure out how to make good sexual decisions against a background of loneliness, insecurities, and social pressures to be "cool."

Three choices

I could see only three choices open to me regarding sex, and the consequences of all of them seemed painful and difficult.

One choice was just not to worry about it . . . just let things happen as they might and not decide before an evening began whether I would allow it to include sex or not. I remember going out on dates in this frame of mind, and I saw quickly that this attitude could lead to behavior which would only cheapen myself, the man, and the very act which God created to have such a special meaning in the bonding of a family unit. To have sex with just any casual date would have been only a selfish kind of "using people" which I felt was an irresponsible approach to life.

A second option was to include sex only in a close, serious relationship, hoping that by including it, the relationship would deepen and allow a better understanding, perhaps leading toward marriage. But it never seemed to work that way in real life.

Time after time I had sat up late with girlfriends who poured out the pain and disappointment of their relationships. The results seemed to be similar. In serious relationships when sex was included, there were other "unspoken" expectations for the relationship that often were not met. This would lead to jealousies and hiding of real feelings, which would cause separation rather than the closeness my friends had hoped for. Also, there was always a nagging debate in our minds over whether this way to live was "right" or "wrong," under the incredible emotional pressures of living life as a single. And I was concerned that I would never really be able to decide for sure.

A third option was not to have sex at all with anyone. I felt that God would like that, but after months of this approach I would feel such pressure about it that my other judgments were clouded. I often felt angry and hostile toward men, feelings which were quickly inflamed if the issue of sex was pressed. I resented the fact that the entire chore of resisting seemed to be mine, and that even Christian guys didn't seem to understand my wanting to live up to this ideal. Sometimes when I'd be unsure of what I really wanted, I'd insist even more firmly that sex not be included in the relationship. Often, this seemed to make men try harder and harder to persuade me, as if they couldn't believe I really meant it. They would use logical arguments, or pleas, or the promise of love, or physical teasing and temptation or threats of rejection. Ultimately, as a rule, a refusal led to the termination of the relationship.

It was a very subtle kind of rejection. No one ever said out loud that a relationship ended because I wouldn't go to bed, but I often felt that was true. Throughout the relationship, the majority of disagreements would be about sex. The man would persist in bringing it up every time, and most dates would end in an argument and negative angry feelings.

I often had difficulty knowing the fine line between showing affection to a man and giving him the idea that even though I was saying, "No," I really would be willing to have sex after all. And I wanted to talk openly with my dates about my struggle, but this only seemed to lead them to believe I was really willing but needed them to persuade me it was all right. I couldn't see any efforts on the part of the man to understand or cooperate with me in trying to live this out. I saw only disappointment, lack of understanding and constant tension when I rejected attempts to become involved sexually.

As I grew more and more hostile, it seemed that nobody at all could understand me, including people at work or my girlfriends. Since I didn't want to tell any of them what was behind my bad temper, it just got worse and worse and even my friends eventually drifted away. There I was, alone again.

I concluded that not a single one of the men I'd ever dated (or would ever date) would want to keep the relationship going if I tried to live out this "no sex without marriage" ideal. It seemed that to live a life with no sex would mean also doing without men. I felt trapped again. Could I withstand the social isolation that I was now convinced would be the price in order to try to follow God's ideals? I was living a thousand miles from my hometown, had almost no social connections with people who had lived long in the city I worked in, and was very lonely. I was afraid I could not stand the isolation. The psychological need for social acceptance was so strong in me that I felt I couldn't make it God's way without some kind of help.

"Okay," I told myself. "Get help. I've done that before through counseling when I've had to deal with tough decisions like my divorce and my career. Why not this?" So I tried to think of somebody to talk to. But everyone I imagined counseling with about facing really tough sexual choices seemed unsatisfactory. They would, I was afraid, either give me "pat" answers from the Bible on the one hand or tell me it was hopeless to try and fight it and to just go ahead, on the other hand. I could picture Christians filled with such moral indignation that they'd never speak to me again, or who would judge me, isolate me, lecture me . . . and the fearful thought process went on and on.

How had I gotten to this state? I felt the two sides of the question—sex or no sex—closing in on me like the two sides of a vise. As I began to feel the crunch, I longed for the ability to make a clean, clear decision in favor of God's ideal and *learn to be happy with it*. Since I believed I would be risking losing all my friends, my good nature, and my composure, I knew I'd have to learn to face life really alone. I was sure I'd never date again if I made this choice irrevocably.

Chastity, the most unpopular Christian virtue

When I had come to this bleak spot in my thinking, I read *Christian Behavior* by C. S. Lewis. In this book there is a chapter about six pages long on sexuality. One of the points Lewis makes is that refraining from sex, or chastity, is one of the most unpopular of the Christian virtues. The Christian ideal is sex within marriage with fidelity and no place else. But this is so contrary to our basic instincts that either Christianity is wrong or our instincts have gotten warped by various factors. He illustrates this by saying that a strip tease act will attract a large audience to watch a young lady slowly take all her clothes off. But suppose you went to a foreign country where you could fill a large auditorium with people by simply bringing a covered dish onto the stage. The cover is slowly lifted so that everyone can see, just before the lights go off, that on the plate is a pizza or a chocolate sundae. Wouldn't you think that something had gone wrong with that country's appetite for food?

Lewis says that sex is nothing to be ashamed of, just as there is nothing to be ashamed of in eating your food. But, "there would be everything to be ashamed of if half the world made food the main interest of their lives and spent their time looking at pictures of food and dribbling and smacking their lips."*

As I read that short chapter, I remembered the propaganda which had affected me in movies, books, and magazines, and in the people

---

*Quoted in *Christian Behavior* from Lewis's *Mere Christianity*, p. 92.

around me. There is a social theory that it is "smart" to experience a relationship fully, including sex, in order to "really know" what you are doing if you decide to make a permanent commitment, like get married.

And the subtle social "comparison game" is also very strong. In this game people imply that you aren't as cool as other women if you behave like a prude and don't allow sex in relationships, especially serious ones. The power of social opinion today is amazing. Such labels as "prude," "frigid," "square," "old-fashioned," or even "boring," "undesirable," "unattractive," could really affect my emotions and thinking when I was trying to deal with these choices. I really cared what my dates thought of me, and I believed that if I stood firm about "no sex," guys would just go away and find someone else to date who was more "liberated."

God understands the difficulties

But Lewis believed that God will not judge us as if we had no difficulties to overcome. He is aware of our situation. What matters is our sincerity and perseverance in *trying* to overcome the difficulties.

When I read the part about God knowing our situation, I must confess that I couldn't really believe that. I didn't think God really knew my situation. I found myself muttering over and over in my mind all the reasons I was going to "have to" agree to include sex in my relationships, hoping to convince God or somebody, maybe myself, that it was acceptable. It never occurred to me then that I could talk directly to God about it. I figured since I kept it all a secret from everybody else, I should also keep quiet about it with God.

I also had a couple of obstacles to overcome in speaking to God. These bother me even now, though I'm learning to go ahead and talk to Him anyway. One is my feeling that I shouldn't ask for forgiveness for anything unless I can *promise* not to do it again. I realized that even if I *wanted* to try to live up to the standard set in the Bible, it was so difficult that I believed sooner or later, if I stayed single, I'd end up breaking such a promise. Since I had broken the biggest promise of my life when I got divorced, I wasn't about to fail again with important promises.

The other obstacle was pride—just plain old stubborn pride about having to admit that I am too weak to handle something without God, and that I would probably be a failure even though I wanted to live out God's best for me.

I can sometimes overcome difficulties when I see fearful enough consequences like, "Don't yell at your boss. Consequence: you'll get fired. Don't steal things. Consequence: you'll go to jail." But the harmful effects of sex outside of marriage are usually hidden and often are seen only afterward, when it's too late anyway, or perhaps they are never seen at all, even though these effects may have taken their toll.

In the last paragraph of the chapter Lewis wrote on sexuality, he said that he believed the center of Christian morality is not in the sexual area. He said that anyone who thinks unchastity is the major sin is quite wrong. Sins of the body, like the sexual ones, are bad, but they are the least of all sins. "All the worst pleasures are purely spiritual: the pleasure of putting other people in the wrong, of bossing and patronising and spoiling sport, and backbiting; the pleasures of power, of hatred."

So I realized that if I could talk to God about my need to control everyone and be boss—which is a pretty major sin—then I could just as well bring Him my struggles with sexual choices!

Lewis said that inside each of us, competing against the human self that God can help us become, there are two things: They are the "animal self" and the "diabolical self." "The diabolical self is the worse of the two. That is why a cold, self-righteous prig who goes regularly to church may be far nearer to hell than a prostitute. But," he said, "of course, it is better to be neither."

Society encourages women—both single and married—to be liberated, cool, sexy, and attractive, to dress and act as if we are not shocked, bothered, upset or disturbed in any way by moral choices and decisions. On the other hand, the church expects us to be pure, blameless, calm fortresses of strength and emotional stability. And above all, "don't talk about it!" Trying to find a zone between being sexually attractive and friendly on one hand and staying committed to the Christian ideal of no sex outside marriage on the other was one of the most difficult areas of my life as a single.

To say that a Christian single has "choices" about sex is a controversial idea among many Christians. But to me, calling the various responses to the human sex drive "choices" does not mean that God approves of all of them or that we are going to choose all of them. One man wrote to us that "having sex outside of marriage is not a choice for a Christian single." And yet, just as we have a choice about whether to lie, whether to judge, whether to steal or whether to cheat on our income tax returns, we have a choice about whether to have sex with someone. God's clear preference on each of these is "No," but He left us free to choose.

In order to make the decisions we feel God wants us to make, it seems to me that we must face these "choices" and their consequences.

To me, it feels horrible to have to face having committed a sin, and doubly horrible if I have to confess that I *wanted* to commit it. Therefore, I believe many of us, as I did, would rather argue about *whether* it is a sin or not than go through the agony of accepting our own weakness and fallibility and the struggle that results if we have any integrity at all.

I believe that God's moral ideals will, if followed, lead me somehow to a healthier life and free me to discover and do His will for me. As I said earlier, I have not always felt about sex the way I do now. But I came to a clear realization that sex outside of marriage is a sin. At that point the question for me changed from "Is it right or wrong?" to "How can I begin to try to live up to this ideal, given my fears and weaknesses?" I had stopped arguing with God and started trying to learn how to do His will. As I began to struggle with this, I also saw that if I were to have any hope of dealing with this area of my sinful nature, then I desperately needed a way to come to God with the *truth* about myself in order to find the courage to face it. When I first saw this, I felt threatened and angry. I could manage to pray only for the courage to face it . . . not about the problem itself.

I felt very alone during this time of struggle because I knew of no one who could understand it. I felt people who had never committed this sin would be shocked that anyone would struggle with it. And people who were involved sexually seemed to have accepted this as a fact of life over which there is no need to struggle.

But the most important (and amazing) discovery I made when I continued to try to bring this struggle to God was that I never felt at any time that He didn't love me anyway—whether or not I had conquered this problem. And I felt that He was glad I was being truthful with Him about it and would help change me in whatever way it took to give me the strength to eventually be able to make a clean, clear decision in favor of God's ideal and learn to be happy with it.

When I finally made a decision to give myself to God, that was the beginning of getting real help with the deep and very personal areas of my life, including the question of sex. He didn't take away the difficulties and temptations, but He gave me a group of people who could understand and identify with the problems and pray with me for courage and strength to live in His way. And He gave me the gift of forgiveness and a whole new beginning.

NOTES

Dear Keith,

The questions concerning sexual choices for
singles and "what to do about them" are very touchy
to talk about these days. You told me some of your
own personal thoughts and feelings about this
area when you first entered the dating world. How
about talking a little about that?

Also, is there anything in the Bible that
tells us about Jesus' attitude toward sex? Since
the biblical ideal is for people to refrain from
sex outside marriage, why do you think it is such
a struggle today for singles to deal with this
issue? Why do you think it is so hard for some to
decide clearly what is right and what is wrong?

I know it is risky to even bring up this
subject, but I think Jesus would have been glad to
lead a discussion group about sex, and would want
His people to understand more about this difficult
area of human experience.

A.

The room was dark except for the slit of light between the drawn shade and the side of the window. If I moved my head on my pillow just right I could see the gas light near the front door of the house. I looked at the digital clock. 3:13 A.M. I had been awake for hours, tossing and turning and trying to decide what to do about sex.

I'd always been protected from the acute agony of this sort of struggle by marriage. But after twenty-seven years of being a sexually active married adult, suddenly I was single. And as a Christian, I was not supposed to have sex—or even lustful thoughts.

As I stared at the ceiling, a scene flashed on the screen of my mind. I was sitting on a porch with an iron railing talking to Cynthia. She was a single Christian woman who'd been divorced several years when I met her. I'd gotten to know her pretty well and I remembered asking her, "Cynthia, you may think this is crazy. But I don't know what the score is about sex in this crazy singles' world. It seems like I've been married all my life, and from the dates I've had lately I *know* things have changed a *lot* since I was single as a kid. Would you just tell me how you see what's going on?"

"Well, Keith, it's wild, given the way I was brought up. Most men push for sex from the first date or two. And if the woman won't go to bed after two or three dates, the man evidently feels like he's not attractive to her, and simply disappears." She paused and stared out over the garden in the backyard. Then she looked back at me.

"Of course, there are a few exceptions—but not many."

I was silent as she went on.

"Most of my close girlfriends," she said, "seem to feel that sex with a single man is all right if you really care for the man and feel that he cares for you." She stopped for a moment and then smiled and lifted her eyebrows as she shrugged her shoulders. "I don't know what else to tell you."

I remembered driving home from that conversation. I knew that Cynthia and her friends were committed evangelical Christians and that they dated mostly Christian guys. The question for me was, "What am *I* going to do about being a strongly sexual single person who is also a Christian?"

The options seemed to be: total abstinence, only relating sexually to women where there was a deep and caring relationship, treating sex with the casualness many people seemed to, or finding someone quickly and marrying her.

I realized that all my background and training as a Christian said that total abstinence was the only Christian answer. But I also realized I'd learned that as a married person with an active and "legitimate" sex life. I saw how naïve and obtuse I'd been in not understanding the nature of the sexual pressure on Christians who, after being married for years, suddenly find themselves alone.

"It's not so simple," I said out loud to the empty room as I stared out the window at the gas light near the front porch.

After floundering around for some months, I thought the problem was going to be solved when I met a woman named Simone whom I was really fond of, and I began thinking about getting married. But, after some months, that relationship broke up, and I was alone again.

I had realized during the time I was dating Simone that it would really be unfair and unchristian to marry someone mainly so I could keep the rules—just to have some legitimate sex, according to the church. I'd seen some Christians whom I'd thought were marrying on that basis. But in my mind that was a triumph of legalism—at the cost of using a person (and the sacrament of marriage) as a ticket to one's own "moral protection." And I felt that Christian marriage ought to be a life commitment for the building of a new family outpost for the kingdom of God.

During the time which followed I found myself repressing my Christian heritage. I "forgot" to pray and read the Bible much of the time. It didn't *feel* like I was drifting away from God, because I *would* pray some, but it got more and more sporadic and the prayers changed.

They were shorter and less personal. I was still praying for my kids, but *my own problems* were less and less a part of my prayers.

I became discouraged about ever finding a woman who would be right for me to marry. I dated a lot with an almost numb attitude. Sometimes it was as if I were watching someone else live my life. There seemed to be little connection between the present and the past or future. And I began to understand something of the sense of lostness in this generation which I had read about—and written about—when I was married. I simply quit dealing consciously with the moral issue of sexual behavior and lived as a "contemporary single."

In a way, this emotional numbness and disconnectedness with home, church and roots was a frightening experience. Besides not teaching a class at church, I wasn't reading the newspapers much or listening to the news. And I saw how easy it would be to move so far from God and the life He'd given me that I could wind up sitting by myself on the outer rim of the Christian world. I felt I'd still be in God's flock, but as a lost sheep in a far corner of the pasture, alone. Somewhere during this time I heard someone say in a sermon that "the lost sheep didn't *run* away. He simply *nibbled* his way out of sight, and woke up lost."

As I began to realize these things, I was asked to talk to a group of Christian singles about the problems involved in living the single life from a Christian perspective.

It was obvious to me that the single Christians who had come to me for counseling were really hurting. Most of them were in relationships which involved sex, even though they didn't believe this was God's best for them. Their questions varied, but the bottom line seemed to be: "I know what I've done isn't right according to the Bible, but what does *God* think of *me?* Is there hope for me to be in a good relationship with Him? Because I can't promise I'll be strong enough not to do it again."

I turned to the Bible to see how the writers dealt with some of the issues singles face—particularly sexuality. And I found some interesting things.

Some observations about Jesus

The early accounts in Genesis indicate that when God had finished creating the world and everything in it (including man, woman, and sex) He saw everything He created as "very good" (Gen. 1:31). I found little evidence that the biblical writers saw sexual intercourse as a bad thing in itself. But the natural next question is, "If sex was invented by God and it is good, when is it permissible for Christians?"

I went through the New Testament and picked out all the references to sex, singleness, fornication, and adultery. And there is no question in my mind that the New Testament standard concerning sexual intercourse is that it is for marriage only with total fidelity to one wife or husband.

But I remembered the men and women who had asked me what *God thought of them* and I tried to see what Jesus' attitude seemed to be toward sex and people who were guilty of unapproved sexual activity.

For one thing, it is clear that sex was very much a part of Jesus' thinking, and that His attitude toward sex and sexual offenders was *very different* from that of the average contemporary religious leader of the first century and those in many modern churches. Jesus' illustrations were often sexual in nature. For example, when He told stories and parables about the kingdom of God, He could have picked any subject matter, but He chose things like the story of the Prodigal Son (who ran away and spent his father's money on whiskey and women; see Luke 15:11–32), the woman caught in the act of adultery (John 8:3–11), and the woman at the well (who had slept with so many men she didn't know what to tell Jesus; see John 4:7–38). And although Jesus obviously did *not* approve of their illicit sexual activities, he also did not *condemn them* for these activities.

In the story of the Prodigal Son, the father not only doesn't *condemn* the son for his illicit sex, he welcomes him back into the family with open arms, and doesn't even mention sex. And although it is clear that the woman caught in adultery broke the cardinal sexual rule and deserved to be stoned to death by biblical law, Jesus refuses to condemn her and, extracting no promises, sends her on her way simply advising her to "go and sin no more." And with the woman at the well, whom Jesus knew to be a loose woman, He had a theological discussion even though it was not lawful for a Rabbi to even talk to any woman in public—even his own wife or daughter.

What I'm suggesting is that while Jesus hated sin of any kind, He had a very different *attitude* about sex and sexual *offenders* than that prevailing in most contemporary churches. He loved the *people* who were involved and gave them forgiveness and the status of first-class citizens in the kingdom—even though there was no guarantee that they could keep His standards.

As I studied the scriptures and thought about modern life, I began to see that according to the emphasis of Jesus' ministry, the crucial point for a Christian to consider is that sin, *any sin,* separates one from God, from other people, and from his or her ideals. But Jesus evidently didn't want people to neurotically concentrate on "not sinning," but rather to focus on loving God and people. He and His disciples broke the rules to meet the needs of people, saying that the rules were made to help the people, not that the people were made in order to keep the rules (Mark 2:23–28). And when anyone sins (lies, cheats, is a religious hypocrite, fails to honor his father or mother, or commits adultery), Jesus has given us a remedy (through the process I'll discuss shortly) to handle the sin and receive forgiveness.

It's a paradox. We're not *supposed* to sin at all. And yet the New Testament is very clear that we *all do sin* ("If we say that we have no sin, we deceive ourselves, and the truth is not in us. . . . If we say that we have not sinned, we make him a liar, and his word is not in us" (1 John 1:8, 10, KJV).

According to the Bible then, all singles (and marrieds) sin. And it is apparent that some are going to sin sexually. I have talked to literally hundreds of Christian singles and have collected almost 1,000 anonymous responses to the question, "What is the most pressing problem you have which keeps you from being the person you think God would have you be?" And although many married church people would be shocked to realize it, I am convinced that a very large number of Christian singles are engaging in sexual intercourse, even though many of them don't feel good about it when they think about God.

What is one to do?

Since the sexual urge is so strong and many Christians are single with no prospects of marriage, every Christian single must deal with his or her sexual urges, and many are going to choose to express their sexual needs somehow. I'm not condoning this or even debating whether this *ought* to be true or not. It already *is* true. The question becomes, "How can we face our strong sexual needs, stay close to God, and make choices and decisions about our lives which will be more likely to bring us closer to God rather than take us further away from Him?"

Since most Christians suspect that sex outside of marriage is not God's best for them, there is a tendency to keep the whole subject "fuzzy," that is, not to examine clearly either the Bible or what they are doing sexually. And that attitude produces the numbness I spoke of having earlier. But if a person does this, he or she may wind up saying, "Well, no one really knows about this, whether it's all right or not," and then move into sexual relations without really having to face God.

But I can't help feeling that it's better for us Christians to try to be realistic with ourselves and face what we are doing so that God can help us. And when I began facing my behavior openly and bringing it to God, the numbness left and I began to move toward a "showdown" with him.

What, then, are the actual inner choices confronting a person when he or she faces the sexual drive imbedded in life?

CHAPTER FOURTEEN
Sexual Choices for Singles

NOTES

Dear Keith,

What are some of the responses people make to the sexual urge? And when a person makes any of these choices, what can some of the consequences be?

I know this is hard to talk about, but I hope God will use what you say to bring some light into a sometimes dark and neglected area.

A.

As I see it, there are eight basic choices one can make regarding the handling of the sexual drive.* As I describe the sexual choices available to singles, I will try to go approximately from "simple" to "complex" in terms of the effects in the life of the Christian making the choice.

1. Suppression

"Suppression" is being aware of sexual thoughts and feelings but for some religious ideal or moral consideration, consciously electing not to act them out. This is historically the preferred choice for Christians.

At times people have tried to push sex away by saying to themselves, "I'm *not* going to think about it! I'm *not* going to think about it!" But as any one considering masturbating knows, if you fight the sexual urge directly, you may give it additional power and are almost certain to lose.

A healthy and more effective way to suppress these urges has been called by the church "sublimation," that is, deciding to concentrate consciously on *another* activity with a lot of effort and intensity.

This notion of sublimation has been spoken of as "the expulsive power of a new affection." For instance, people have sublimated their sexual desires by concentrating on being artists or musicians. Some work hard at their jobs or get a lot of exercise, or fill their lives with good deeds, or evangelism, or prayer. By concentrating on something

*We realize that some Christians reading this book could say, "There is only *one* sexual choice for a committed Christian single. But, as Andrea has said, in real life God *always* seems to leave us free to choose other options than those which are best for us. Our feeling is that to examine the *truth* about *any* situation *can* lead to greater wisdom and better choices for a Christian.

besides the sexual feelings, the sexual consciousness and intensity sometimes abate and a sense of peace may replace them.

The saints have always said that by loving Jesus with all their hearts, concentrating on Him and doing His will, they were better able to avoid the competing desires. This is how committing one's whole life to Christ can help the sublimation process. The commitment can substitute a new focus and affection for one's whole life.

Contrary to some people's opinions, conscious suppression through sublimation is *not* harmful psychologically. If you can suppress your sexual needs through sublimation, that is the preferred Christian choice according to the church in light of the Bible.

Many Christian singles have already made the choice to remain totally chaste until or unless they find the right person to marry. And if you are one of these, I hope you can stick to your guns in the face of other singles' attempts to make you feel weird or abnormal. Chastity, if freely chosen, is a perfectly valid choice psychologically. And according to the Bible, it is the best choice spiritually.

2. Repression

On the surface, "repression" may seem to be the least complex way to handle sex, because to repress means to deny *to our own consciousness* that we have any sexual needs. Freud discovered the phenomenon of repression, and it seems to work something like this.

If a thought that is very threatening to my self-concept is about to come into consciousness, my mind can actually capture that thought *before* it reaches the conscious level and "push it out of sight" into the unconscious regions of the mind. And as far as my conscious mind is concerned *I never had the thought at all.*

At first, repression of sexual thoughts would seem like a blessing from God. But the consequences of repression are not quite so simple. It seems that the unacceptable and threatening thoughts have energy connected to them. They are in some way struggling to come out in the open where we, in whose lives they exist, can "see" them. And even though we are not conscious of the inner struggle, it takes a lot of psychic energy to hold the unacceptable thoughts out of consciousness. As I said earlier, repression is like pushing a large beach ball under water and out of sight. The beach ball cannot be seen, but your emotional hands are tied up holding it under so you can't do other psychological work. And this diversion of energy in order to look righteous to ourselves can make us very anxious "over nothing," tired and enervated for no apparent reason.

Some Christians who repress their sexual desires believe they are more holy or righteous than those who struggle with them. (This is natural if they don't understand about repression and the fact that every healthy adult has sexual drives.) These people sometimes count their lack of conscious sexual drive as righteousness, and they tend to look down on people who struggle with their sexual desires. In effect, the repressers are saying, "I'm so sorry you have all these sexual problems. Perhaps you aren't praying enough." And the tragedy is that Christians who are conscious of their sexual needs tend to believe that the one repressing really *is* more righteous. But this is not the case at all.

For example, let's say that you and I are in a room alone and there are one hundred pounds of gold on the table. Let's assume that I am blind and you can see. When they lead us in the room with the gold and neither one of us takes it, which one of us has made a moral decision? Only you, because one has to *see* and *recognize* the possibility of doing something wrong before choosing *not* to do it has any meaning at all. And people who repress their sexuality are psychologically blind with regard to their sexual feelings. They simply are not aware that they have sexual desires, and of course there is no "moral justification" in that. It's not even a conscious choice.

What happens to many people who repress their sexuality is that they often become tense and nervous. They may become very judgmental and edgy, vindictively condemning people who have sex. And more serious consequences can result from sexual repression—like impotence, frigidity and various kinds of neurotic behavioral symptoms.*

So if you are *conscious* of sexual needs and struggling with how to deal with them in a healthy way, you are in a more whole (and holy) condition psychologically and as a Christian than if you have repressed your sexuality from your own view. God is so gracious that He will not

---

*It is often helpful to talk to a competent counselor if one has no sexual feelings and also has compulsive behaviors he or she doesn't understand.

meddle with us unless we ask Him, and if we don't know we have a problem we have nothing to confess, nothing to ask Him about. Jesus indicated to the Pharisees and Scribes that even God couldn't help them if they didn't know they needed help (see Luke 5:31, 32).

It is true that some people have such a low sex drive that they are seldom conscious of sexual feelings, and they are not repressing. But of course this lack shouldn't be mistaken for "moral fiber" either.

3. Platonic friendships

There have been many deep friendships between men and women in which the sexual desire has been suppressed or sublimated. Such relationships can be very loving without any physical contact. These have been called "platonic friendships," and they can be wonderful.

But it is wise not to count on the assumption that a friendship between a man and woman which starts out to be platonic will remain so. Although it is possible to have deep friendships across sexual lines, it's best not to be naïve. This is true because the kind of closeness which comes from a good loving friendship is the prerequisite for the best expression of sex. And since humans are strongly sexual beings, the change from platonic to sexual relations can be sudden and unexpected. And if you don't want marriage or sex, just be aware that the consequences of platonic friendship can be surprising.

One of the best ways of finding healthy platonic friendships is in small Christian sharing groups, like those for singles in many churches. In these groups people can learn to express the problems, hopes and joys of life at an intimate level of sharing and prayer. Some people have complained to me, as an exponent of such small groups, that such sharing sessions *cause* people to have sex together, because they may have heard of a group through which two people wound up having sex. But I am convinced that small groups in which Christians can talk and pray about their real feelings have *saved* thousands of people from having to trade their bodies for a little human warmth. As a matter of fact, such groups represent one of the only places singles can go anywhere in contemporary society without having to face the question of "Are we going to have sex?" as a matter of course.

4. Lust of the eyes

Lust is an intense sexual desire. Living a life of lust is to titillate one's self by focusing one's attention on sex or sexual objects. This might mean filling your life with pornographic pictures or literature and/or concentrating on mentally undressing every attractive person you see.

Many singles who have decided not to actually engage in sexual intercourse choose to live a life style of lusting, thinking they will be "within God's law." But trying to *gain God's approval* by legalistic compliance in this area can hardly be justified by the New Testament.

In the fifth chapter of Matthew, Jesus said in effect that if you look at someone lustfully you have already committed adultery with that person in your heart (see Matt. 5:28).

Some singles get very discouraged by Jesus' comment, thinking He was saying that lusting is as serious and harmful in God's eyes as committing adultery. But it is almost ridiculous to think that "thinking a thought" in your mind is as bad as breaking a lifelong commitment and possibly destroying a family. It seems obvious that Jesus was not saying that. He was saying, it seems, that legalistic compliance with the outward rule is not enough to gain the kind of purity God has. And He was telling His listeners that they had all sinned when compared to the purity of God, even those who thought they were pure because they had outwardly kept the rules.

Recognition. Many sincere Christians go through a lot of unnecessary guilt in the area of lust because they mistake the *recognition* of sexual compatibility for sexual lust. For years I thought that if I saw an attractive woman and the thought flashed into my mind, "Wow, I'll bet she would be neat to be with in bed," that I was lusting and sinning. But I now believe I was wrong. *Recognizing* sexual compatibility is normal and healthy. If we quit *recognizing* beauty and sexual compatibility in the opposite sex, this would be the last generation. In fact, if you do not *recognize* sexual compatibility in someone of the opposite sex you may need a physical examination instead of a spiritual one.

Recognition is not sin. Sin has to do with what one *does* with that recognition. Thomas à Kempis, in his book *The Imitation of Christ,* describes the process of sexual temptation. First, there's an awareness of somebody out there who is attractive. Then you invite that awareness into your imagination and you begin to live out your sexual fantasies with the person you have seen. That's when lust begins. And the only place to stop this process is at the point of recognition. That is, when you recognize somebody of the opposite sex who might be compatible sexually, I believe what you do with that awareness at that moment determines whether or not it becomes sin in the sense of Matthew 5.

If I am walking along the street and I see a sexually attractive woman, in my mind I am saying "Hi there." That is recognition, and that is not sin. But sin would start if I would mentally say "Hi there, *come on in.* I've got an offer for you." And in my imagination I would take her down to that room in my life that I keep walled off from everybody else where these kinds of activities take place and begin to have a sexual encounter with her. *That* would be what I think Christ was describing as committing adultery in your mind.

So what can one do at the point of recognition if he or she wants to stop the lusting process? When I am walking down the street and see an attractive woman, at the moment of recognition I say, "Thank you, God, for making beautiful women," and then walk right on down the street looking at other things.

When I fail and lust, I say, "God forgive me for filling my mind with lust," and walk right on down the street.

Since sin is anything that separates us from God, other people and our best selves, the consequences of a life of constant lusting can be very isolating. And if a person wants to remain chaste, then consciously choosing to keep himself or herself obsessively stirred up sexually is hardly the best approach. As C. S. Lewis said: "Anybody who has an obsession has very little sales resistance of any kind."

5. Masturbation

Masturbation seems to be the most general sexual expression of Christian singles. The consensus of people we asked was that the church sees masturbation as evil. This view has led to some sad and unnecessary tragedies.

Some time ago when I got home from a speaking trip, I found a letter in the mail. It had been there several days, and it was from a Christian man who was in a tragic condition. This person was in Canada living in a motel. He had sold everything, moved out of an apartment and gone down to this motel to commit suicide. The owner of the motel, seeing that the man was distraught, had given him a copy of a book I had written.

So the man wrote me a letter in which he said, "I am going to commit suicide." And he continued, "The owner of this motel says that God doesn't want me to commit suicide, but I know that my sin is so bad that God will never accept me. I went to my minister and he told me that God won't accept me. And so," the letter concluded, "if you don't answer me within two weeks I am going to commit suicide."

I looked at the date and I got in touch with the guy right away. The bottom line was what he said in a P.S. "You may not even want to answer this, since I am so horrible, because my problem is *I cannot quit masturbating!*"

Obviously this man's perspective was badly skewed because of ignorance—his own and that of the person he went to for help. Most ministers would not have been so insensitive, nor given him such counsel. But how is a Christian supposed to view masturbation as a sexual choice?

Masturbation is a practice which is evidently virtually universal. If you have never masturbated, don't think you are an oddball, because I understand there are some normal people who have not. But I repeat, almost all single adults and many married people of all ages masturbate or have done so.

Many children have a scene etched in their memories from when they were very young. They were exploring or playing with their genitalia and a mother or father said in a shocked loud voice, "NO, don't play with yourself!" I can still remember the horrified look on my mother's face she said these words when I was about four years old. From that time on I had the notion that even touching myself was somehow wrong. And I think many people translate this notion into a theological context later by saying, "God says masturbation is evil."

But there seems to be little in the Bible, Old Testament or New, to substantiate the view that God considers masturbation an evil in itself, and because it doesn't involve another person, the consequences of masturbation are much less complex than those of the choices I am about to describe. But if masturbation and thinking about it become obsessive and occupy all one's waking hours, then neither God nor doing His will can. And in that sense the consequences would be a real separation from God, a sin. If you have made the choice not to masturbate, you have made a good Christian choice. But to relieve sexual tensions periodically by masturbation would seem to be for most Christian singles a basically normal sexual outlet.*

6. Sex with another single

The sixth sexual option is a single person's having sex with another person who is not married. The New Testament witness is clearly that sexual intercourse is supposed to take place within marriage, with total fidelity.

Limits short of intercourse. In order to keep from failing to meet this standard, some single Christians decide to set arbitrary limits on how far they can go sexually (short of sexual intercourse). Some people decide that touching anything below the chin is out of bounds. Others decide "below the neck" or "below the waist."

At one conference a young man said to me, "Mr. Miller, my girlfriend and I sleep together all night but we don't have intercourse." And he said, "What would Jesus say about that?" I said that I wasn't sure what He would say.

But the young man said, "I don't think you understand what I am saying, Mr. Miller. We're naked."

And when I was silent for a moment, he said, "I guess you don't

---

*Many people are under the impression that masturbation is a phenomenon of early youth. But Andrea and I were at a national conference for singles in which a seventy-year-old lady came up to me in tears and said, "Oh, thank you for telling me about that. I have lived in an inner horror-chamber of fear and guilt since I was thirteen years old because I still masturbate." It seems that older people make the sexual choice of masturbation a lot because of being widowed and/or living alone. Sometimes as Christians they feel terribly guilty about this. But I would hope God could free them from that.

really hear me. We have oral sex, but we don't have intercourse. What would Jesus say about *that*?"

Before I could answer, somebody sitting in the back of the room said, "You're asking the wrong question. You're trying to find out to what point you can have sex and still keep your righteousness with God." And, he continued, "If righteousness is really a gift of grace, then you cannot *win* your righteousness with God by drawing a line around your waist or around your breast or anywhere else. God does not give His love *in exchange for keeping any rules!*"

But as a practical matter, I think singles who are strongly attracted to each other do have to set definite limits if they do not intend to have intercourse. And it's probably a good idea to do this before starting to make out. *Any* touching can escalate sexual feelings pretty fast if two people of the opposite sex are in a close, loving relationship. And it's hard to stop at the point of intercourse.

But whatever decision you make, I'd suggest you make it *before* the evening begins, since the sex drive is so strong that it may be impossible to make a decision to set limits after you begin touching in a potentially loaded sexual situation.

What if you decide to have sex with another single? We know some Christian singles who have chosen to have what they honestly believe to be "responsible sex" with other singles. Their reasoning is that there are circumstances in which sexual relations between two loving, concerned singles are not bad in any way. (And there was a long time when I felt that way.) Even though these people are aware that their behavior is counter to the biblical witness, they feel that the psychological and emotional reasons they give make their behavior O.K. in God's sight.

But while I recognize that as adults we are certainly free to choose any lifestyle we want to, I think we should not try to change the biblical witness to fit our needs. In other words, if I as a single Christian choose to have sex outside marriage, I think I should face the fact that this is not the biblical way to go, and be responsible enough to say that I am choosing to have sex anyway. I think God can deal with this sort of honesty better and more compassionately than with my trying to change the message to make it fit my choice.

Let's say that you have made the choice to have sexual intercourse with another single. What are the possible practical consequences?

Some people feel terribly guilty. But other people are amazed to discover that they don't feel any guilt at all. Still others feel no guilt at the time, but *after* they are married—even to the same man or woman—they suddenly become impotent "for no reason." It's as if their mind had an internal regulating system. If they feel at an unconscious level that they should be punished and weren't, their own psyche will see that they are. And then in all honesty it must be said that there are Christian men and women who have had sex with a number of people and who apparently experience no negative psychological or physical consequences.

The spiritual consequences of any act one believes to be a sin is that it separates one from God, from other people and eventually from himself or herself. This process of separation may be subtle in terms of the experience of the one sinning. But it can deeply and negatively affect the believer's integrity and growth as a Christian and a person.

Talk about the meaning of your relating. A possible tragic consequence of two singles engaging in sexual intercourse is that one may break the other's heart if they do not communicate what they are "saying" by engaging in the sex act.

When some people are approached about having sex, they consider it as an invitation to marriage. They've always been told that "if you have sexual intercourse then that's the person you are going to marry." And other people in our society today think of sexual intercourse as about the equivalent of a movie ticket. In other words, for them it's an "entertainment" venture.

So if those two people meet and go to bed together but *do not discuss* what they are doing, one may think they are going to get married while the other thinks they are having an entertaining evening with no future commitments involved.

So whatever you decide to do about having sex with another single, it's surely serious enough to discuss with that person. In other words, if you decide to have sex as a single Christian, then find out what you both think you are saying by this act. Because it is very weighty to have intercourse with somebody. It may not be easy to talk about this ahead of time, but it's a lot easier than crippling people's lives just to get your needs met for an evening.

Several of our single friends who read this book in manuscript form complained that by our saying that sex between singles is not right according to Christian tradition, we are *creating guilt* in people who think differently. But we want to emphasize that we do *not* want to create guilt in anyone. All we are trying to do is to tell it like it is.

If single Christians choose to relate sexually to other singles, I think God can forgive them. But the facts are that they will be choosing to go against the traditional biblical position. There is no way I can get around that—and I have tried. In real life there are many ways in which we all go against what we've been taught is right. And these times are when we know how much we need the grace and forgiveness of God. Sometimes I wish life were easier, but I didn't invent it.

In conclusion, the New Testament ideal is that sexual intercourse is for marriage only. And if you are trying to live that ideal, I believe God will help you. If you elect to have sex with another single person, I believe that God will continue to love you and help you, but that you may eventually feel separated from Him and from important aspects of your self, and that this choice can hinder your growth in Christ.

7. Adultery

Adultery (voluntary sexual intercourse between a married man and someone other than his wife, or between a married woman and someone other than her husband) is something both the Old and New Testaments are very clearly and strongly against. The Old Testament penalty for adultery was death by stoning. Besides all the risks and possible negative consequences of sex between singles, adultery is a direct attack on perhaps the most basic of human institutions (marriage) and can affect the lives of many people besides those committing the act.

But in spite of these things, some single Christians choose to have sex with married people because they feel it is "safer" than being with another single. If a single man chooses a married woman, and the woman breaks up with him later, he can say, "Well, of course, she had to reject me because she is married." So he thinks he is getting away from the pain of being rejected.

Or others have told me that having sex with a married partner is safe because "she's not going to come running after me, since she is already married, so I am free to step in and out of that relationship without the risk of her expecting a commitment."

But this way of relating is not really "safe" at all, because one's *emotions* don't understand all these clever reasonings, and a person can get deeply involved emotionally with somebody who is married. Then without realizing how it happened, the single may cripple his or her life and the married person's and his or her whole family's. And if someone is having sex with a married person whose husband (wife) "just doesn't understand me," he (she) is often giving that person a sexual and emotional outlet so that she (he) can more easily avoid facing the marriage and possibly getting it healed. And the fact that the adultery has taken place may make it that much harder for the person to face her (or his) marriage partner openly.

8. Homosexuality

The biblical record—Old Testament and New—is clearly against homosexuality (exhibiting sexual desire toward a member of one's own sex). As in the case of adultery, the penalty for homosexual acts in ancient Israel was stoning to death (see Lev. 20).

In contemporary Christian society I don't suppose any sexual option mentioned so far comes even close to homosexuality in terms of the censure and rejection it elicits from the church. This does not mean that God does not love the homosexual person or will not forgive him or her. But it can mean that a homosexual may have a great deal of trouble finding Christians who can understand or accept him or her. Consequently the pain and rejection experienced by many Christians who are homosexuals is often intense.

What happens when we fail?

Let's say that you start out with the best intentions, wanting to be a fine chaste Christian. Then due to loneliness, temptations, or whatever, you go to bed with someone. What should a Christian single do then? As I have mentioned, the temptation is to run away from God, to back away from Him—especially if you feel you can't promise not to do it again. But I think that is a mistake.

I think one can get up, confess,* and tell God, "You know I can't promise You that I won't ever do this again, but I offer myself to You, and I ask You to change my desires or to help me find a way to express them that will be right with You."

Or let's say you are sexually involved with someone regularly and you make a commitment today, "I'm not going to ever do this again because I want to give my life totally to Jesus Christ." And then next Thursday you call and say, "Hey, can I come over?" And you have sex with that person. Then Friday morning you start to give up the whole Christian faith because you failed again.

Don't do it. Stay very close to God at that point. Get up Friday morning and say, "God, forgive me, I have done it again!" and then don't dwell on it, just go about your business and try to stay away from the tempting circumstances. And over a period of time, if you pray for Him to change your desire or "take away these needs I have for relating sexually with other people or give me the right way to channel them in a marriage," then you are putting yourself and your future in God's hands. And in the last analysis that is all any of us can do—put our futures in His hands and do our best.

I believe with all my heart that God loves us all and understands what we are going through. He hates sin because of what it can do to harm us and separate us from Him, from other people, and from our best selves.

But although God hates sin, He has amazing love and patience with us sinners. And whether the sin involves lying, stubborn pride, religious hypocrisy, or sexual sins, if we bare our hearts to Him, confessing where we are and what we are doing, it will not make Him angry, but will bring His loving care and strength into our struggles to be His persons. And if you can't change your behavior instantly, He's not going to be shocked. It may take you months or even years to get your life in order the way you want it. But His presence can help you work much faster than you might if you turned your back on Him because you were embarrassed about your continuing failure to be what you want to be.

---

*By confession, I do not mean a light "acknowledgment of sin," but rather the whole process leading to forgiveness described in chapter 16.

CHAPTER FIFTEEN
Faith in God and the Single Life

NOTES

Dear Andrea,

This chapter is, for me, the bottom line for everything we've tried to say so far. The only reason I care enough to risk being embarrassed or misunderstood in this book is that I feel God loves us and wants us to reach out to other people who are going through what we have.

How about describing your own spiritual journey through the single experience? How did you think about God? When, if ever, did you try to make a commitment to Him? What happened to bring you to an understanding that He really does love you and understands what you've been through?

Add any other pictures or insights which have been helpful to you as you've wrestled with the problems of having faith in God as a single person.

It has really been fun doing this book with you. I was a little skeptical at first about how we could work it all out. But here we are—at the next-to-last chapter!

K.

Although I'd drifted away from my childhood faith in college, I turned back to the church when trouble came in my marriage four years later. And the counseling and support I received helped me survive the shocks of separation and divorce as I stumbled into a new life. But after the divorce I desperately wanted to make it on my own. And besides, there wasn't much room for a faith which would permeate my whole experience since I was living four separate lives, only one of which pertained to Christianity as I understood it.

After about four years of the struggle to prove I could handle my own life without any outside help, I was sitting at home one night feeling very restless and disassociated from people and from God. I had no good books, and the TV schedule looked awful. I was wishing I was out to dinner with a man, laughing and talking and having a good time. I realized I had not "kicked the habit" of needing male companionship. I was also thinking that I wasn't sure if I ever *wanted* to numb myself from the need for male affirmation, and I hated myself for having the need.

As I wandered through the rooms of my apartment, I sensed that old feeling coming over me of being trapped there alone, and a deep anger welled up inside me—anger at fate or the situation or whatever had me trapped. In spite of all that I'd done about my apartment, my wardrobe and my job, I wasn't happy and I wasn't where I wanted to be. I realized that I wasn't even sure *where* I wanted to be. Then the frustrating thought came out of my mouth, "So, if you don't know where you want to go, how would you know if you *ever got there?*"

That was when I heard myself talking out loud, angrily, to God. "Look, God, if you're really there—and sometimes I seriously doubt it!—show me a way to find some peace of mind. If there's some man I'm supposed to meet, show me who he is. If there isn't, then help me get over this restless feeling of needing to be with a man and help me to learn to live a happy life with purpose and meaning some other way!"

After saying that, I felt silly. I flopped down in my big chair. The room seemed strangely silent. There was no audible answer, no knock on the door, no great revelation in my head, no missing puzzle piece to solve my dilemma.

But something did happen. My mind slowly began to turn away from the problem of being with or without a man to that of living a meaningful life with purpose. And that certainly made a difference in my attitude! It was one of the first times I had seriously considered my own life as an entity in itself . . . not just an incomplete part of a dual life with someone else. I started to feel excited, and stood up! "So this is how I might deal with my depression and anger," I thought. I began to think back through my relationship to God as I went to the kitchen for a Fresca.

I had kept God tucked away as if He really were stored on the top shelf in the cabinet above the refrigerator for all these years, along with all the other things I needed but didn't use very often. So I hardly understood what I was talking about. But I realized now that I wanted to know more.

A big step: Commitment to God

I popped the top of the Fresca can and returned to my chair. My mind wandered back to a summer evening two years before when I had been driving toward Waco from a weekend at the Gulf Coast. It was night and I couldn't see much except for the occasional double pin-points of light coming at me from down the highway, only to flash by and leave me alone again. I had been talking about God a lot and even praying directly to Him some. I felt ready to take some kind of step toward a deeper relationship with God.

I puzzled over how to do it and realized that up until now I had treated my relationship to God as if I were dating Him in the singles' world. He was a friend whom I could accept or reject depending on what other plans I had in my life at any given moment. And I knew that if our relationship became "too uncomfortable," I was prepared to cut it off again, as I had in college.

But now as I watched the broken white line on the highway slipping silently under the left front fender of the car, I knew I wanted a permanent relationship. I saw at last that for me, the only way toward a whole, meaningful life whether or not I *ever* got married was through a permanent commitment to God. So I formed the thought carefully in my head and said out loud, "God, I want to be Your person. I'm not even sure how to go about it, but I want to stop putting You off and arguing about whether You are good or even exist. I believe You are the only hope I have for a meaningful life, and I ask You to come into my mind, emotions, and soul and teach me how to become the person You had in mind when You created me."

When I finished talking, there was a lump in my throat and I felt very tense. But as I drove on through the night, I gradually relaxed. Again, as I had felt at age nine when I was baptized, I knew I had made a big step toward God. And I was now determined to find out what it all meant.

But during the next few days, nothing happened as a result of that specific commitment. I had done it because a friend had suggested that making the commitment might help. "The main point," he had said, "is to begin *living* as you believe God wants you to, as much as you can. You'll learn as you go along." So I started living the way I thought God wanted me to, but I forgot about the actual commitment I made that night.

Learning as I went—The next two years

About a year after the verbal commitment, I had joined a prayer group and started reading the Bible. And during the three months that Keith and I were apart, I'd had a deep experience of how different life is with God in it. At last I had somewhere to turn besides to another human being with all my pain, fear, anger, loneliness, and even happiness. I was finally convinced that even though people might let me down, God would not. That, I had realized, is the "promise" to which Christians had kept referring. And in my loneliness I was beginning to experience it personally.

In some ways I began to feel God's presence in my life as a loving Person. I'd come home from work in the evenings and feel a welcoming coziness in my apartment, as if I weren't alone. I looked forward to more time there to read and think and pray—instead of working late and running errands to avoid facing those empty walls. It was as if God's Spirit were there in the apartment somehow, and that I was safe at last—safe enough to relax, to feel peaceful, and even to endure the painful times of loneliness, fear, anger, and depression with the hope of coming *through* the pain to happier times.

I'd also realized that God had been available to me those other times I'd been miserable, only I hadn't "felt His presence" because of all the walls I had built which shut Him out . . . walls of doubt, cynicism and of selfishly trying to prove to the world (and myself) that I could survive on my own without *any* help.

It was still important to me to know that I could survive without clinging to a relationship with a human being (like a man, or my friends, or my parents). But it had begun to seem stupid for me to try to live without God's help. And then, when Keith and I had broken up, I had been able to turn to God in a new way. And I felt that at last I might be able to let Jesus Christ into the center of my life.

The inner door opened at last!

As I sat in my big chair in the living room thinking about God and this new relationship I'd begun with Him, I looked around at all the familiar things in my apartment and thought, "How like the inside of my life this place is."

Often I had come home from a business trip to find the same mess I had left behind me a few days before . . . newspapers and magazines thrown around, dirty coffee cups, clothes I had decided not to take thrown on the couch, glasses filled with melted ice, and my shoes thrown on the rug beside my favorite reading chair.

When I came home, I usually dropped my suitcases on the bedroom floor and climbed into a comfortable, ratty old robe and big fluffy bedroom slippers. I would roam around the living room, gazing mournfully at the mess, too tired to do much about it. I usually wound up in my chair thinking, reading, or watching television.

A couple of times I remember sitting in that kind of careless disorder and the thought had occurred to me, "What if someone knocks on the door?" The idea of being caught in that kind of a mess sent waves of panic through my stomach. But that day, as I was comparing my life to the inside of my apartment, I imagined that it happened. In my mind there was a knock on my door. And I realized that the visitor outside my door was Jesus Christ.

In my fantasy I considered the various options. One was just to sit still and pretend that I was not at home. The embarrassment of having anyone see my messy apartment and sloppy clothes was stronger than my desire to have a visitor.

But in this fantasy I could see Him outside the door, dressed in the long white robe and dusty sandals of the biblical pictures. He looked patient, tired, and concerned. One hand was scratching His shoulder, and His head was lowered and turned to one side as if He were listening for an answer. I was still ignoring Him. He kept knocking, patiently. I felt my heart pounding as I continued the fantasy.

Irritated, I felt like shouting, "Come back later when I have cleaned up in here and I'll let you in!" Suddenly I knew it would *never* be clean enough for me to feel comfortable letting Jesus inside. Finally, I decided to risk it.

I went to the door with a mixture of feelings. I felt embarrassed, and I thought, "I wish things weren't in such a mess, and I wish You hadn't come just now." Then I felt more anger. And I could almost hear myself saying, "Couldn't You have called first and given me a chance to get things straight around here?" And then I felt apologetic. "I haven't had time to clean up yet, but I really *wanted* to."

Braced for the worst

I opened the door, and Jesus walked in. He didn't seem to notice the mess, sloppy clothes, and smeared make-up. He looked into my eyes with a smile and, passing by me, He sat in my favorite reading chair, throwing His sandals into the pile with my shoes. He said, "I'm so glad you finally opened the door. I love you. I've missed you. What can I do to help you?"

A wave of relief came over me, from as far back as I could remember. And then I finally got the picture. God *isn't repulsed by my messy life!* He *knows* about loneliness. And it dawned on me what people mean when they say that God is lonely for our love. He'd been standing out there knocking for a long time. He knew about heartbreak and broken hopes and feelings of rejection. We taught Him that when He was here on earth. He knew about drinking and overeating and laziness and bossiness. People have had those problems for thousands of years. And He knew about sex... God invented that, too.

Then I realized that He wanted to *help* me clean up. But I still couldn't quite believe it. So I started with something small, the dirty coffee cups all around. As we talked about that, I saw that it wouldn't be so hard to clean them up, and so I did. Next I went through the messes, one by one... the surface ones, and then those just below the surface.

Finally, His nonjudgmental listening helped me find the courage to say, "Boy, you aren't going to believe this, Lord! Look at this awful stain here—I'm almost sure it's permanent!" And I rolled back the throw rug and let Him see my worst mess of all. Instead of cringing, He pulled out some cleansers that I couldn't even have imagined. And I saw that He could remove even the stains I feared were permanent, if only I could find the courage to show them to Him.

God's love is forever, even if mine isn't

And before long I realized that once I had allowed Jesus into my life, He was planning to *stay* with me. Sometimes He has to lead me through experiences that I can't go through by myself because I am just too scared. And if I do get too frightened, or forget how much I need Him, and throw Him out again, I can ask Him to come right back in, and He always will. Jesus never says, "No, not this time, kiddo. You threw me out, and I'm staying out!"

I can't imagine any human friend taking that kind of garbage from me, and I certainly couldn't take it from anyone else. If you never cleaned your house, never took a bath, and ignored me when I came to see you and knocked on your door, I would quit trying. Or I might try to discuss it with you and demand an explanation, or judge you and try to get you to become acceptable according to my terms—clean and cheerful. I realized then, that I had been braced for God to do one or all of those things to me, because I had lost touch with my faith in Him during the trauma of trying to find out what to do as a single person. And as I sat thinking about these things I realized that, thanks to Jesus, God isn't like that for me any more. I believe He not only keeps up His end of our relationship, but when I drop *my* end and behave rudely, *He* keeps *my* end up *for* me until I am able or ready to come back.

And now, much of the time, I have a feeling of communicating with a Person who is patient and understanding, and not judgmental. I believe Jesus would seat me at a formal banquet table with velvet-covered chairs and elegant guests, even if I were totally covered with mud—and never even wince.

The thing that broke through to me while I imagined this scenario in my living room is—*I don't have to wait until I am all straightened out to invite Jesus into the center of my life!* He *is* in it, and He expects me to be honest about what the messes are (He doesn't seem to help me clean them up unless I point them out). And although He appears to want me to be responsible for doing all I can, He helps me. Each time I let Him in, I am motivated to clean up just one more mess. And the experience of His love and acceptance makes me want to keep trying forever!

NOTES

Dear Keith,

    As I've said, a lot has changed for me with regard to my relationship to God. It's been very moving for me to write this chapter and to see how the changes occurred.

    What was going on in your spiritual life? You had been very close to God for years and instrumental in showing Him to other people. Was it possible for you to stay close to Him? And were there new and deeper levels of trust you found through the experience of being single?

    I think many people may have felt you were lost as a Christian when you became single. What new things did you learn during that time?

A.

It was April, early morning. Through the open window I could hear a robin singing in the tree outside my apartment, and I could smell the earth after the spring rain of the night before. The curtains billowed softly in the breeze. Something was different, but at first I couldn't tell what it was. Then I knew! I felt *at peace* with myself for the first time in a *long time!*

As I lay there, I thought back through what had happened during the two and a half years since I'd been divorced. The scared, angry and bruised middle-aged boy driving toward the beach in the rainstorm, crying, was only a memory. In the almost three years since, I had walked through a kaleidoscope of emotions. I'd tasted loneliness in a different form. I'd experienced the *fear* of failure—and *failure,* love and friendship in new ways, financial problems I hadn't known in years, anger, and even hatred. I'd found the freedom of having made the parent break with my long-dead father, faced alienation from the experience of a home, and gone through a whole reappraisal of my relationship with my children and of the question of my identity as a man.

I felt tougher somehow, stronger. The pain of being single and taking responsibility for my life at long last had made my mind begin to feel more lithe and creative. The mistakes and sin had been stark and painful, but through them I'd learned a lot about what I did *not* want to be and do. So I was almost grateful for even the worst experiences. Out of what had appeared to be the wreckage of my life was awakening a different person.

I thought about my spiritual journey, my relationship with God. Near the end of my first marriage I had backed away from God when the rush of formerly repressed feelings had begun to come out of my unconscious in a raging torrent. I couldn't feel God's presence. It was hard to pray. The heavens were brass. I felt very detached and alone. But when I knew the divorce was inevitable, I turned again to God in an intimate way. Divorce was unthinkable . . . yet after two years of all kinds of counseling, talking, prayer and intense agony, the shadow of divorce was standing at the door.

I spent days alone in the Texas hill country in prayer and fear, trying to decide what to do. Then I realized that I was going to have to trust that God would love me anyway, even divorced . . . my greatest act of faith. Then resignation. Divorce. Hurtling through space into the single experience.

As I became a single, I held on to God very closely. But my world was suddenly like a giant tumble dryer filled with cascading people and paradoxes. Brief meetings . . . loneliness . . . love . . . partings . . . insight . . . rest . . . gratitude to God for survival . . . fear of loneliness . . . love . . . guilt . . . forgiveness . . . comfort of God . . . not belonging . . . meeting Andrea . . . falling in love. The "dryer" began to slow down, and finally came an awareness that I needed to confront my disconnected life.

I realized that after more than two years of being single, I was approaching a real spiritual crisis. The time had come once more to face myself and God and see if I could trust Him with the future, particularly the intimate sexual part of me.

For months I had avoided thinking about the inner personal part of my life in the presence of God. But as I've mentioned, some singles asked me to do a series of talks on "being single as a Christian." As I went through the Bible in preparation for the series, I tried to see what it really said about things like singleness, identity, and sex. I became convinced that *I* needed to come to God with the most personal and (I felt) vulnerable part of my life—my need for a loving relationship with a woman. That was where I was stuck spiritually. Before, I had said in effect, "Don't worry about that part of my life, God. I'll handle that." But now I saw that God was saying to me, "No, Keith, I want to be with you in that search, too."

And I'd been protesting, "No, Lord, You wouldn't like it out there! You wouldn't understand!" But He had kept nudging me. And I realized that I was at a new threshold in my relating to God . . . one I'd never heard anyone talk about.

Could I possibly *trust God* to sustain and guide me so that I could find and marry the right woman? And if marriage was not God's will for me, would I be resigned to a life of sexual unfulfillment? I know this may sound terribly impious to some readers (but not, I think, to those who have been there).

The question was, could I "turn loose" of the control of my life enough to trust God *that much*? Paul Tournier had said that growth often takes place in the Christian's life when he or she becomes ready to let go of something. It's as if we are hanging on a trapeze bar. God swings another trapeze toward us, just far enough away so that we can't hang onto this bar and reach the next. We have to turn loose of our present security and reach out in faith for the next one. And somehow I heard God calling to me, "Release the control of your intimate life and hold on to Me, and trust Me with it, with *everything in your future!*" and it scared me to death.

Andrea and I quit dating for two months that fall, and I was miserable. I loved her very much. But I knew I had to settle some things in my own life before I could consider going on with our relationship . . . which meant a great deal to me.

One night everything seemed to be wrong. I was afraid I'd lost Andrea. And I realized that I had made an idol out of our relationship—in some ways wanting her more than God. I knew that was wrong but I couldn't seem to help it. I'd tried to escape but the hound of heaven kept coming. I tried to sleep, but sleep wouldn't come. I looked at the clock: 4:50 A.M. I'd been sweating, tossing for hours, wrestling with God in that miserable semisleep world, telling Him to get off my back and at the same time wanting to know the peace of being right with Him. More twisting and turning. The sheets were knotted ropes. Finally I said out loud, "*All right, God!* All right! I *do* trust You with my life—*all* of it! I'm scared, and I can't make any promises about doing it all right, but I want to be Your person and to trust You about the future, *including a relationship with the right woman!* I'm tired of struggling to control everything and everyone around me so I'll be happy. *I surrender my life to You!*"

I looked at the clock again. It was 5:20 A.M. I fell into a deep, dreamless sleep. I'd like to say that I woke up and everything was easy and all worked out immediately. But it wasn't, and there was a period of wrestling and of continuing to try to face my needs and my lifestyle.

But somehow things changed at that point, and I began to see that a lot of my striving and driving to get my needs met had been because of my fear that they would never be met. And the night I started to trust God with my whole future, I began to trust that even if I never found the right woman to marry and if these needs weren't met, at least there would be a purpose in my life that would make it worth living—to be God's person.

Then I went through a rough period of trying to decide about my whole future, vocationally and personally. As I began to become more aware of how I wanted to live, I was able to make better decisions about my life. And I knew that even though it might take a lifetime to get to be the person I felt God wanted me to be, for now the war was over somehow. By committing my whole future as a single Christian to Him, I had a foundation on which to build a new life.

CHAPTER SIXTEEN

The Mystery of the Gospel

NOTES

Dear Keith,

After discussing these various areas of life
from the perspective of being single, would you
elaborate a little about the message of the Gospel
and how it relates specifically to people who are
single?

For several years I had gotten so caught up in
things like discovering my identity, surviving on
a small income and dating that I almost lost touch
with the one thing that offered meaning and purpose
for my life... my relationship with God and the
whole meaning of Christianity. For me,
rediscovering the renewing process God has given
us through Jesus Christ deeply changed my
perspective on life—both the day-to-day problems
and my long-range hope.

A.

It was very quiet, although there were nineteen of us sitting around the room. Betty Lou had just admitted that she'd engaged in sexual intercourse as a single—after implying for ten weeks in our group that she simply never thought about sexual problems. At least that's the way we had read her. No one knew what to say.

We'd been discussing "forgiveness." As I looked around the room some people were staring at the floor and others at the ceiling. But no one was looking at anyone else. We were all deeply touched by her trust, and I felt a wave of love for her from the group for her vulnerable honesty.

Betty Lou finally looked up at me.

"Keith," she said, "I know God will forgive me." She stopped and then with an anguished look, continued, *"But how many times?"*

The question of our sin and God's forgiveness for all sins is at the heart of the Christian message. And yet many people have some strange preconceptions concerning God's demands and the practical application of His forgiveness for our not meeting them, especially in certain areas of life where we aren't quite sure they apply.

The Gospel seems to be telling us that we were made in God's image for a close and loving relationship with Him and each other. But the difficulty is that *He* is totally *pure* and *righteous* and can't tolerate the presence of impurity or unrighteousness, whereas we are all sinners and impure. So, the Gospel tells us that He provided a way for us to get "cleaned up" so we can be in a close relationship with Him—even though we are all sinners.

The Christian view of the solution to this difficulty is that somehow through God's action in the life, death, and resurrection of Jesus Christ, there was an atonement (at-one-ment) between God and us.

Through this atonement, for all practical purposes, we are as pure as God and can be in relationship with Him again.

But the problem of human sin is so deep that we, His people, continued to sin even after the atonement. So God, it seems, has given us a process whereby we can come to Him again and again and be made clean and free.

The process works something like this.

Let's say we set out in a new relationship—with God or with another person. We want to be loving and honorable. But since we all have a flaw in our nature (sin) which makes us "miss the mark" and foul our own nest, we fail . . . we sin.

At first we try to deny to ourselves and God that we have sinned. We rationalize and say we didn't realize what we were doing, or the temptation was too strong, or it was someone else's fault. But pretty soon we get sick of our own dishonesty and the separation we feel from the One we love.

So, we *repent,* that is, we "turn from" the bad behavior. We confess that we have sinned and tell God we don't want to do it any more.

After we repent and confess, an amazing thing happens. *God forgives us completely—as if we had never sinned!* It's as if our sinful mind were a cluttered blackboard on which three classes had written and no one had erased. And when we confess and ask God's forgiveness, He takes a damp cloth and wipes the mind's slate clean. Then He hands us a piece of chalk and says, "Here, you're free to write the next chapter of your life on a clean slate."

And at that time, if it's appropriate, we are to go and make restitution to the person we sinned against—if doing so won't harm them.

These faced-and-forgiven sins are transmuted by the alchemy of faith into what the world calls wisdom and nondefensive understanding. People who have been hurt by and freed from failures and sin have a deeper understanding of life than those who have never faced their sin.

How many times will God forgive us? When Peter asked Jesus how many times a person should forgive, Jesus said "seventy times seven," which is the Hebrew way of saying an *infinite number* of times (Matt. 18:21–22). Andrew Greeley has said that if one person were to forgive another the number of times God forgives us all, we would consider that person mad. The love and grace and forgiveness of God are so far above our ability to even grasp that they seem like madness.

What does this mean to us in practical terms?

1. God hates all sin and can't tolerate its presence.

2. We all sin and continue to sin.

3. He's given to those who love Him and commit their lives to Him a way to continually come to Him and be made fresh and clean.

4. But though the process of repentance, confession, forgiveness and restitution sounds easy, it is heartbreaking for those who really love God to fail Him and have to come back again and again, especially having been forgiven before for the same sin.

5. The miracle is that God, unlike us, evidently isn't as interested in scorekeeping the *number* of times we sin as He is in winning us to a close, honest relating with Him and each other (however long it takes). He has a process through which we can become free from guilt and sin so that we can fulfill our creative potential with Him as agents of His kingdom.

So whatever our failures or sins, Jesus Christ invites us to come to God and confess our sin and our baffling inability to quit sinning. We can ask Him to change our desires, our situations, and for strength to make it through one day at a time.

And if we fail—we can *come to Him again*! And again. And again! He will not forsake us. That's the good news of Jesus Christ!

I heard a story not long ago that is going around the Catholic church. It was about a bishop somewhere in Europe whose name was Sin, and a young nun who claimed to have had a vision of Jesus. As was the custom when someone claimed such a vision, she was called before the bishop and he interviewed her.

"Sister, did you talk to Him?" he asked.

"Yes, I did."

Then, after talking to her further, he said, pointing to himself, "All right, if you ever have another vision of our Lord, would you ask Him this question: 'What was the bishop's primary sin before he became a bishop?' " (He knew that only God and his confessor would know.) "I'd like for you to come and tell me His reply." He was testing to see if she had had a real encounter with Jesus.

About three months later, the nun made an appointment with the bishop.

When she came in he asked her, "Sister, did you see our Lord again?"

"Yes sir, I did."

The bishop's expression was suddenly very serious and almost apprehensive as he said, "Did you ask him, 'What was the bishop's primary sin before he became a bishop?'"

"Yes, I did," she replied.

Hesitantly, he asked, "What did He say?"

The young woman looked up toward the corner of the room, remembering her Lord's face. Then she replied to the bishop, "He said... 'I don't remember.'"

* * *

It seemed strange to be back at the coast again. The light predawn breeze coming in from the Gulf had only a tinge of the salt-marsh smell of the sea. The atmosphere was heavy, another hot June day coming. As I walked the block from where I was staying to the water, in the grayness I passed our old beach house crouched on top of the big dune. A family from Canada owned the house now. A hundred ghosts of the past seemed to come out and dance around on the long front deck—the ghosts of children laughing and playing, and a big white dog smiling through the railing at me with his tongue lolling out from running. They all seemed to be beckoning to me to go back in time with them. As I stopped for a moment and watched them in my imagination, I felt a real tugging from the past. But then I turned and started on toward the beach. And I saw a slit of light, high above the gray rolling surf. The sun had already risen, but it had come up *behind the clouds!*

By the time I'd walked the water's edge to the old wooden pier where I'd shouted so many of my questions at God, the sun had broken through in a dozen places, creating in the leaden sky a towering pink and white castle with shafts of gold and silver coming down to the sea in front of me from all around it.

I stood on the end of the pier and let the spray hit my face as I felt and heard the thud and boom of the waves crashing into the huge pilings below. And then I felt tears of happiness mingled with the fine salt mist on my face. Since early that morning—long before dawn—I had been wrestling with the question, "What has the single experience meant to me?" And now, although I wasn't sure I could write it down, I knew.

With all my struggles and questions concerning "What kind of a person am I, really?" and "How can I risk relating to God and to people intimately and just be myself?" the "answers" were not at all what I had expected. Instead of finding "coolness" and wisdom which could guide me around the problems and pain of life, God seemed to be saying to me in that sunrise, "Keep walking *right through* the hard things to where you can see Me. Leave the past behind and look up at Me above all the anxiety and grayness. I've already risen above them and am about to show you a new day. You'll find out who you are as you face the pain and help other people through it. And intimacy comes when you quit running from the truth about yourself and decide to turn loose . . . and walk into the future with Me."